CRISIS OF SOCIALISM—
Notes in Defence of a Commitment—Vol. 4

THE RIGHT LESSON
AND
THE WRONG CONCLUSION

CRISIS OF SOCIALISM—
Notes in Defence of a Commitment—Vol. 4

THE RIGHT LESSON AND THE WRONG CONCLUSION

Randhir Singh

AAKAR

The Right Lesson and the Wrong Conclusion

First Published, 2011

ISBN 978-93-5002-153-8 (Hb)

Published by
AAKAR BOOKS
28 E Pocket IV, Mayur Vihar Phase I, Delhi 110 091
Phone : 011 2279 5505 Telefax : 011 2279 5641
info@aakarbooks.com; www.aakarbooks.com

Printed at
Mudrak, 30 A Patparganj, Delhi 110 091

Contents

Publisher's Note

Professor Randhir Singh's *Crisis of Socialism—Notes in Defence of a Commitment* (Royal size xiii+1087 pages) was originally published by Ajanta Books International in 2006. A response to the collapse of the Soviet Union's 'actually existing socialism' and dealing with the basic issues of the why and how of this collapse, its implications and where it leaves the question of socialism in our time, the book has been hailed as a pioneering work—'one of the most important, if not *the* most important book we have ever read', 'a key to all that is going on in our world today', 'if there were a required reading list for the U.S. left, this should be on it', and so on—and there has been a persistent demand for its argument to be available in a form easier to handle and access. Therefore, with the consent of the author and in consultation with him, we at Aakar Books have decided to publish it as a thematically reorganised 6-volume edition : Volume I (chapters 2 and 3, titled **Of Marxism and Socialism** — available in the author's **Marxism, Socialism, Indian Politics—A View from the Left**, published by us); Volume II (Prologue, chapters 1, 4, 5, 6, 7, 8, 9, 11, 12, 13 and Epilogue, titled **What was Built and What Failed in the Soviet Union**); Volume III (chapters 10, 14, 15, 16, 17, titled **The World after the Collapse of the Soviet Union**); Volume IV (chapters 18 and 19, titled **The Right Lesson and The Wrong Conclusion**); Volume V (chapter 20, titled **Contemporary Ecological Crisis—A Marxist View**); Volume VI (chapter 21 and 22, titled **Struggle for Socialism—Some Issues**).

—K.K. Saxena

In Lieu of a Biodata*

There is a certain inevitability about it. Sooner or later someone was bound to ask me, again, for my biodata.

A 'biodata', now, has been a source of perennial embarrassment for me. For I simply don't have any—I have no credentials at all so far as scholarship in the academy goes. I have only a life to speak of, lived somewhat differently, and on a generous interpretation, maybe a little more meaningfully too. Here, very sketchily, then, is some of the more public part of the story, for whatever it is worth.

Childhood, they say, is important, always and in many ways. For me it was a rather unhappy childhood, very bleak and altogether lonely. I literally lived and survived on books, which partly explains my lifelong love for and involvement with them. This childhood, possibly, also left me with a certain sensitivity for the reality of suffering in the human condition of our time.

Over this childhood loomed large the heroic figure of Bhagat Singh. A morning is still vividly etched on my mind, the morning after he and his comrades were hanged. I was detained, briefly, while passing in front of the Lahore Central Jail on my way to the Borstal primary school in the neighbourhood. The

* An 'autobiographical note' written in response to a request for biodata for a felicitation volume (1988).

army and the police, a surging sea of humanity, tears in each eye and the proud faces, portraits, of the martyrs everywhere—and the defiant unending cry of '*Inquilab zindabad*'.... That morning was born a dream which, I believe, in some form or the other, has always stayed with me. Years later I was to spend a few months, among the happiest in my life, in the 'Terrorist Ward' of this very prison with some of the surviving comrades of Bhagat Singh—Kishori Lal and others—who had in the meantime joined the Communist Party.

Thus I grew up. And in due course, on the eve of the Second World War, I again came to Lahore, this time for my studies at a college there. My father, a remarkable man in his own mixed sort of way—a brilliant physician and surgeon, profoundly religious and puritanical, with a rather deadly combination of Gandhi and Lenin in his head—sensing the turbulence inside me, his only son, had advised: 'Do anything out there but don't join some illegal organisation'. Predictably, this was the first thing I did on reaching Lahore. Even as I was searching for it, the Communist Party found me. When my father admonished me that I had shown scant regard for the family, I wrote back: 'I have found my real family'. The Communist Party meant this and very much more in those days, to many of us at least. Besides, there was a certain pride in being a Communist. I still remember from those times two lines from the poet C. Day Lewis. A question and an answer, they went something like this:

> Why do we on seeing a Red feel small?
> For he is future walking to meet us—

Fifty years later, badly buffeted, some of this pride yet remains. Incidentally, this is also how I came to Marxism—beginning with whatever Marxism was then available with the Comintern and permitted or possible in our country under the British rule.

Followed years of hectic activity in the students' movement and in the underground with the Communist Party, including entire vacations spent with workers in factories away from Lahore or with peasants in their villages.

We were good students, among the best in the University. I

duly qualified for admission to the Medical College. But it was clear that the demands of ever-increasing political work would be impossible to reconcile with those of a study in medicine. I decided to shift to a 'soft' discipline. I was advised that Political Science was, possibly, the easiest subject to get your master's degree in. That, perhaps, is one reason why I could never take it seriously. Later I was to discover that it is also, possibly, the poorest among the social sciences. And if I may suggest, one important reason for its poverty as a social scientific enterprise is its near-universal ignorance of or hostility towards Marxism as social science; though, in recent years, it has not been averse to recognising Marxism as 'political thought'.

Be that as it may, in a couple of years even the pursuit of Political Science had to be given up for full-time work with the Communist Party—on the party wage of, I think, rupees twenty or twenty-five per month. For most of the next five years and more, till after the Partition, I moved around the villages and towns of Punjab, organising people and persuading them to move through their struggle for freedom towards a social revolution in this country, which I believe still needs to be made.

Soon enough I landed in prison, charged with opposition to 'the war effort' of the British Government in India. (Incidentally, it was 'the people's war' period!) Released, after nearly a year's imprisonment, I was for some time put under the usual restrictions on movement, meetings, etc. I filled up the time with a stint on the editorial staff of the Party's Punjabi weekly, *Jang-i-Azadi*. I also started work on a biography of the still active legendary revolutionary, Baba Gurmukh Singh, a fragment of which was later published as *Ghadar Heroes: A Forgotten Story of the Punjab Revolutionaries of 1914-1915* (1945). My professor at the University—he was none other than Dr. J.N. Khosla—who was rather fond of me, insisted that I use this opportunity to at least finish my studies. The Party gave me the required leave for a couple of months, and my professor provided me with the necessary certificate of attendance at classes—which partly overlapped the period I was in prison! I duly took the examination—and was soon back in the villages.

(The degree, a first-class-first, was to come in very handy later in my life, at Delhi.)

Came the great popular struggles, the near-revolutionary upsurge of the mid-1940s, the haggling and compromising presided over by Imperialism, the consequent riots, the Partition, and more riots—and Indian independence. A faith had been kept *and* betrayed. Those were glorious yet ignominy-laden years, the years at once of victory and defeat for the Indian people. More specifically, it was the final success, however ambiguous, of a Gandhi and bourgeois-led politics, and a definitive failure, only temporary we thought, of our Communist politics, which included that last adventurist flourish with B.T.R. as well as the heroic struggle in Telengana. One lived, shared and fought through it all—and survived. Some of this experience, intensely personal as well as political and collective, found expression in a small collection of poems in Punjabi—*Rahan Di Dhoor* (1950). In one of these, I recorded:

> A caravan has reached the destination,
> And yet lost its way—

I never wrote poetry again—don't ask me why. Only very recently I have learnt that early in 1951 itself, a distinguished critic had, in a review, hailed my book as a truly significant piece of work. A contemporary scholar even considers it to be the best poetry of that period, though, as he told me, he had difficulty in locating its author!

It would appear that, as in scholarship, so in poetry, and may be in much else besides, I am a genuine 'might have been'.

I came to Delhi sometime after the Partition, having lived with death the previous few months and on the way. Uprooted, a refugee, everything around me, including my politics in a shambles, I sought a new foothold in life—only temporarily, I had then thought, mistakenly. I started teaching at what was then known as Camp College, an institution set up by the Punjab University at Delhi for refugee students and teachers. Even as I began to enjoy my new vocation, the Party, passing through a series of crises, both internal and èxternal, finally opted for 'peaceful', 'parliamentary' ways. And so it came to pass, with other tangible and not-so-tangible factors contributing, that, over a period of time—during which I still edited from Delhi its theoretical monthly in Punjabi, *Sada Jug* (till removed, charged with 'individualism' and 'intellectual arrogance' for refusing to publish a BTR criticism of Mao Tse-tung), and translated *Communist Manifesto* and some more Marx into Punjabi—I just opted out of the Party. [Later, soon after its formation, I was to spend a few years in the Communist Party (Marxist)]. For me the comforting rationalisation was that in our society, after 'revolution-making', teaching perhaps holds the maximum possibilities for a non-alienated life. Here, if you want, but only if you *want,* earning your living can be at the same time living your life. So teaching it was to be for me for the rest of my life. Soon I moved from Camp College to Delhi College, where I was to teach for nearly two decades; then, after a brief stint at Jawaharlal Nehru University, in 1972 I joined Delhi University, rather late in life, as Professor of Political Theory.

Thus it is that having spent some of the best years of my life elsewhere, away from the academy, and the rest only teaching, scholarship has simply passed me by. Hence, as I said in the beginning, 'biodata' has been a perennial embarrassment —for I never managed to acquire one as a scholar. I have no research degrees and no publications except some odd entirely casual exercises, including the book, *Reason, Revolution and Political Theory,* which was an ad hoc response to a provocation in the classroom when my students wanted me to explain and defend an observation I had made. I have had no string of scholars working 'under' me, no fellowships, no research projects, no study or other academic leaves, no 'seminaring', national or international, nothing—not even a visit abroad that has come to certify any sort of achievement or standing as a scholar these days!

Recently, the Indian Council of Social Science Research, perhaps wanting to be helpful, more than once extended me invitations involving 'a foreign visit' each time. Having somehow missed or evaded every such opportunity or activity in the past, I thought, I would make a virtue of it—and declined. Besides, it seemed a bit too late in life for me to now get started on this. Perhaps I also wanted to make certain that there is at least one professor in this country who has not been abroad!

Incidentally, the Council have also very generously offered me a National Fellowship which I have accepted. So I may yet end up as a scholar, though, I am not too sure. For the subject on which I have chosen to write a brief monograph is rather away from what have been my major concerns as a teacher—Western Political Thought, Contemporary Political Theory, Marxism. My subject is so obviously *political*, not 'scholarly'; I seek an understanding of Indian politics which may, it is hoped, help towards 'a more effective people's intervention in what is happening in our country'. What is more, contrary to the current fashions in the world of Marxian scholarship, where 'orthodoxy' is almost a dirty word, and a comfortable and comforting 'post-Marxism' is abroad, I visualise my work as an exercise in Marxist orthodoxy!

If I have, most of the time, done none of the things that scholars are normally supposed to do, I have been, most of the time, busy with what they are normally supposed to keep away from. Which is as well, for life has been such fun this way. I have thus functioned, in the profession and in the university, more as a militant on the Left—even when revising the syllabi in Political Science whenever or wherever I got the opportunity to do so, or putting in a rather noisy plea on behalf of Political Theory in general and Marxism in particular on the campuses of Indian universities. As a militant, the aim was always *hegemony* and not factional or mere economic or organisational gains.

Over the years, teaching and related work apart, I have, along with many others of course, spent a great deal of time helping build up the teachers' movement, fighting for democratic rights and reforms in the university (with the vice-chancellors and against them), carrying on socialist education among workers, students and teachers, including school-teachers, running Marx Clubs and putting together Socialist Groups (one such effort, incidentally, went into the making of the Communist Party (Marxist) on Delhi University campus), writing and publishing pamphlets and bulletins, editing and producing, distributing or circulating journals like *Enquiry*,

Socialist Digest, The Marxist Review, Monthly Review, Science and Society and *New Left Review*, campaigning on issues like Vietnam and Czechoslovakia, collecting signatures for Iranian students and others, mobilising and marching for all sorts of popular causes, associating with almost any radical initiative on the campus and every revolutionary venture off it, an association which on occasions, quite understandably, even ended in a love–hate relationship, —and so on. That is how it has been for the most part over nearly forty long years.

But if scholarship has passed me by, I have not done too badly as a teacher. At least that is what my students, colleagues, and many others tell me. And I am inclined to believe them; maybe because I very much want to. I have taught in the departments of History, Political Science, and occasionally Philosophy. Students have come to my classes from other disciplines and other universities, from Economics and Sociology, Law and Literature, Mathematics, even Chemistry and Physics. (Perhaps Commerce and Business Management alone have been missing!) And they have given me abundantly of their love and affection, and thoughtful appreciation. This has been compensation enough for whatever I may have missed out on not being a scholar. It was compensation enough especially during periods of bitter conflict and controversy which, inevitably, have been a persistent feature of my long career as a teacher. It is the students who first spoke of 'a legend in Delhi University'. And it is, above all, to them that I trace the real source of an observation Bertell Ollman has made, though it is also expressive of his own characteristic generosity. After his recent visit to Delhi and Jawaharlal Nehru Universities, he writes: 'If I wasn't already over 50, I would probably say something like: when I grow up I want to be a Professor like Randhir Singh.' Yes, teaching has been compensation enough.

At one of the farewell meetings at Delhi University, they questioned me on the subject of my teaching. I responded that, given the 'functional rationality' governing the organised structures of teaching and research, so that scholarly writing is increasingly addressed not to problems or publics but to peers and to prestige and preferment in the needlessly bureaucratised academic professions, and given the growing, and often mindless, specialisation in the social sciences (including Political Science) which is resulting in a situation where fewer and fewer people are hearing more and more about less and less—given all this, a certain lack of conventional academic scholarship can even be an advantage in that it may help one see the social reality as a whole, see the wood and not just the trees, and thus address, as teacher or scholar (or activist), the real problems of society.

Incidentally, I also told them, my students and colleagues, that, for one speaking up for Marxism, my knowledge of Economics is shockingly poor and that I have always regretted it. But this lack, perhaps, has made me that much more sensitive to the humanist, philosophical, and above all political dimensions of Marxism. Of course, I added that 'politics as revolution' is central to Marxism, at least to Marxism as Karl Marx practised it. 'Marx was before all else a revolutionist', as Engels put it.

These are, however, somewhat peripheral considerations. I had gone on to suggest that its strictly academic aspects apart, my teaching could be viewed as a form of 'robinhooding' which, even as it functions within the system, yet seeks to stretch it to its limits. Of course, this 'robinhooding', this functioning as a radical or a Marxist inside the classroom, has its problems and its risks too. The most important problem is that it needs to have a certain quality about it which, above all, demands a genuine and acknowledged familiarity with the mainstream scholarship in the concerned field or discipline, one's reservations about it notwithstanding. Lacking this, it can easily degenerate into vulgar propaganda or empty moral rhetoric. As a student coming from the discipline of English literature, in a complementary reference, once said: 'One needs to have that rare combination of idealism and intelligence.' As for the risks, the most important ones concern the security of job and the denial of promotion. I must admit that I have been rather lucky in this regard. It is true that whenever interviewed, the selection committees invariably turned me down. Yet appointments came, by invitation, including the professorship in 1972, when, incidentally, seeing everyone making a beeline for Jawaharlal Nehru University, I chose instead to opt for the University of Delhi.

'Robinhooding' has its minor risks also. For me it has meant another continuous struggle from the day I started teaching. At the very outset they asked for an undertaking 'not to teach subversion'. Later, they stopped you, again and again, from teaching, or teaching a particular course. For long years, they would let me teach only Plato and not Marx—so that you learn to teach Marx via Plato, which is not only possible but is in some ways far more effective also, for obvious reasons. They can organise harassment and humiliation for you in diverse ways, with the lumpen elements in the academic community thrown in.... One has struggled against all this and *them* all along, and with a reasonable measure of success. My only regret is for the students and teachers who, now and then, had to suffer for their association with me.

There are problems and there are risks. And for better credibility here one must learn to say 'no' to at least some of the innumerable benefits, the cooptive attractions the system has to offer even to a radical teacher, though this 'no' is only of symbolic value. But the most important thing is to be aware of the limitations, even ambiguities, inherent in the very nature of 'robinhooding' as an academic exercise. And for this reason one needs to be very modest about what one is doing or achieving here.

What is more, in so far as it is an exercise *within* the system, it is always in danger of itself becoming a form of cooption into it. In fact, the more you succeed in what you are doing, the more you are also, in an important sense, lending legitimacy to the system as a whole. Such is the dialectics implicit in this mode or style of teaching. That is why its quality is of decisive importance. Even so, how effective it is in its own modest manner, and how it contributes to any qualitative departures in the system, will be determined by other, larger social forces at work in the historical process in this country. We can only recognise and try to help these in whatever way we can.

I will only add that what goes on within the discipline of

Political Science or its classrooms, or, for that matter, within the universities and the social science institutes of this country, is only of marginal relevance to the problems and prospects of the Indian people's struggle for a better future. But this is where we work—teachers, students, scholars, all others. And it is axiomatic, for most of us, that we make our efforts where we work, or we shall make no effort at all.

Preface to the Original Edition

This is a book which ought to have been published more than a decade back when its argument was first delivered as a series of lectures in memory of my friend and political associate Professor Moin Shakir at Marathwada University, Aurangabad, in February 1991. The writing naturally bears its mark but the delay has taken nothing away from the validity or relevance of my argument.

I had spoken from detailed notes and was supposed to produce a written version of these lectures. Associated with the communist movement for more than half a century, and mindful of Moin Shakir's concerns, I proceeded to write them down as a militant's response to what had happened in the Soviet Union, addressed to fellow militants in the movement and radicals at large. Part of what I wrote was published from time to time in the following years. The opening section was published in 1992 itself – in *Economic and Political Weekly* – entitled 'Crisis of Socialism – Notes in Defence of a Commitment'. This piece of writing, conveying something of my 'journey through communism' since 1939, was much noticed and appreciated at home and abroad and was reproduced and translated in many places, including an Urdu journal in Pakistan. Victor G. Kiernan, the distinguished historian, called it a 'splendid article'. Paul Sweezy and Harry Magdoff were equally appreciative. Sweezy noticed its appeal for readers of *Monthly Review* – 'many of whom (perhaps too many!) have been through similar experiences in their own lives' – and wrote to me: 'I read the piece with great interest and found it both eloquent and moving. Different as our experiences have been during the last half century, there is still much we have in common in reacting to the collapse of the revolutionary experiment in which and for which we had such high hopes'. This article soon came to be viewed as a document of the times. I have included it here as a *Prologue* to the book.

I had begun writing this draft but could not, or did not, complete it for reasons as diverse as my diffidence or lack of discipline when it comes to writing things down, more pressing or welcome academic engagements or political work, bouts of personal ill-health and, not the least, the hassles and harassments of ordinary middle class existence in the corrupt, communalised and mafiaised polity that much of India is today. The most important reason, however, was my awareness that scholars far more competent than me were writing on the subject, making it unnecessary for me to carry out the essentially secondary exercise of putting on paper what I had said at Aurangabad. And I was not wrong. We have since, for example, Istvan Meszaros' magisterial *Beyond Capital – Towards a Theory of Transition*, which has been rightly assessed as 'the definitive Marxian synthesis for the present moment, the phase of what Meszaros calls capital's *structural crisis*'. I have myself found it most useful for my argument in several places while completing these notes.

I however kept speaking on the subject or its sub-themes, discussing them with radical groups, at universities and other formal and informal gatherings; and pressure kept mounting, as much from the old-generation friends of socialism as from the new crop of young activists, that I put down my argument, such as it is, in writing. A National Fellowship at the Institute of Advanced Study, Shimla, finally persuaded me to take the plunge. But for this fellowship I would have made no progress at all with the completion of these notes. But the unexplained termination of this fellowship proved equally disruptive and delayed the completion of even this first draft by a few years. The writing is therefore obviously flawed in many ways. It bears the mark of being written, or completed, in bits, over a long period of time. That its sub-themes were the subject of separate treatment or lectures at different times or places has also contributed to uneven writing and to repetition in parts of the book. The format of Notes, with its need to provide the context of and complete the specific point being made has also added to the problem of repetition. I had expected my student and friend Arvind N. Das to take care of all this, edit and put this draft in proper shape for publication. But his premature death ruled this out. I thought of doing the needful myself, but somehow this has not been possible. In the meantime, the publication of some parts in the weekly *Mainstream* had created a constituency for what I have to say. The desirability of a better organised, more rigorously argued, and linguistically felicitous book notwithstanding, there was a growing demand that these notes be published, as they are – in their present rough form, even without references or footnotes – without any further delay. S. Balwant at the Ajanta Books International having agreed to do so, I, for myself, can only seek reader's indulgence, ask her or him to bear with the many inadequacies of this publication. What is important or really matters is its basic argument.

Occasional use of my earlier writings, particularly *Reason, Revolution and Political Theory* apart, these notes are based on my necessarily limited reading, rather what I remembered of it. I have borrowed freely from other scholars, taken their analyses as my own, used their arguments, at times in their own words, and not hesitated to quote them at length for the simple reason that they had expressed the idea or the argument better than I could have done. My debts are far too many to be acknowledged. Those familiar with the literature will easily recognise them. For me it is enough to rationalise it all by saying that these are scholars who are, so to speak, more or less on my side of the barricades.

There is one debt, however, which I would still like to explicitly acknowledge – to *Monthly Review*. It is the journal I have felt most comfortable with, intellectually and politically, over the past 50 odd years, and my debt here is writ large over several important parts of this book. For Marxist theory and sustained revolutionary commitment, there has been indeed nothing else like *Monthly Review*. Its authentic Marxist analysis of developments across the globe, easily accessible yet sophisticated in the best sense of the word, its unwavering commitment to the cause of socialism and principled support to revolutionary struggles everywhere, have educated, encouraged and inspired socialists and radicals throughout the world. Paul Sweezy and Harry Magdoff have been a constant source of enlightenment and inspiration. For me personally, Paul Sweezy was and remains a model of what a Marxist intellectual should be in our times. In recent years I have much benefited from the wide-ranging work of Ellen Meiksins Wood and John Bellamy Foster's writings in the field of ecology.

The original impulse for this writing lay in my long-time interest in understanding why and how things had gone wrong with socialism in the Soviet Union. As the crisis in Soviet society deepened in the 1980s, the subject became a matter of still more serious concern. Sometime before 'the earthquake of 1989', in my Preface to Bertell Ollman's Indian publication, *Marxism: A Uncommon Introduction*, referring to Macpherson's view that 'the utility of Marxism as a means of understanding the world is increasing over time', I had added: '"the world" includes.... not only the advanced capitalist countries or India and the so-called Third World, but the world of "actually existing socialism" also, with its troublous past, continuing problems and the truly historical predicament today'. The predicament soon ended in the ignominious collapse of Soviet socialism and then of the Soviet Union itself. But no viable Marxist explanation of what had happened was forthcoming from within the country's communist movement – a situation that still persists; even the later, more informed or updated 'official' efforts are a string of eclectic propositions: 'serious mistakes'; 'wrong notions of the role of the Party and the state'; 'the failure to effect timely changes in the economy and its management'; the failure to 'deepen socialist democracy'; 'the erosion of ideological consciousness'; etc. In this situation, as the enemies' explanation – 'socialism has failed', 'Marxism is dead', etc. – held sway, there was a demand on me to share my understanding of what had happened. The opportunity to put my ideas together for the purpose came in the form of the invitation to deliver the Moin Shakir Memorial Lectures at the Marathwada University. As originally written or rather loosely expanded or updated in many places, these lectures – my 1991 response to the interrelated set of issues involved in the collapse of the Soviet Union – constitute the core of these notes, now being published as a book.

This response is obviously not an academic exercise, a work of scholarship or historical research, and it makes no claims, absolutely none, to originality. As the sub-title indicates, my response has a strong personal dimension to it. But this does not make it merely a declaration of faith. On the contrary, what is presented here is a serious argument in behalf of the continuing validity and relevance of socialism as a historically necessary, superior-to-capitalism, social order, and the need for the common people everywhere to struggle for it. Even as each chapter stands by itself, different chapters well hold together in support of this argument. The text apart, evidence in support of my argument is there, scattered all around us, only if we are willing to see; a little reason and ability to interconnect is all that is needed.

Not an academic exercise, these are notes of a militant in the movement, 'a small "C" communist', to borrow that most helpful self-description from E.P. Thompson. And the argument is addressed to fellow militants in what is left of the communist movement, to 'social democrats' who still remain socialist, to the new crop of radicals, in the social movements or outside them, struggling to find their bearings in a world now almost universally dominated by capitalism, and to all those on the Left who share my concern with the present and future of socialism. Even others may find it of interest for their present and future too is now involved in the present and future of socialism in a way that was never the case before. If anything, these notes are an exercise in theory, a plea to parties and activists on the Left for a return to the basics. Theory, it may be added, does not directly yield a political programme which is the task of political parties or activists on the ground. But it serves to provide a basic understanding of things, a perspective or sense of direction, most necessary for the success of any popular struggle. A struggling people will not get very far without some substantial knowledge of the structures they need to overthrow for their emancipation and a sense of direction in their struggle.

[The format of Notes has enabled me to deal with a wide range of issues in this regard, many of them raised with me by the concerned activists or friends on the Left. (The chapter on Marxism, for example, in its overall thrust and detail, is very much a response to an express request from two such friends, most eminent in the fields of literature and people's theatre in Punjab). The way the original lectures were planned and delivered, there is little direct reference to India, but relevance to India is more than implicit in the argument throughout these notes. The language (English), I know, is a handicap in reaching out to a larger readership, especially at the level of activists on the ground. I hope translation will help out as has already happened with some already published parts of these Notes.]

I have already regretted the repetition that marks these Notes and offered an explanation, not justification, for it; though even a justification is not to be entirely ruled out. Gunter Grass has said: 'In politics you have to repeat and repeat, like a parrot, ideas you know to be correct and proven as such, which is exhausting – you constantly hear the echo of your own voice, and end up sounding like a parrot even to yourself. But this is evidently part of the job, if one is to find any listeners at all in a world so full of different voices', or, I may add, when the noisy voice of those currently dominant in society seeks to drown all other voices and wants us to forget what was said earlier and has been proved to be true, or forbids what needs to be said or repeated anew today.

If my experience with the sophisticates of the academy or bourgeois ideology, or plain anti-socialist propagandists, is any guide, 'crudeness and simplification' is a charge sure to be brought against my argument. I will not here argue or complain over it, but borrow from Marcuse to suggest that, at times, crudeness and simplification also help to make the truth of an idea more visible. And truth of the socialist idea is my main concern in these Notes.

During the heady, rebel days in the late sixties, students of Paris used to ask of everyone who would address them to first tell them: 'where do you speak from?' For every speaker, and for that matter every writer, inescapably speaks or writes from a particular philosophical-political standpoint and owes it to his audience or readers to publicly state it. It is only fair to acknowledge that I have written from the standpoint of Marxism, rather Marxism as I understand it. For I have no pretensions to scholarship in Marxism. I picked up some on the way and have found it useful not only in my politics or profession as a teacher but in living my life as well. This last is not just a formal statement. Knowing Marx does make a difference to what sense you make of life, how you understand, live and act in the world. 'Indeed, I must confess that Karl Marx made a man of me', is how George Bernard Shaw once put it. Marx, therefore, is important to me and, I believe, he is important to all of us, today more so than ever before, if for no other reason than this: the world we are living in is a capitalist world, more capitalist than ever before after the Soviet collapse, and Marx more than any other human being, then or now, devoted his life to explaining the reality of this world and his achievement here remains unrivalled. In one sense, this is what this book is about.

I know that the way I have been speaking or writing about Marx, about capitalism, socialism, and such other things, in recent years, not a few have thought of me as someone woefully out of sync with our post-modern, neo-liberal or globalised times, a 'dinosaur', as it were, from another age. Many will think the same of this book and will be similarly dismissive about its argument. This is nothing to be surprised at or complain about, only something that even the best among us have to endure. Paul Sweezy and Harry Magdoff had the distinction of being referred to as 'paleolithic sectarian survivals' in the aftermath of the Soviet collapse because they continued to argue and speak up for socialism. Recently we have had the example of the Nobel

Laureate Gunter Grass and the world famous sociologist Pierre Bourdieu. Holding that neoliberalism is 'simply a return to the methods of nineteenth-century Manchester liberalism', 'a strange revolution that restores the past but presents itself as progressive, transforming regression itself into a form of progress', they have said: 'It does this so well that those who oppose it are made to appear regressive themselves. This is something we have both endured: we are readily treated as old-fashioned, "has-beens", "throwbacks"..."dinosaurs".' Grass and Bourdieu have nevertheless insisted that one must continue to speak up.

So have Paul Sweezy and Harry Magdoff, all along. Some years back, apropos post-Soviet capitalist triumphalism, they had written: 'Capitalism's victory settles nothing. In its global form, it encompasses ever more people and intensifies their exploitation and oppression. History shows that there have been alternatives in the past, and reason tells us that there will be others in the future.... It is of the greatest importance to keep the radical tradition alive and vigorous, ready to undergrid and give direction to the revolutionary struggles that lie ahead'. This is how I too had conceived this writing in 1991. Since then, the euphoria over 'capitalism's victory' long over, the struggles that lay ahead are already on the agenda of the peoples everywhere. This is where I locate whatever relevance this book has.

I would like to thank the Institute for Development and Communication, Chandigarh and its Director Dr. Pramod Kumar, for providing the facilities to complete and put together the manuscript of this book and getting the book itself into shape for the printer and publisher at Delhi. I can never be too thankful to Ashwini Kumar for the hard work he personally put into all this. I am grateful to my wife, Mohinder Kaur, for bearing with me as I struggled with this writing in Delhi, Shimla and Chandigarh. Not exactly thanks but something more is due to Priyaleen, Shimareet, Meenakshi Gopinath and Bertell Ollman who, each in her or his own way, sustained me in writing these notes. The responsibility for the argument, of course, remains mine.

Randhir Singh

March 2004

1

The Single Most Important Right Lesson: Democracy

What has happened in the former Soviet Union does not in any way invalidate Marx's argument for the necessity and possibility of a socialist negation of capitalist social order. Only the struggle for socialism is turning out to be far more complex and difficult than he ever visualised. Not prepared to build, the Soviet communists and people yet sought to build socialism. They have failed. This failure demands of socialists that they be self-critical and draw the necessary lessons from the Soviet experience. Here issues of theory are of course central, and we have discussed them. But beyond them, it needs to be recognised that while questions of economy, of what should be done or, at the very least, what should *not* be done in matters of planning and organisation of economic life remain important, the failure in Eastern Europe and Soviet Union occurred essentially on the political terrain, as a consequence of the politics practised in these societies over a very long period. Insofar as it is politics that commands economy under socialism, even the economic failure, whatever its autonomous causation, cannot be dissociated from the politics that ultimately governed it. Therefore, it is here, in the realm of politics, that the more basic lessons of Soviet experience lie. More specifically, the most decisive of these lessons concerns the issue of democracy in a socialist transition. Whatever their economic and social achievements or failures, the greatest failure of the societies of 'actually existing socialism' was in the area of building socialist democracy, a self-governing society of the associated producers and reproducers that socialism postulates. Instead, though born of socialist revolutions, they became each a grossly undemocratic system whose authoritarian politics bred extraordinary corruption of power at the top and became a decisive factor in the ultimate collapse of the system itself. If, issues of theory apart, we were looking for *the single most important right lesson* to be drawn from the Soviet experience it can be legitimately located in relation to democracy, which 'Soviet socialism' signally failed to practise, even though it is enjoined by classical Marxism as absolutely integral to a socialist transition anywhere. It is indeed so integral to socialism as a value and as a necessity that one can say: socialism will be democratic or it will not exist.

II

Even as we take note of Soviet or East European failure on the terrain of democracy, it is important to reject simple caricatures. It needs to be noted, though it is very unfashionable at the present time, that the men and women who led the socialist revolutions and took power in these societies were not unprincipled careerists or adventurers, and thus naturally given to authoritarian exercise of power. They were gifted and sincere people, moved by the highest of human ideals and values, and had long fought against the authoritarian and oppressive regimes in their own countries, in Czarist Russia or Fascist Europe, spending years in prison, concentration camps or exile, staking their very lives in pursuit of their ideals. And they had taken power with the determination to build what they believed to be socialism as classically understood, to ensure a better life for their long-suffering peoples. These revolutions not only brought large masses of people into political life as actors in history, in some cases at least also pioneered political forms which demystified things and allowed for direct popular participation, leadership and control in the governance of society, for grass roots democracy of a kind much deeper than bourgeois democracy. In the initial years these forms were most certainly not devoid of real content or effectiveness. In the Soviet Union 'democracy of the Soviets' flowered as part of the revolutionary process in the immediate post-October period, and elements of political pluralism and workers' democracy continued to exist during the years 1918–1923. But the compulsions of historical circumstances of these years – backwardness, threat of counter-revolution and civil war, famine, foreign intervention, etc. – combined with certain theoretical limitations of Bolshevism itself, some of them carried over from classical Marxism – its elements of contradictions or ambiguity, 'silences' or 'empty spaces' – led to a precipitous decline of this early revolutionary democracy, giving way to the adoption of authoritarian measures. Even where old forms persisted or new ones were put in place constitutionally, they lacked content. Even when the 'force of circumstance', which had compelled the initial departure from the democratic principle inherent in socialism, relatively eased, there was no returning to the principle, the construction or reconstruction of a viable socialist democracy. Instead, the departure itself became the principle, and was even rationalised as what it most definitely was not, a 'dictatorship of the proletariat'. A bureaucratic malignancy arose which spread throughout the state apparatus and in due course undermined and then destroyed the Bolshevik Party itself. The upshot of it all was an authoritarian, bureaucratic political system which did not admit of any checks at the top and dispensed with all critical debate and accountability. A gross caricature of socialist democracy it claimed to be, it was really the monopoly of power by the *nomenklatura*. The utterly undemocratic character of this system, first established in the Soviet Union in the late 1920s and 1930s and imposed on Eastern Europe after the second world war, was one of the most crucial reasons for the grossly distorted socialism that came to be built in these countries and for its ultimate collapse.

III

This is not to suggest that democracy, *by itself*, could be the solution to all or most problems of socialism as it was built under

Stalin or maintained by his heirs till it collapsed. ('Democratisation' in the former 'socialist' regimes, in Eastern Europe or Russia, it is evident, has neither solved their problems, nor even remotely yielded any real advance over the past. Rather, there has been grave regression in most spheres of life). The former 'socialist' regimes indeed faced serious problems and these problems had their own autonomous reality and compulsions. What is being suggested is that as against the *instrumental* nature of such issues as the place of market in a transitional socialist society, etc., democracy is an issue of *foundational* nature in the construction of socialism, which involves not only the abolition of class-dichotomy between the owners and the dispossessed but also the ensuring of political equality and shared freedoms for the people as a whole. This, the overarching importance of democracy is evident in the fact that it was basically political mismanagement which led to mismanagement of economy as of social life in general in the societies of 'actually existing socialism'. In the absence of democracy, necessary correctives to bad planning and mismanagement of social and economic life were simply not forthcoming. Lack of democracy not only made for personal corruption; it also fostered gigantic errors of policy, harebrained adventurism, productivist megalomania, environmental vandalism, just as it sanctioned purges and political repression, which no one in a position of responsibility dared oppose. Again, it was not simply a matter of authorities suppressing discussion or bypassing the legal or formal democratic structures. The denial of democracy, of individual rights and political freedoms themselves intersect in complex ways with the economy and social life. Democratic participation requires such things as providing people with the requisite time and information to participate, encouragement to critical and independent thinking, a constant ideological struggle to root out the long inherited attitudes and beliefs including deference to authority, dependence on outstanding leaders, timidities and 'under reaching' that are built into the socialisation of people in class societies – all of which by and large came to be neglected in the former 'socialist' societies. Marx-enjoined transformation of people through revolutionary practice, that is their active participation in the revolutionary transformation of their societies, simply failed to take place, resulting in people's lack of self-confidence, a loss of their creativity. There is certainly a link between the denial of democracy and the political and cultural inertia which came to characterise these societies after the efflorescence of early years. Conformism and stupor of so much of their official culture, including official Marxism, was no doubt an important contributory factor in the degeneration and final collapse of their established social systems. Indeed, it can be argued that it was precisely the denial of democracy over a very long period, the prolonged powerlessness of the people and the consequent apathy, indifference and alienation among them, which made it possible for the rulers in these societies (or for that matter in China now) to take the capitalist road so easily without any immediately significant resistance by the people in defence of the gains of their socialist revolutions.

What this means, rather obviously, is that the process of building a socialist society will be deformed, perverted, and ultimately blighted out of existence, if it is pursued outside a reasonably democratic context. In her early critique of Bolshevik departure from democratic principles, Rosa Luxemburg had rightly argued that under a dictatorship, without multiple parties, freedom of the press, speech and association, workers could never learn how to become a ruling class, and that in the absence of political freedom there is no way to generate the 'thousand solutions' that need to be discovered in face of the 'thousand problems' that a transition to socialism inevitably entails. As has been well put: 'The failure of communism was not only due to the strength of global capitalism. It was also due to the Communist Parties' and regimes' lack of understanding that democratic rights alone provide socialism with the political air it needs to breathe.'

IV

Its economic and social achievements notwithstanding, the failure of 'actually existing socialism' in the area of democracy, its repressive undemocratic character, not only proved disastrous for it, it has also grievously harmed the image and cause of socialism everywhere, in the west where capitalist democracy for all its crippling limitations has been not only immeasurably less oppressive and far more democratic than former 'socialist' regimes but also beneficial to the people in many ways, and in the third world where fight for democracy and its defence are today integral to peoples' struggle for economic and social liberation.

In the last century socialism and democracy were invariably seen to be positively interlinked. Today the link is tenuous, almost no more, in large part because of the Soviet experience. This experience – its lack of political freedoms and gross abuse of power, its Terror and Gulag and lawless destruction of millions of lives (including those of communists), its official 'truth' and official lies, and the travesty of every democratic notion – has left the democratic credential of socialism badly damaged. In the popular perception, socialism and democracy have become dissociated. Even for well-meaning people socialism has come to be linked with the ideas of a strong, not to say all-powerful, state and with centralised regulation of all aspects of social life. The undemocratic nature of 'Soviet socialism' has enabled the opponents of socialism, in a hegemonic offensive, not only to argue, ever more effectively, that socialism is inherently authoritarian and oppressive but also to counterpose democracy to socialism and appropriate it for capitalism, even restore capitalism in the name or under cover of democracy. It is significant that the upheavals in Eastern Europe and Soviet Union were guided not by a futuristic vision or by ideals of the past summed up as 'democracy'. 'It was 1789 taking revenge on 1917 in 1989', as a commentator has put it. The 'normal society' sought by those who carried out or supported these upheavals may have meant prosperity of 'free market' and liberal democracy, but in effect democracy came to be identified with the 'free market' so that the 'new democracies' of Eastern Europe, for example, were 'democratic' in proportion to their progress in 'marketisation'. Given this identification, it has become possible to so bypass the issue of capitalism that the question of seeking an alternative to it, of its transcendence in socialism, simply does not arise. In a clever, confusing use of terms, ideologues of capitalism, in the media and the academy, on occasion helped even by some 'progressive' critics of the Soviet system, present the issue as democracy versus socialism. Thus instead of socialism being an alternative to capitalism, democracy itself is frequently put forward as an alternative to socialism – a view that has been superficially strengthened by the return of 'multiparty democratic politics' to Russia and Eastern Europe in conjunction with the drive towards full restoration of capitalism. The ideologues proclaim that in opposing 'communism', they are defending democracy against its enemies on the left, whether those enemies called themselves Communists, socialists, or whatever. The Western campaign in support of democracy becomes an attack on socialism. Perhaps the greatest of all successes which capitalist ideologues and politicians have scored in their struggle for hegemony has been in the appropriation of democracy as their particular cause and concern.

The cynicism of it all is indeed remarkable. At home capitalism, its ideologues and politicians have always fought tooth and nail against all democratic advance; and when forced to retreat, they have invariably striven to narrow as far as possible the meaning and scope of the concessions that had to be made. Abroad, the world over, western capitalism is notorious for its interventions to aid or set up dictatorial regimes – Somoza in Nicaragua, Batista in Cuba, Duvalier in Haiti, Pinochet in Chile, Marcos in the Philippines, Idi Amin in Uganda, Suharto in Indonesia, Ayub Khan in Pakistan, the Korean generals ... the list is endless. In fact Western capitalist powers are, in principle, neither for nor against democracy. Their overriding, all determining interest is maintenance of their capitalist exploitative order at home and an imperialist order abroad that reserves to them the right to exploit all the riches of the planet for their own profit, to the detriment of its other people. If this order can be better served by a 'democracy', they are for it, but they never hesitate to subvert it or support or even install a dictatorship, if this better serves their needs. (Just as they are not, in principle, either for or against peace. If peace does not menace their capitalist or imperialist order, they are for peace. If it does, or their interests demand it, they choose war, as fierce as is necessary).

However cynical their argument, bourgeois ideologues' successful use of democracy against socialism makes it all the more necessary for us to recover and assert democracy's integral link to socialism. Of course, democracy is no *substitute* for socialism. In fact it cannot really come into its own without social equality for which socialism is a prerequisite. But, especially after the Soviet experience, democracy needs to be asserted as a foundational value for socialism. To grow, develop and realise its potentialities socialism has to be democratic in the root sense of the word, that is it must really empower people in the economy and outside. And it is not a matter of socialism being thus democratic in its ultimate outcome. The 'transition' itself has to be similarly democratic. Marx and Engels had, for good theoretical reasons, described this democracy of the transitional period as 'dictatorship of the proletariat' and saw it exemplified by the Paris Commune whose democratic practices remain unrivalled till today. We need to rescue this profoundly democratic concept from its vulgarised interpretation and exercise as a dictatorial form of government.

V

Compulsions of objective historical circumstances were of course there but, as suggested above, the failure of Soviet socialism in the sphere of democracy also points to a certain persistent inadequacy of Marxist theory in the realm of politics as a whole. What we have here is a neglect, non-development or backwardness relative to other areas like economics or history or philosophy. The classical writings are simply silent or extremely perfunctory over major issues of politics and political theory. Even otherwise there has been noticeably limited systematic theorisation of Marxist politics, so that, in a sense, politics could indeed be described as the Achilles heel of Marxism. This is rather remarkable for as a revolutionary doctrine, contrary to conventional understanding, Marxism postulates the primacy of not economics but politics, it puts revolutionary politics at the centre of social practice for our times. And the most distinguished of Marxists have been themselves revolutionaries, highly gifted men and women who were totally immersed in political struggles and who at the same time attached the highest importance to theory as an indispensable part of revolutionary politics – 'without a revolutionary theory, there can be no revolutionary movement', as Lenin has put it. Though remarkable, this theoretical 'absence' is not entirely accidental.

Part of the reason perhaps lies in the exceptionally complex nature of the subject, politics (including politics of capitalism), which, with its additional, historically specific difficulties in different lands, climes or conjunctures is not amenable to law-like tendencies comparable to what Marx discovered in the capitalist economy. There is also the fact that Marx's own work, as we have already suggested, remained very much an 'unfinished project', it had all too many 'empty spaces' and 'silences'. Viewed in terms of practical implications, most important of these, arguably, relate to politics, an ever present 'absence' as it were in his Marxism. Marx's proposed work on *The State* never came to be written and whatever else he wrote or said on politics was for the most part a response to particular historical episodes and specific circumstance, including problems faced by the international working class movement. Often times it was a part of some other work or concern. Therefore so far as theoretical exploration of politics is concerned it was mostly unsystematic and fragmentary. This is true of what are now referred to as Marx's 'Political Writings' (including such classics as *Eighteenth Brumaire of Louis Bonaparte* and *The Civil War in France*). Much the same can be said of Engels' work including his theoretical and practical interventions in the German and European socialist movement after the death of Marx. Full of valuable political insights as the writings and utterances of Marx and Engels are, they did not come to be theorised by them to provide at least an initially necessary basis for a Marxist theory of politics.

Such or similar extraneous considerations apart, reasons for Marxism's relative theoretical neglect of politics or political theory are to be found within Marxism itself, most importantly, as pointed out by Ralph Miliband, in the conceptual status of politics in Marxism.

On the most general plane, Marxism's view of social life rejects the separation between the political, economic, social and cultural parts of the social whole as essentially artificial and imaginary, really an 'ideological' misconception. Thus, for example, there is no such thing as 'economics' free from 'politics'. There is only 'political economy', in which the 'political' element is an ever-present component. This interconnectedness of things, the pervasive and ubiquitous presence of 'the political' in social processes and phenomena tends to rob politics of its specific character and make it less susceptible to particular treatment, save in the purely formal description of processes and institutions which Marxists have precisely wanted to avoid.

Again, at the very beginning of his political life Marx made a distinction between 'political emancipation' and 'human emancipation'. Political emancipation, with its civic rights and political freedoms was always important for Marx. 'Political emancipation is certainly a big step forward' wrote Marx in his essay *On the Jewish Question* (1843), but only as 'the last form of human emancipation *within* the prevailing scheme of things'. 'It is not, to be sure, the last form of universal human emancipation' which, going beyond political freedoms, requires the revolutionary transformation of the economic and social order. For Marx 'the whole content of law and the state lies beyond constitutions' and therefore human emancipation can never be achieved in the political realm alone. Implied is the Marxist insistence that sense could not be made out of political reality without probing beneath political institutions and forms. This insistence has indeed been the great strength of Marxist political analysis and sociology. But, as Ralph Miliband has put it, 'while this in no way requires the conclusion that political forms "within the prevailing scheme of things" are of no great consequence, it produces a tendency to draw just such a conclusion; and the tendency has been very strong within Marxism to devalue or ignore the importance of 'mere' political forms and to make very little of the problems associated with them.'

This tendency was, in its own way, reinforced by an associated aspect of Marxist tradition. Viewing politics as an expression of man's alienation and political power as a matter of class domination or oppression, 'human emancipation', among other things, also came to mean, as it were, the end of politics. In the *Poverty of Philosophy* (1846), Marx wrote that 'the working class, in the course of its development, will substitute for the old civil society an association which will exclude classes and their antagonism, and there will be no more political power properly so-called, since political power is precisely the expression of antagonism in civil society'. More than thirty years later, in his *Anti-Duhring*, writing about the state, Engels said: '... when at last it becomes the real representative of the whole of society, it renders itself unnecessary. As soon as there is no longer any social class to be held in subjection; as soon as class rule, and the individual struggle for existence based upon our present anarchy of production, with the collisions and excesses arising from these, are removed, nothing more remains to be repressed, and a special repressive force, a state, is no longer necessary... State interference in social relations becomes, in one domain after another, superfluous, and then withers away of itself; the government of persons is replaced by the administration of things, and by the conduct of processes of production. The state is not "abolished". It withers away.'

This optimistic view was reaffirmed in the most extreme form in Lenin's *The State and Revolution* – written on the eve of the October Revolution – where we have an extraordinarily complacent view of the ease with which political problems (other than mastering bourgeois resistance) would be resolved in post-revolutionary societies.

We have earlier discussed how, when after the revolution these problems came up in the form of a bureaucratic degeneration that threatened the revolution itself, the Bolsheviks found themselves most ill-equipped to cope with the situation, how Lenin recognised the threat but failed to avert it, and how it all ended up in the denouement of 1991. In the immediate context the significant thing to note is that while Lenin and those around him did take up many theoretical and organisational problems in the years before 1917, from economic analysis and philosophy to the organisation of the party, they never thought it necessary to seriously consider the problems of the exercise of socialist power, the practice of socialist democracy or the 'dictatorship of the proletariat'. Making this point Ralph Miliband has written:

> It is symptomatic that it was only after 1917 that one of the most alert minds among the Bolsheviks, Bukharin, should have become aware of the import of the challenge posed by theories of elite and of bureaucratization which had been posed to Marxists – and left unanswered for a good many years past. Much of the reason for this must be sought in the absence in Marxism of a serious tradition of political inquiry; and in the assumption commonly made by Marxists before 1917 that the socialist revolution would itself – given the kind of overwhelming popular movement it would be – resolve the main political problems presented to it. *The State and Revolution* was the ultimate expression of that belief.
>
> There did occur very extensive and passionate discussion of all such problems after the Russian Revolution, in Russia and in the socialist movements of many other countries; and this would undoubtedly have produced in time a strong Marxist tradition of political thought. But the debates were overtaken by Stalinist 'triumphalism' from the mid-twenties onwards; and this required agreement that the main *political* problems of socialist power had been solved in the Soviet Union, except for the problem presented by the enemies of socialism. To suggest otherwise was to cast doubt on the socialist and proletarian character of Soviet rule, and thus to turn automatically into one of the very enemies of the Soviet Union and socialism. The impact of such modes of thought on the history of Marxism in subsequent years cannot be overestimated.

An important reason – 'more particular and direct' Miliband has called it – for the Marxist neglect of political theory has to do with the concept of 'base' and 'superstructure', or rather with the implications which have tended to be drawn from this metaphorically formulated concept which, variously interpreted or misinterpreted, touches upon some fundamental issues in Marxism. We have discussed this concept in other contexts but the issues involved – including the status of the political element in Marxism – are important enough to give it a quick-look over again. Here two crucially important, and often quoted, references in Marx are the famous passage from his 'Preface' to *A Contribution to the Critique of Political Economy* which goes as follows: 'In the social production of their life, men enter into definite relations that are indispensable and independent of their will, relations of production which correspond to a definite stage of development of their material productive forces. The sum total of these relations of production constitutes the economic structure of society, the real foundation on which rises a legal and political superstructure and to which correspond definite forms of social consciousness. The mode of production of material life conditions the social, political and intellectual life process in general. It is not the consciousness of men that determines their being, but, on the contrary, their social being that determines their consciousness'; and the equally important formulation in the third volume of *Capital*, which reads: 'the specific economic form, in which unpaid surplus-labour is pumped out of direct producers, determines the relationship of rulers and ruled, as it grows directly out of production itself and, in turn, reacts upon it as a determining element... it is always the direct relationship of the owners of the conditions of production to the direct producers – a relation always naturally corresponding to a definite stage in the development of the methods of labour and thereby its social productivity – which reveals the innermost secret, the hidden basis of the entire social structure, and with it the political form of the relation of sovereignty and dependence, in short, the corresponding specific form of the state.'

Miliband has commented: 'Clearly, these texts can easily be interpreted as turning politics into a very "determined" and "conditioned" activity indeed – so "determined" and "conditioned", in fact, as to give politics a mostly derivative, subsidiary, and "epiphenomenal" character. At its extreme, this turns Marxism into an "economic determinism" which deprives politics of any substantial degree of autonomy.'

But, as we have pointed out earlier, and Miliband goes on to underline, Marx and Engels explicitly rejected any rigid and mechanistic notion of 'determination' and Engels specifically repudiated the idea that Marx and he had ever intended to suggest that 'the economic element is the only determining one', which he described as a 'meaningless, abstract, senseless phrase', though he admitted that 'Marx and I are ourselves partly to blame for the fact that the younger people sometimes lay more stress on the economic side than is due to it. We had to emphasise the main principle, *vis-à-vis* our adversaries, who denied it, and we had not always the time, the place or the opportunity to allow the other elements involved in the interaction to come into their rights.' Again, for Marx, the 'determination by the economic', if we must use this phrase, is never unique. It is essentially a *correspondence* and, therefore, variable. For example, speaking of 'the political form of the relation of sovereignty and dependence', that is, 'the specific form of the state', Marx wrote: '... due to innumerable different empirical circumstances, natural conditions, relationship among races (tribes, & c.), historical influences, etc., the same economic basis – same in terms of the main conditions – can show endless variations and gradations in the phenomenon, which can be made out only by analysis of these empirically given circumstances.'

What is really involved in this issue – of 'economic determination' – is the dialectics of science and revolution in Marx. As science, Marxism's insistence on the 'primacy' of the 'economic base' – the 'main principle' as Engels called it – cannot be understated. Without its emphasis on the special role of the economy in the shaping of social and political relations, Marxism would be theoretically indistinguishable from any other 'sociology'. As a revolutionary doctrine Marxism accords primacy to politics. Engels indeed wrote of 'the economic' as decisive or determining 'in the last instance'. But given the fact that Marxism's socialist project postulates a transformation of the 'economic base' by revolutionary politics, it is more apposite and meaningful to treat the 'economic base' as a starting point, that is, as a matter of the first instance. For Marxism, within the necessities and constraints of a given objective, economic-structural situation, that is, a 'determination by the economy in the *first* instance', whatever happens, including a revolutionary transformation of the economic base or structure itself, is *ultimately* determined by the activity of human beings in pursuit of their ends.

Marxism is no 'determinism', economic or any other. In the immediate context, however, there is no denying that the entirely legitimate emphasis which Marxists have placed on the importance of the 'economic base' and the 'mode of production' has also been the cause of a persistent 'economism' in Marxist thought and social analysis, and this has involved a related neglect of the importance of the 'superstructural' sphere, and therefore of politics and political theory.

VI

There are reasons within classical Marxism which tended to relegate questions of politics and political power to a secondary role. But some of the reasons also lie in the subsequent historical development of Marxism, of the movements and parties inspired by it or the regimes built in its name.

The unavoidable concern of mature Marx with what he called 'Economics', and its high visibility in his published work, together with the achievement it embodied, had its own consequence in reinforcing the tendency to 'economism' in Marxism, which was, it must be noted, a very minor element in Marx's theoretical work as a whole, and never figured in his lifelong revolutionary practice. But a far more potent factor here was the turn to reformism in the European socialist movement. Though specifically disowned by Marx – 'all I know is that I am not a "Marxist"' – an easy economistic view of Marxism took over. The Second International put its stamp of authority on a scientistic economic-determinist Marxism which pushed politics, revolutionary praxis, completely into the background. Kautsky, for example, saw socialism made 'something inevitable' by 'irresistible... natural necessity'. Lenin broke away from this Marxism, put revolutionary politics firmly back on the agenda of contemporary socialist movement. But even as he repeatedly affirmed the integral linkage between socialism and democracy and proclaimed 'all power to the Soviets', the problems of democratic exercise of political power in post-revolutionary society remained unaddressed. He recognised these problems in the malignant growth of bureaucracy in the Soviet state and even warned that if it was not taken care of 'one day the Russian people will hang us with stinking ropes, and deservedly so'. But in the few years still left to him he could not think beyond the essentially Jacobin solution of the Workers and Peasants Inspectorate. After him, ritual references to Lenin and his legacy notwithstanding, even a recognition of these problems – really the problems of democracy in a socialist transition – disappeared. An economistic dogmatism became the hallmark of Marxism in the Soviet Union, and consequently in the Third International. Logic of backwardness and compulsions of survival in a most hostile capitalist world naturally made for economism in Soviet thought and practice. A mechanical, rigidly scientistic and determinist interpretation of the base-superstructure metaphor provided the necessary justificatory theory – 'the theory of productive forces' as Mao later called it. The pseudo-scientific fiction of 'laws of socialism' and concern with (not socialist but) 'scientific management of society', each in its own way helped in the evasion of issues relating to alternative politics *within* socialism, issues which should have been the staple of Soviet Union's 'socialist democracy'. 'Socialist democracy' in fact stood reduced to a mere honorific word. As Marxism ossified into a legitimising ideology of the Soviet system, dictatorship in the country was by definition proletarian and centralism in the Party by definition democratic, making it senseless even to formulate demands for proletarianisation of dictatorship or democratisation of centralism. As the world communist movement, via the Third International and afterwards, became subordinated to the requirements of Soviet foreign policy, and the historically specific Russian experience, before and after the revolution, universalised as a guide for the Communist parties abroad, the Soviet model of politics was imposed or copied in the communist countries and much lauded by communists elsewhere. But significantly enough, *Marxist* study of its politics remained tabooed in the Soviet Union throughout its seventy odd years of existence. As Academician Vladimir Kudryavtsev has informed us (in 1990), 'Marxist political science (was) not at all considered as a science in our country'. Writing of 'ways of combating bureaucracy' he points out that 'the only national monograph devoted to this subject was published in Moscow in 1906'. The amazing sterility or cretinism of Soviet Marxism on the subject of politics is well expressed in his admission: 'Not a single serious study dealing specifically with the issue was carried out during all the years of Soviet power'. To think that Lenin had died fighting precisely this bureaucracy as the greatest threat to the construction of socialism in the Soviet Union!

Moscow's 'official Marxism' was in fact an important reason why there was no significant development of Marxist political theory even outside the Soviet Union. Miliband has written:

> At least a part of the answer must be sought in the experience of Stalinism and of Stalinism's domination of Marxism over a period of some thirty years and more from the late twenties onwards. The point is not so much that the Stalinist version of Marxism was a dreadfully impoverished affair, though it was certainly that; but that its version of Marxism, and style of approach to it, were accepted, largely because of extraneous political reasons, by the vast majority of people who then called themselves Marxists, not only in Russia but everywhere else as well.
>
> A particular quality of Stalinism, in this realm as in all others was its imperative and binding definition of 'the line' to be followed. This served to decide, in catechismal form, what were the 'fundamentals' of Marxism, or rather of 'Marxism-Leninism' and it also served to specify who was and – even more important – who was not to be regarded as having made a contribution to Marxist thought. Those who were not so regarded constituted a great host – in fact most of the people who have in this century (that is the 20th century) made a serious contribution to the development of Marxism. So they were banned in the Soviet Union and greatly neglected or altogether ignored by most Marxists outside.
>
> Marx and Engels were not banned. But they were read very selectively; and probably less than their accredited interpreters, Lenin and Stalin. The accent was on authoritative interpretations and non-arguable propositions; and on the capacity of 'Marxism-Leninism' and dialectical materialism (another term

> which Marx never used or even knew) to resolve all theoretical problems, or at the very least to provide a sure guide to their solution. These were not perspectives in which Marxist thought could be expected to flourish, least of all in the highly sensitive area of political theory and political analysis; and it did not.

It may be here added that if Soviet Marxism went stagnant and sterile on politics in an increasingly authoritarian regime and under party-grip, outside of Soviet Union, equally authoritarian communist party leaderships claimed an ossifying monopoly or custodianship on questions of politics, laying down 'the party line' whose dogmatism was immune to any questioning, and intolerant of all dissent, within or without. Buttressed with democratic centralism, which was more central than democratic, so far as Marxism or 'Marxism-Leninism' was concerned, party leadership was the sole qualified arbiter on matters political. So far as parties of social democracy were concerned, abandoning all pretensions to theory, Marxist or any other, they simply accommodated practice to the requirements of bourgeois democratic politics. As for the communist formations committed to revolutionary politics that have survived the Soviet collapse, they are for the most part still dogmatically holding on to their yesterday's orthodoxies, scientistic Marxism and 'party lines' duly buttressed with selective quotes from Marx and Lenin, but more from Mao – all of which is no substitute for a Marxist political theory they need for our changed times.

VII

These are some of the reasons for the lack of development or relative backwardness of Marxist theory of politics. There are other reasons too, within or without the Marxist tradition, including constant hostility and persecution by the dominant political and academic establishments of the bourgeois social order. Before concluding I would like to refer to an aspect of development of Marxism in our times which has its own relevance to the subject under discussion.

The post-war world – initially marked by high prestige of the Soviet Union and communist parties for their role in the struggle against fascism and the success of Chinese revolution under Marxist leadership – witnessed an 'efflorescence' of Marxism in the West. In countries where Marxism was not the official ideology and there was no 'recognised' Marxist orthodoxy commanding general obedience or which could be imposed, it was a period of intense probing and questioning in Marxist thought without parallel in its history, involving 'the proliferation of coteries and fashionable trends, with different sects and schools proclaiming their own version of Marxism as the only authentic one, or as the only one appropriate to the times we live in, or whatever.' But the significant thing to note about this deluge of interest in Marxism is that it was a 'theoreticist deluge' of largely academic Marxism with little concern for politics, least of all revolutionary politics. Lacking any vital relationship with living working class or other popular movements, even the best of this Marxism went in for ideological-philosophical or cultural critiques, idealist or humanist conceptualisations, or exegetical and analytical exercises. This certainly revived the libertarian and humanist concerns of Marx's concept of socialism, focused on the important issues of ideology and class-consciousness, and introduced much-needed rigour in the study of Marxism. But politics proper remained a poor cousin – a fact whose implications evoked diverse comments from scholars. William Dowd said: 'the upsurge of Marxism has just as unquestionably coincided with – not, one trusts, caused – a noticeable decline in the overall political effectiveness of the left in the United States'. Another friendly critic, Hugh Stretton, was compelled to write: 'I do not believe the workers of the world can expect much benefit from the feuds which entangle some contemporary Marxists in the concerns of Althusser, Habermass, and other obscure but rigid elaborators of Marx.' Taking note of the fact that scholars have been more interested in history or philosophy or elaboration of 'grand theory' and not politics, except as an appendage to this theorising in other areas of Marxism or as a most general theory of the state, 'dictatorship of the proletariat', etc., Hal Draper wrote: 'If no attempt has previously been made to reconstruct the whole picture of Marx's views on political theory and political struggle, it can scarcely be doubted that prejudicial interest has stood in the way. The "grand theory" precisely because it seems to soar above current struggles, can sometimes be discussed with an air of tranquillity. When the subject is the political realm of power, the knife cuts deeper. Politics in the broad sense is only one aspect of social revolution, but it is its cutting edge'.

(For Marx, it may be noted, this 'cutting edge' was throughout a matter of vital concern, even though he could not find time to theorise it. 'He was above all a revolutionary', as Engels emphasised. His intense practical activity throughout his life, his political work with small working class groups as well as the International Workingmen's Association (the First International), his association with revolutionary struggles in France, Germany or Russia, his active advice to diverse working class movements in Europe and America, his interest in liberationist movements the world over, his treatment of politics in what are now referred to as his *political writings*, all this and more bear ample witness to Marx's lifelong concern with politics.)

That politics has been something of 'a poor cousin' in Marxist theorisation of recent times does not, however, mean that serious concern with political theory has been entirely lacking. Contributions have come from scholars whose significance must not be underestimated. Classical tradition, however fragmentary its insights, has been critically examined and books written on 'Marx's Politics'. Many hitherto neglected or underestimated problems have attracted greater attention and many old problems have been perceived in a better light. However controversial in parts, there is the pioneering work of Ralph Miliband, especially significant for its Marxist treatment of a whole range of political experience of our times – involving such issues as capitalist state, structures and working of bourgeois democracy, parliamentary politics, pluralism, Soviet model of politics, socialist democracy, human rights, etc. etc. – about which classical Marxism is, in any direct way, naturally silent. Miliband's famous debate with Poulantzas, with Left intellectuals across Europe and North America lining up with the 'instrumentalists' or the 'structuralists', provoked a flood of argument about the nature of the capitalist state and the relative importance of what we would today call structure and agency in the struggle for a socialist transformation of society. Another outstanding example which I would like to mention is Hal Draper's multi-volume *Karl Marx's Theory of Revolution* with its extraordinarily rich, truly pathbreaking exploration of political theory of Marx and Engels. One can therefore legitimately suggest that the beginnings have been made of theorisation on politics in the Marxist mode.

Only the beginnings, however. There is still a vast amount of ground to make up. Classical Marxism may have only fragmentary insights to offer but not so its known political practice. The resources of classical tradition still remain to be tapped to provide a firm basis to a Marxist theory of politics. It is no exaggeration to suggest that the theoretical and practical work of Marx and Engels as of Lenin and Mao, Ho Chi Minh and Che Guevara as well as other practitioners of revolutionary Marxism like Rosa Luxemburg, Trotsky or Gramsci contain greater wealth of political theory than is to be found in the bulky tomes of the discipline called political science. But this work has remained historically textured and underlined. Repeated, copied or quoted to no end, it has not been adequately theorised. Gramsci, whose writings are wonderfully suggestive on the subject of a Marxist, that is, revolutionary theory of politics for our times, in fact now even needs to be rescued from being reduced to a theorist of 'culturalism'.

A vast amount of ground indeed still needs to be made in developing an adequate Marxist theory of politics for our times. Much work has been done and important gaps have been filled in. But there is no denying that a basic inadequacy remains. Witness to it are the difficult problems that practice of revolutionary socialist politics faces in the post-colonial third world countries or in regimes of bourgeois democracy. But Marxist political theory as such is not my concern at the moment. My immediate concern is with the question of democracy as part of this theory. And the inadequacy here is equally evident in the highly unsatisfactory state of Marxist theory on the question of democracy in general and democratic exercise of power in post-revolutionary societies. As Norman Geras has put it: 'Marxism has had too little to offer towards a theory of political institutions necessary for any genuinely democratic community'. A crippling inadequacy at all times, it proved disastrous when such a theory was most needed, that is in the post-revolutionary societies of our times. Of course the inadequacies of Marxist theory of politics or democracy, the gaps or errors in what Marx or Marxists had to say about, for example, the rule of law, or the rights of the individual, or the need for checks and balances in political structures, etc. do not constitute the essence of Marxism as some are busy claiming today. But they certainly contributed, directly or otherwise, to the undemocratic practices of what came to be built as socialism in the Soviet Union.

VIII

It has been suggested that, in a profound sense, we simply do not have a Marxist theory of political democracy. This is meant in the same sense that Althusser insisted that 'there does not really exist any "Marxist theory of the state"'. What he was anxious to stress was that Marx was so intent on avoiding all bourgeois conceptions of the state that he ends up with the purely negative demarcation line, producing what Althusser describes as 'the classical negative definition'. The history of Marxist discussion of representative democracy, it is pointed out, has been dogged by a similar negativity; it has been constructed, as it were, out of criticism of 'bourgeois democracy' and warnings against 'bourgeois illusions'. The suggestion has a great deal of validity. And it points to an initial inadequacy or flaw in Marxist theorisation on democracy which has persisted over time.

Deeply committed to democratic principles which can only be realised in socialism, Marx was apt to scoff at freedoms and civil liberties of the bourgeois state and its supposedly democratic structures. In his conception of politics as *radical negation* of the established order, Parliament usually appears in its 'almost grotesque negativity' as Meszeros has called it, summed up in the dictum: 'To delude others and by deluding them to delude yourself – this is *parliamentary* wisdom in a nutshell! Tant mieux!'. This is at least partly due to the fact that Marx lived and wrote at a time when liberal democracy really didn't exist yet. There were a few liberal states but they weren't anything like 'really' democratic even in the contemporary conventional sense. The liberalism of 19th century capitalism didn't much extend to the working class. Few of them had the vote, and freedom of organisation and assembly had to be bitterly fought for. The locus of political power of the bourgeoisie visibly lay in the extra-parliamentary realm – in the civil-military-police apparatus of the state. The actual work f the state was admittedly carried out behind and outside the representative institutions. Such being the reality of the times, Marx had reasons enough to dismiss 'democracy' and its civil liberties as a capitalist convenience.

Marx's approach to bourgeois democracy here can also be seen as linked to a basic epistemological principle of Marxism which makes a distinction between *form* or *appearance* of things and their *content* or *essence*. Marx had pointed out how capitalism's *essentially* exploitative social relationship is *formed* and *appears* as a free and equitable exchange between owners of capital and the labour force in the market place. In the same way, for Marx, the form and appearance of democracy concealed its content or essence as bourgeois dictatorship – the rule of the bourgeoisie as a class. This was reason enough for Marx to be generally dismissive about bourgeois democacy.

Focussing on the *essential* nature of democracy under capitalism, ignoring that in Marx's materialism a certain reality also belongs to the realm of appearance and form, Marxists have long continued, and not unconvincingly, to characterise democracy as a form of covert rule, even dictatorship, of the bourgeoisie. This, for example, is how Lenin described 'bourgeois democracy': '...this democracy is always restricted by the narrow framework of capitalist exploitation, and consequently always remains, in reality, a democracy for the minority, only for the possessing classes, only for the rich. Freedom in capitalist society always remains about the same as it was in the ancient Greek republics: freedom for the slave-owners. Owing to the conditions of capitalist exploitation, the modern wage-slaves are also so crushed by want and poverty that "they cannot be bothered with democracy," "they cannot be bothered with politics"; in the ordinary peaceful course of events the majority of the population is debarred from participating in social and political life.'

Given the persistence of this approch – 'the classical negative definition' – positive Marxist theorising on the subject of political democracy has been largely missing, certainly the elaboration of a theory of socialist democracy. As already suggested, neither Marx, nor the tradition after him, even remotely offered an adequate theory or sketch of the political institutions of a post-revolutionary transitional society, much less of an ultimately postulated class-less communist society. And when the successful October Revolution put the issue on the historical agenda, for the first time in the Soviet Union, this turned out to be a grievous lack.

IX

Marx and Engels, it may be noted, never showed much concern with the political (for that matter even economic) organisation and functioning of a post-revolutionary society. The means or mechanisms to ensure a just organisation or exercise of political power during the period of a socialist transition, through multiform institutionalised structures of democracy – genuinely democratic elections and popular control over elected representatives, appropriate distribution of functions and powers among different organs of government, the election and removal of judges and civil servants, a semi-independent structure of rights of individuals as well as minorities, independent press, freedom of political dissent, checks on arbitrary exercise of power by the state, and so on – was never a matter of much interest to Marx and Engels, occasional hints to the contrary notwithstanding. In another context, Marx was devastating in his criticism of bureaucracy but both he and Engels tended not to be worried about the power that would come to be vested in the controllers of an economically planned society in transition to socialism/communism. They spoke of 'dictatorship of the proletariat' and recognised the necessity of breaking up the old entrenched political power and forcible suppression of the resistance of the former possessing classes. But even as they viewed it as a transitional phase, this 'dictatorship' for them did not even remotely mean a dictatorial form of government involving the disciplining or forcing into obedience of the working people. On the contrary, for them it meant 'democracy carried to its fullest' – with the Paris Commune as its example – in the sense of the majority class becoming the ruling class for the first time in history. Nevertheless insofar as, even as a transitional phase, it meant a period of centralised and repressive rule entailing strict measures to finally defeat the old ruling classes and prevent counter-revolution, Marx and Engels never thought of the risk that coercion might become institutionalised and overwhelm the democratic dimension of the process of socialist transformation of society. They never felt concerned about the problem of transcending or superseding this phase, more particularly, of 'the withering away' of the 'revolutionary absolutism' of 'the dictatorship of the proletariat'. Marx indeed understood a communist society to be the only possible realisation of democracy. He saw political power essentially as the direct manifestation of class antagonism and contrasted it with its opposite: the abolition of political power properly so-called in a fully realised socialism in which there can be no room for separate organs of political power, since 'the social life-process becomes... production by freely associated men, and stands under their conscious and planned control'. He also wrote of 'converting the state from an organ superimposed on society into one thoroughly subordinate to it'. But he never came to canvass the important problem of how this was to be secured. The fact remained that the *concrete* problems of the exercise of political power in a transitional socialist society were never seriously posed, discussed or answered by him.

X

The absence or lack of concern with these problems in Marx is not too difficult to comprehend. I have already spoken of the quite understandable 'empty spaces' or 'silences' in Marx's work, the 'unfinished' nature of his theoretical project. That apart, part of the reason perhaps lies in the way Marx visualised the building of socialism which according to him is not feasible without the necessary material foundation, a series of material conditions of existence, which in their turn are the natural and spontaneous product of a long and tormented historical development. In other words, it was Marx's major assumption that socialism would be consequent upon a revolution in a mature bourgeois society, to be built, and that too early enough, on a material basis created for it by the economic, political and cultural achievements of capitalism. This building also assumed accelerated material abundance that a transition to socialism will ensure, the abundance of means of production, of consumption, of human skills, abilities and experience, of tools and technologies, and above all an abundance of culture and so on. History's trick on the doctrine of Karl Marx, that we have noted, falsified this assumption, confronting a single 'underdeveloped' country, a country with extremes of economic, social and cultural backwardness and without any worthwhile tradition of political democracy, with the task of effecting history's first socialist transition. It has failed, unable to resolve the difficult and unanticipated problems of such a transition, overwhelmed finally by global capitalism. These problems now remain as part of the dilemmas facing the revolutionary socialist movements in the more or less 'underdeveloped' countries of the third world; just as 'overdeveloped' late capitalist societies of the first world will confront equally difficult and unanticipated though different problems, when sooner or later they face the task of attempting their own socialist transition. Be that as it has been or may, the immediately relevant point is that given classical Marxism's assumption or anticipation of abundance of a developed capitalist social order as the basis of a successful transition to socialism after the revolution, political freedom is an element that it could well take for granted. This possibly is one reason why Marx, even as he took a positive view of it, but rarely spoke about political freedom. As Issac Deutscher put it: 'Precisely because he assumed a revolution amid the abundance of a mature bourgeois society, he took political freedom so much for granted that he discussed only, so to say, the higher mathematics of freedom, those refinements of genuine freedom of which only socialist society would be capable.'

Part of the reason why Marx does not say much about the political institutional forms of the period of the 'dictatorship of the proletariat', about the way freedom would be institutionalised during this transitional period or beyond it, perhaps also lay in Marx's attachment to the ideal of direct democracy, the vision of a democratic order in which popular power would be barely mediated by representatives who would be delegates constantly accountable to and revocable by those who had chosen them, political mechanisms of direct democracy – such as immediate recall, workers' salaries for political leaders, the rotation of tasks, popular courts, a people's militia, etc. – are deemed necessary and enough to protect leadership from the temptations of power, secure authentic popular control over administrators as 'servants' of society, and ensure people's effective participation in public affairs. This was of course the vision evoked by Marx in his glowing defence of the Paris Commune in *The Civil War in France* in 1871 – later advanced in much greater detail by Lenin in *The State and Revolution* in 1917, and even sought to be realised by him through democracy of the Soviets in the period immediately following the October Revolution. This ideal or vision of democracy postulated a regime in which the power hitherto appropriated by the state would be more or less directly re-appropriated by those in whom it should by right be vested, namely the people, who would not merely rule, but also govern, with the state in a process of rapid decomposition. There was a Rousseauesque criticism of principle of representation and the associated Saint-Simonian perspective on society of the future where, in Engels' words, 'administration of men' will be replaced by 'an administration of things' which reduces the expectation or the need for a democratic form of resolving conflicts or other problems to such an extent that the spontaneous self-organisation of the people, as described by Rousseau, appears to be sufficient.

However attractive Marx's vision of democracy and whatever its viability in a far-distant future, it has little relevance to the problems of political organisation a regime would immediately face in the construction of a socialist society after a successful revolution. Of course such a regime would need or seek to radicalise political processes, foster new avenues of collective choice or decision-making and in general extend popular participation and power. But this raises the procedural and related issues of providing forms for the purpose, which would at the same time ensure that popular power is not exercised arbitrarily. On the other hand, however much the perspective of its 'withering away' is held on to, the state would continue to be with a great deal of power, for at least a pretty long transitional period, to take care of diverse class and non-class functions, not the least being the settlement of conflicts that would still arise or the protection of rights of individuals and minorities. This would call for not only a radical democratisation of state apparatuses but also mechanisms to ensure that the state is representative of and accountable to the working people and duly controlled and circumscribed against arbitrary use of its power. Indeed popular power and state power, even as they would complement each other, would also need, under agreed procedures, to check each other. In other words, a post-revolutionary society would need multiform well-mediated institutionalisation to ensure its practice of socialist democracy. This is precisely the missing concern in Marx's vision of democracy. He never addressed such or similar problems of institutionalisation of socialist democracy in a post-revolutionary social order.

As a matter of fact Marx's attachment to the ideal of direct, unmediated democracy was problematic in another way too, in that it carried within it a tendency to class reductionism in matters of political power in sharp contrast to his (or Engels') more balanced critique of capitalism. This found a typical expression in Lenin's *State and Revolution*, where he speaks of socialism as *unmediated* class rule. This view is certainly infused with a profound democratic spirit and is in line with Marx's vision of the distant future, but it also tends to obviate the need for agencies of working class power in the *transitional* post-revolutionary society. For, as Benglesdorf has put it: 'If the political arena is defined as the stage upon which one class enforces its will on another, then the end of class domination effectively means the end of politics. The beginning of 'real history' was to be marked by the absorption of political society by civil society. Therefore questions of political society – of the form and nature of political institutions – are almost by definition no longer relevant. This was true, even if somewhat problematically, of Marx and Engels, and no less true of Lenin, it certainly contributed towards what was a major inadequacy in the theory of Bolshevism in power – its inability to coherently articulate an alternative vision of a democratic socialist society. In other words, the vision of an entirely new social order based on direct or semi-direct democracy has tended to make Marxists oblivious to the need to explore seriously the ways in which socialists ought to tackle the vast problems which the notion of a genuinely democratic system is bound to pose. This gap, as part of the 'empty space' that is the Marxist theory of socialist democracy, still remains, waiting to be ultimately filled up by concrete socialist practice.

A couple of final observations on this 'gap', so far as Marx himself is concerned, will not be out of place. It needs to be borne in mind that Marx had tremendous amount of confidence in the working class and its ability to govern as the ruling class by methods much more democratic than anything in the most democratic bourgeois regimes. He certainly overestimated the revolutionary potential of the working class as it was developing in Europe in the 19th century. Perhaps, under the direct influence of the Paris Commune, he was much too optimistic here too and gave too much credit to its capacity for innovative democratic governance. It was not that he was simply idealising this working class. Using 'civil war' as a metaphor for 'class struggle', he had told this working class that it had '15, 20, 50 years of civil war to go through in order to alter the situation and to train yourselves for the exercise of power'. Even so his immense faith in the creativity of the working people was very much there and he had always assumed a revolutionary, class conscious and free proletariat in power during the socialist transition, which would be capable of finding answers to problems as they emerged. This apart, given the scientific as against the utopian mode of his thinking, Marx never saw the problems of the future, of socialist democracy in a post-revolutionary society included, as his problems. His method simply excluded any such inclination. He had categorically stated: 'It is not our task to build up the future in advance and to settle all problems for all time'. These were problems for revolutionaries of the future to be faced and resolved by them when history confronts them with the task of building socialism. That they, on the whole, failed to do so is another matter.

XI

The failure occurred first in the Soviet Union and was then repeated in other post-revolutionary societies, with the possible, qualified exception of Cuba. The inadequacy of theory when combined with the exceptionally adverse historical circumstances proved disastrous for the cause of socialist democracy in the Soviet Union. The consequences were a steady bureaucratic degeneration of the revolution, of socialism that was sought to be built, including the gross excesses of the Terror of the thirties; the failure to make a clear distinction between the justified violence of the period of defence of revolution and immediate consolidation of power, and the need for its democratic transcendence in the consequent period of socialist construction even provided a certain legitimation to these and other excesses. The concept of 'dictatorship of the proletariat' was simply vulgarised. Marx had spoken of it as both a state and a non-state to pinpoint its essential democratic dimension. Lenin reminded the proletariat of this contradiction between the state and the non-state in the midst of setting up the dictatorship of the proletariat. But Soviet practice after his death (and to a certain extent during even his life) denied this understanding and rejected its essence, the 'withering away' of the state, to degenerate into a dictatorial form of government. That rejection – this bourgeois baggage – was then passed on to the other revolutions of the century. Socialism and democracy had parted ways with disastrous consequences for the present and future of socialism.

Whatever else was wrong in the economic and other spheres, lack of democracy turned out to be the single most important factor contributing to the ultimate collapse of the Soviet system. The issue of democracy was in fact never squarely posed after Lenin's early initiative with 'All Power to the Soviets' and last desperate effort with *Rabkrin* (Workers' and Peasants' Inspectorate). If some forms of democracy persisted from the early period or new ones were added, they were empty of content, there never was a return to the original inspiration. Instead, with the collateral degeneration of Soviet Marxism, a major shift of emphasis occurred within Soviet 'Marxist' thinking in this area which reduced the issue of democracy in the Soviet Union into a non-problem. While classical Marxism's unambiguous commitment to democracy continued to be repeated, it was grossly violated in practice, and in a truly fetishist exercise, it was simply declared to have been already realised in the extant Soviet system, described as 'Soviet Democracy'. The emphasis shifted to a criticism and rejection of bourgeois democracy, by focussing exclusively on its *bourgeois* aspect, rather than learning a few things from the Western liberal tradition as a whole and focussing on the need to achieve a superior socialist democracy in the Soviet Union. Classical Marxist understanding of bourgeois democracy as another form of class rule was reduced to regarding it as only that and nothing more, and democratic and civic rights as merely bourgeois rights, only 'bourgeois-democratic freedoms', and thus their suppression in a regime of 'proletarian democracy' was viewed as not incompatible with the socialist project. It is thus that Soviet Marxism served to condone and sanctify as democratic and socialist the ruthlessly authoritarian class system that come to be built in the Soviet Union, a model which was later imposed or accepted elsewhere with equally sad consequences.

Outside of the Soviet Union, the left responded to this development in different ways. Social democracy, while highly critical of 'Soviet democracy', uncritically endorsed bourgeois democracy, adapting and adjusting to it as part of its overall acceptance of capitalism and adjustment with it. Communist parties, however, generally denounced bourgeois democracy as a sham, upholding and defending the Soviet model as immeasurably more democratic than any bourgeois democracy. Such an understanding may not have prevented these parties from accepting the framework of bourgeois democratic politics all too often on bourgeois terms, but it certainly served to blind them to what should have been their indispensable concerns, namely, criticism and correction of the political course in the Soviet Union which in moving away from democracy had moved away from socialism, and confronting the concrete problems of practising revolutionary politics in their own regimes of bourgeois democracy where socialism has remained as far away as ever.

XII

A currently fashionable tendency is to trace every evil in the Soviet System back to Karl Marx. Marxism itself is painted as an essentially anti-democratic doctrine. It is necessary, therefore, to return to the question of Marx's commitment to democracy. I shall do so by touching upon a few related issues, including his argument over bourgeois democracy which, contrary to the view hawked by the critics, upheld its 'political freedoms' and sanctioned its usefulness for working class politics, even as it sought its transcendence in socialist democracy – a transcendence not of democracy but its bourgeois dimension or character.

We have more than once noticed Marx's celebration of the working class democracy of the Paris Commune. Later, in a discussion of the programme of his party in Germany (in *Critique of the Gotha Programme*) Marx wrote: 'Freedom consists in converting the state from an organ superimposed upon society into one completely subordinated to it.'; a formulation which suggests not only the continuance of a kind of (converted) 'state', but also its democratic foundations. This transitional state of the socialist period, the 'dictatorship of the proletariat', is visualised by Marx as an exercise of power so completely democratic as not to be a state at all in its repressive aspect so far as the working people are concerned. This democratic theme recalls and reaffirms the substance of some of Marx's earliest theoretical reflections, on Hegel or on the Jewish question, where Marx championed democracy as the highest form of government, mounted a powerful critique of the absolutist state and bureaucratic government and argued in defence of 'political emancipation'. Early in his journalistic career he penned one of the most brilliant defences of the freedom of the press that we possess. In a series of newspaper articles written in 1842, Marx attacked the Prussian state's 'censorship instruction' and spiritedly defended the freedom of the press. Freedom of the press, Marx wrote, 'is itself an embodiment of the idea... of freedom, a positive good, whereas censorship is an embodiment of unfreedom'. Further, the 'essence of the free press is the characterful, rational moral essence of freedom. The character of a censored press is the characterless monster of unfreedom; it is a civilised monster, a perfumed abortion'. Again: 'The free press is the ubiquitous vigilant eye of a people's soul, the embodiment of a people's faith in itself, the eloquent link that connects the individual with the state and the world, the embodied culture that transforms material struggles into intellectual struggles and idealizes their crude material form. It is a people's frank confession to itself, and the redeeming power of confession is well known. It is the spiritual mirror in which a people can see itself, and self-examination is the first condition of wisdom.' Marx concluded: 'The absence of freedom of the press makes all other freedoms illusory. One form of freedom governs another just as one limb of the body does another. Whenever a particular freedom is put in question, freedom in general is put in question. Whenever one form of freedom is rejected, freedom in general is rejected and henceforth can have only a semblance of existence, since the sphere in which absence of freedom is dominant becomes a matter of pure chance...' As Marx supported himself through journalism in the 1850s and 1860s he never failed to advocate freedom of the press. In writing on the Paris Commune in 1871, he praised the Communards for publishing accounts of their deliberations and their proclamation of freedom of the press. He proudly wrote: 'The Commune did not pretend to infallibility, the invariable attribute of all governments of the old stamp. It published its doings and sayings, it initiated the public into all its shortcomings.' Freedom of the press remained a lifelong concern and commitment of Marx.

Within the movement, however uncompromising Marx may have been on matters of theory, pluralism and criticality have been quite important components of the classical Marxist tradition. For example, there is no plea for a monolithic opinion to be represented by the party of the working class or suppression of dissent. Evident in Marx's early journalistic writings where he makes an impassioned plea for freedom of the press, this is as much evident in his treatment of his anarchist opponent, Bakunin, in the debates of the First International. The anarchists were not denied the right to argue their case. About the party, Marx and Engels were particularly specific about the need for collective check on the leadership of the party. Marx, writing about the rules of the Communist League, stressed that '...every thing promoting the superstitious worship for authority should be deleted from its Rules'. Engels had argued: 'The working class movement rests on the most scathing criticism of the existing society; how can it avoid criticism or try to ban debates if criticism is its essential element? Can it be that we demand freedom of speech from others only to destroy it again in our own ranks?'

As parties of socialism grew up in Europe, this issue came up specifically in a controversy within the German Social Democratic Party over the publication of Marx's Critique of the Gotha Programme (*Gothakritik*), suppressed for 15 long years with the 'justification' – sadly familiar to members of the socialist movement ever since – that criticism of party leaders helps our enemies, and even then published, in the face of powerful opposition, at the insistence of Engels, earning him the ire and hostility of the 'socialist bosses' as he called them. Engels' concern with issues of discussion and self-criticism within the Party, of conducting matters under *public* scrutiny, clearly comes through in the following extracts from his correspondence of the period: 'this fright (of publication) was essentially based on the consideration: what will the enemy make of it? Since the thing was printed in the official organ, the exploitation by the enemy will be blunted and we put ourselves in a position where we can say: See how we criticize ourselves – we are the only party that can allow itself to do this; try and imitate us! And this is also the correct standpoint which should have been taken in the first place'; again: 'The fear that it would put weapon in the hands of our opponents was unfounded. Malicious insinuations, of course, are being attached to anything and everything, but on the whole the impression made on our opponents was one of complete bewilderment at this ruthless self-criticism and the feeling: what an inner power must be possessed by a party that can afford such a thing!'; yet again: 'The *Vorwarts* is always boasting about the inviolable freedom of discussion, but one does not see much of it. You just don't know how strange such propensity to coercive measures appears here abroad, where one is accustomed to seeing the oldest party chiefs duly called to account in their own party (for instance, the Tory government by Lord Randolph Churchill). And then you must also not forget that in a big party discipline can by no means be so tight as in a small sect'. Taking note of the dangerous trend of bureaucratisation and suppression of criticism within the Party, Engels commented with bitter irony: 'It is indeed a brilliant idea to put German socialist science, after its liberation from Bismarck's Anti-Socialist Law, under a new Anti-Socialist Law to be manufactured and carried out by the Social-Democratic Party authorities themselves.' Putting his finger on a most delicate matter, in a letter to Kautsky Engels warned: 'it is also necessary that people finally stop treating Party functionaries – their own servants – with the eternal kid gloves and standing most obediently instead of critically before them, as if they were infallible bureaucrats'.

(In view of what later went wrong with the socialist movement, including the Communist Parties, especially the Communist Parties in power, it is instructive to note what Meszaros, dealing with the *Gothakritik* controversy in some detail, describes as 'the dangers' that Engels 'soberly identified at the time of their emergence': '(1) the transformation of a *moral* authority into the dictatorial powers of a "bureaucratic" *ex officio* authority; (2) the suppression of the *freedom of discussion*; (3) the introduction of a system of *coercive measures*; (4) the assertion of the *infallibility of party chiefs* (which put the socialist party below the level of the bourgeois parties, though it was supposed to exercise a "ruthless self-criticism" as a demonstration of its "inner power"); (5) the imposition of the *artificial* discipline of a *small sect* on a *mass party* (in other words: the triumph of *enforced sectarianism*, functioning through the multiplication of coercive measures and the religious cult – the "personality cult"? – of "infallibility"); and (6) the artificial cultivation of the crisis mentality of a *state of emergency* as the self-evident and unquestionable justification of the most blatant, systematic violation of all principles, organisational forms and practices of any conceivable socialist democracy').

Marx and Engles never made a serious theoretical analysis of democracy as it was developing in the advanced capitalist societies. It really came into its own long after them. They indeed recognised it as *bourgeois* democracy, a democracy both expressive of and limited by the logic of its economic context, a capitalist system. But they never discussed it as such. The few comments and observations they made are in relation to particular events and situations or problems and prospects of the ongoing working class movement. These are often ad hoc, only isolated insights, at times ambiguous and even seemingly contradictory. There is nothing dogmatic about them. But what clearly emerges from this textual evidence and associated political practice of Marx and Engels is their unquestionable democratic commitment and a critical but favourable view of 'bourgeois democratic freedoms'. There may be an occasional purely functional or instrumental view dismissing, for example, the 'vulgar democracy' of the French Third Republic, but they did not despise such freedoms as some of the more unwise of their followers have done or still do.

Marx and Engels welcomed the achievement and extension of 'bourgeois democratic freedom', they were enthusiastic supporters of wider suffrage and, in practice, of the workers obtaining their full rights within the bourgeois social order. That is how the Social Democratic Party, their party in Germany, gave a call for the democratisation of the German state – to include not only universal suffrage, broad civic liberties, and trade union rights, but such advanced democratic proposals as votes for women and proportional representation. Engels was very happy with this, the first 'Marxist programme', though he would have liked to see a further commitment to republicanism and federalism. Marx's address to the CC of the Communist League had insisted: 'Even where there is no prospect whatsoever of their being elected, the workers must put up their own candidates in order to preserve their independence, to count their forces and to bring before the public the revolutionary attitude and Party's standpoint.' Engels wrote of universal suffrage as the gauge of the maturity of the working class, and together with Marx, fought against sectarian advocacy of 'boycotting Parliament'. They wanted the working class to make the fullest use of the extensions of suffrage and the democratisation of political institutions as avenues of class struggle, to pursue their immediate and long-term interests. It was even possible, under certain conditions of developing capitalism to transform political democracy 'from an instrument of deception – as up to now it has been – into an instrument of emancipation'. The importance of democracy or democratic republic was not that in itself it provided all the means by which transition to socialism could be effected, but that it was the form in which workers could wage the widest and freest struggle for political power – not excepting the electoral struggle but by no means limiting the struggle to that and nothing more.

Of course Marx and Engels never supposed that electoral victory was synonymous with revolution, as the 'reformists' thought, or that socialism could be achieved by electoral means. The point rather was, without abandoning the use of revolutionary force in principle and without entertaining illusions about the exploiting classes and the class character of bourgeois democracy, to make use of legality and the possibilities offered by bourgeois democracy. In a view fully sensitive to the complex or even contradictory possibilities of bourgeois democracy, or democracy in a bourgeois democratic republic, Marx wrote of bourgeoisie being forced 'into democratic conditions, which at every moment help the hostile classes to victory and jeopardise the very foundations of bourgeois society' – thus suggesting the possibility of victory of socialism through, not ballot box or elections but democracy, the enforcing political power of the people. He was prepared to allow that working class might gain political supremacy, at least in some countries, by democratic, relatively peaceful means.

In *Communist Manifesto*, Marx wrote of 'forcible overthrow of existing conditions', which remained a general *tactical* proposition for him in legitimate recognition of the historical ruthlessness and resistance of the ruling classes. Marx, like all his contemporaries, had the example of the French Revolution sixty years earlier very much in mind, and thought 'the forcible overthrow of existing conditions' would be necessary in order to achieve the social revolution in most countries, given the predictable resistance that would be offered by the bourgeoisie and its allies to any fundamental change in relations of production. But later, in the 1860s and 1870s, we have a more subtle expression of his position which allowed that in countries with long traditions of democracy, the workers might 'achieve their goal by peaceful means'. In an important but little known speech (in Amsterdam in 1872) Marx said: 'The worker will some day have to win political supremacy in order to organise labour along new lines: he will have to defeat the old policy supporting old institutions... But we have by no means affirmed that this goal would be achieved by identical means. We know of the allowances we must make for the institutions, customs and traditions of the various countries; and we do not deny that there are countries such as America, England, and I would add Holland if I knew your institutions better, where the working people may achieve their goals by peaceful means.' Though, even so, Marx did not expect the ruling classes to submit without 'a pro-slavery rebellion'. This is certainly linked to his awareness not only of the variability of circumstances which working class or revolutionary politics must take into account, but of the need for 'approaching the situation in their own particular way', and making allowances for '*the institutions, customs and traditions* of the various countries', which by implication allows democracy or peaceful means as the vehicle of revolutionary change.

Revolution for Marx, it must be clearly understood is not about violence or the use of arms, it is about revolutionary change in social production relations. And his position was: 'peaceful way where that is possible for us, and with weapons if it should become necessary'. Marx's attitude here was practical. The right to revolution – 'the only really historical right', as Engels said just before his death in 1895 – was a democratic right, the right of the majority to make their own history; it would be exercised peaceably if possible, forcibly if not. Marx's profoundest political commitment was to this democratic right. It was from the opponents of socialism that he anticipated violence, and not without cause.

Engels was equally practical in his attitude. He recognised that with the passage of years the conditions of struggle had changed – due to technical reasons, but most importantly due to the changed conditions of bourgeois hegemony, something that Gramsci was to emphasise later – and wrote: 'The time of surprise attacks, of revolutions carried through by small conscious minorities at the head of unconscious masses, is past. Where it is a question of a complete transformation of the social organisation, the masses themselves must also be in it, must themselves already have grasped what is at stake, what it is they are going for, body and soul. The history of the last 50 years has taught us that. But in order that the masses may understand what is to be done, long persistent work is required...' At the same time, if Marx was scornfully dismissive of socialists within his own party in Germany who 'keep themselves within the limits of the logically presumable and of the permissible by the police', this is how Engels admonished the German Party leadership. 'I cannot suffer the thought that you intend to pledge yourselves body and soul to absolute legality, legality in all circumstances... no party in any country goes so far as to give up the right to render armed resistance to lawlessness'. Engels complained about Liebknecht selectively quoting him to support 'the tactics of peace at any price and of opposition to force and violence' and criticised Kautsky for showing 'excessive deference to the "respectable Fabian brand of socialism".'

It is true that Engels himself on occasion tended to read more into electoral successes of Social Democrats, their entry into national governments or elections to local offices than a century of experience of the 'parliamentary road to socialism' has justified, but there is no denying the political correctness of his insistence on utilising to the full the possibilities of the available parliamentary processes to win the legitimacy and mass support for revolutionary change in society, however peaceful or violent it may ultimately turn out to be.

XIII

If, fed by a superficial and ahistorical interpretation of the Soviet experience, it is a mistake to look for authoritarianism or violence in Karl Marx and his commitment to social revolution, it is equally a mistake to so charge Lenin, as quite a few, who are willing to spare Marx, still insist on doing. However fashionable these days, there is no justification for it in Lenin's life and work as a whole.

We have already noticed Lenin's repeated insistence on the indissoluble relation between democracy and socialism, as also the extraordinary degree of democracy practised inside the Bolshevik party, underground or in power, even under conditions of civil war, till almost the very end. As a Marxist, he indeed recognised the bourgeois character of democracy under capitalism, often criticised it in the sharpest language and may have even used the not always unjustified term 'pigsty' to describe its legislatures. But he also wrote: 'This domination of finance capital, however, does not in the least nullify the significance of political democracy as a freer, wider and clearer form of class oppression and class struggle'. Recognising this significance, following Marx and Engels, Lenin underlined its positive value for the Russian workers' movement, while remaining firm, like them, in a revolutionary's resilient awareness of situation-dependent other options. In a statement of more than merely tactical importance, he wrote: 'there is not, nor can there be, any other path to real freedom for the proletariat and the peasantry, than the path of bourgeois freedom and bourgeois progress'. He argued against 'the hoary

Narodnik theory that... we do not need bourgeois political liberty' and against 'anarchism which denies any participation of the proletariat in bourgeois politics... in bourgeois parliamentarism'. In his *State and Revolution,* he spoke of the benefits to the proletariat of the 'wider, freer, and more open form of class struggle' vouchsafed by the democratic-republican type of bourgeois state. For this very reason he upheld 'the viewpoint that it was... obligatory to participate even in a most reactionary parliament,' that 'participation in parliamentary elections and in the struggle on the parliamentary rostrum is obligatory on the party of the revolutionary proletariat.' Of course, this has to be a subordinate part of the proletariat's more basic, society-wide extra-parliamentary struggle for emancipation.

Again, following Marx, Lenin did not rule out the possibility of the old society being more or less peacefully superseded by the new, of a 'gradual, peaceful, gentle' road to socialism in Russia. He indeed contemplated it in his famous *April Thesis* (1917), which charged the Bolsheviks with the task of winning a majority in the Soviets and using the precious opportunity of leading the workers to power peacefully without civil war. Precisely because this was 'the least painful' course, Lenin considered it 'necessary to fight for it most energetically'. He wrote: 'A possibility very seldom to be met with in the history of revolutions now faces the democracy of Russia, the Soviets and the Socialist Revolutionary and Menshevik parties,... to ensure the peaceful development of the revolution, peaceful elections of deputies by the people, and a peaceful struggle of parties inside the Soviets; they could test the programmes of the various parties in practice and power could pass peacefully from one party to another.' It needs to be noticed that along with 'peaceful development of the revolution', this perspective expressly envisaged the existence of several parties and competition for power between them, 'a peaceful struggle of parties inside the Soviets', that is within the system of working-class power. In fact Russia of the Soviets from 1918 to 1921, certainly not a bourgeois democracy, had nonetheless several parties, and that too in the midst of a civil war. (For that matter, the Paris Commune – Karl Marx's 'dictatorship of the proletariat' – far from being a bourgeois democracy – too had several parties).

But counter-revolution's armed attack on the revolution not only foreclosed the option of 'the peaceful development of the revolution', it also effectively destroyed the prospects of 'a peaceful struggle of parties' for power in pursuit of their programmes. The progress of revolution and counter revolution, the increasing polarisation of forces during the civil war, led to the Mensheviks and Socialist Revolutionaries aligning themselves with the counter-revolution and foreign intervention and therefore to their being pushed out of power and eventually suppressed along with the counter-revolution. Even critics of the Bolsheviks, like Otto Bauer, recognised this later on. History has always been a cruel mistress.

Yet again, following Marx's endorsement of the Paris Commune, Lenin argued emphatically in *State and Revolution* that socialism was to be built by way of a system of near direct democracy, with popular rule at all levels, with representation kept to a minimum and representatives as delegates strictly subservient to the wishes and dictates of their constituents, and with very little if any constraint on popular rule itself. This may be a visionary option, not possible at any rate for a very long time to come when a new breed of people will have been produced by a prolonged lived experience of socialist relations of life. But it is still to the credit of Lenin that this is precisely what he sought to achieve in the immediate aftermath of the October Revolution. That Lenin failed does not take anything away from his commitment to democracy. And if democracy is what he fought for on the very morrow of the revolution, his dying years again saw him fighting the last battle of his life for it, against the emerging authoritarianism of a malignant bureaucracy in the Soviet Union.

Lenin failed. Principles were indeed departed from in the practice of democracy in the Soviet society and the Bolshevik party. But these departures were viewed as temporary, compelled by the objective circumstances, by the need, as perceived by Lenin and his comrades, to defend and save the revolution and to consolidate the Soviet power against its internal and external enemies. They were not born of any Marxist theory, it was history impinging upon the practice of Marxists. They, including Lenin, could certainly have done better. It is always possible, but what ultimately happened must not be allowed to obscure the basic, principled commitment of revolutionary Marxism, that Lenin well represented, to democracy as the only adequately humane and legitimate form of economic, social and political organisation and practice in our society.

Departures from principles were made, to themselves become principles in the post-Lenin period. But, it may be noted, not without a powerful protest affirming democratic values from within the revolutionary Marxist tradition itself. We have, in an earlier chapter, already taken note of what Rosa Luxemburg wrote in 1918 by way of fraternal criticism of these departures. A fellow Marxist, ardent admirer of Bolsheviks and active supporter of Russian Revolution, she had warned: 'Without general election, without unrestricted freedom of press and assembly, without a free struggle of opinion, life dies out in every public institution, becomes a mere semblance of life, in which only the bureaucracy remains an active element.'

XIV

Closely associated with the question of democracy is the question of power in society, which has been a much, though poorly, discussed subject in contemporary social theory. I am here concerned with only one particular aspect of the question. With a renewed focus on the 'evils' of the now collapsed Soviet system, we are again being told that power always and necessarily corrupts, that it can never be trusted, no matter who is in control of it. It has its mechanisms, which regardless of the intentions or determination of those 'in power', have their own effects or consequences and these tend to go counter to individuality, spontaneity and independence of human beings. Power not only makes for 'normalisation' and conformity, enforced sameness and standardisation of life, it is, per se, anti-democratic, a source of authoritarianism, an enemy of freedom. At the end of such a discourse, Marxism, which seeks power for the working people, for the poor and oppressed of the world to change this world into a more humane place, is seen as the main culprit, responsible for most authoritarianism and its evils in our time. This however is nothing new. With varying interest or emphasis over time, it has been a feature of bourgeois discourse on power in recent decades. By associating power with the authoritarian danger, it has regularly sought to question and undermine people's aspiration for power to be able to change society in their own interest.

It is significant that this questioning of people's aspiration for power has been accompanied by efforts to obscure or hide the reality of rulers' own power in capitalist society which, again, has been a feature of bourgeois discourse on power in recent decades. We may well take a quick look at this before proceeding with the main theme.

It has always been dangerous to look too closely at political power in class-divided societies. Hence mystifications have abounded. Bourgeois democracy, as we shall see, in its own way hides or mystifies the reality of power in capitalist society. But typically for our times, this is also done in the name of social science and has been a distinct feature of recent political theory. In the heyday of behaviouralism, for example, one supposedly scientific study after another was made – really so many exercises in 'barefoot empiricism', which focusing on 'facts', on 'the visible' and 'the obvious', analysed the decision-making by different lobbies, interest groups, 'society notables', etc. – to reach the conclusion that power in capitalist society is not concentrated in a single more or less homogenous 'power elite' or 'class', but is rather competitive, fragmented and diffused; everybody directly or through organised groups has some power and nobody has or can have too much of it, etc. etc. Arguing along these lines, we had the almost bizarre achievement (or evasion) of bourgeois political science where, with Robert Dahl and others, no one has political power in the USA, or at the very least, we cannot legitimately speak of any one having it.

That this is a grossly mistaken view of things is obvious. It was pointed out at the time that such studies of 'concrete cases where key decisions are made', neglected the power of 'non-decision-making', the role of 'institutionalised bias' or the 'mobilisation of bias' of the structure, in other words, the structural conditions of social behaviour or decision-making. More to the point, this 'pluralist' view ignores the fact that political power or domination in capitalist society primarily grows out of its economic or class-structural constitution. Power in such a society is essentially concentrated not so much in its individual capitalists (or groups of them) but its structures. Decision-making is not just limited by this capitalist context, it is dominated by it in the sense that it decisively influences the range of both choices and roles of individuals. The power inhering in the structures of capitalism determines, within a range of possibilities, particular acts of decision-making. Capitalism's private property regime is installed at the very heart of productive apparatus of capitalist society and its structured exigencies are decisive in determining the 'decisions that matter' – unless, of course, we are prepared to overthrow it. Though it is well to remember that this regime, the economic structures of capitalism are always well-protected by the capitalist state, however democratic it may be. (Incidentally, the state as a subject of political study became unfashionable with the pluralists and the question of state playing any such class role virtually disappeared in their discourse on power. Wrote Ralph Miliband: 'Its first result is to exclude, by definition, the notion that the state might be a rather special institution, whose main purpose is to defend the predominance in society of a particular class. There are, in Western societies, no such predominant classes, interests or groups. There are only competing blocs of interests, whose competition, which is sanctioned and guaranteed by the state itself, ensures that power *is* diffused and balanced, and that no particular interest is able to weigh too heavily upon the state'.)

The myth of bourgeois pluralism has been well cultivated. In a pleasing euphemism capitalism is described as 'the plural society' and the pluralist asks 'Does anyone have power in this society?' – the answer is 'No'. And the implication is obvious: the more powerful you want to make the capitalist class, the less powerful you see it. Yet if the scholars are unclear about where power lies in capitalist society, those who rule have no doubt whatsoever. Nor those who actually exercise power in their behalf. Way back in 1913, Woodrow Wilson had said: 'The masters of the United States are the combined capitalists and manufacturers of the United States'. Again, in the early 1960s, in his final address after eight years as President, Eisenhower warned Americans against the danger from the 'military-industrial complex whose total influence – economic, political, even spiritual – is felt in every city, every State House, every office of the Federal Government', indeed, 'reaches into every American family'. The bourgeois social scientist refuses to see what the presidents of the United States have long known and acknowledged!

If the bourgeois discourse on power has, indirectly or otherwise, sought to obscure or hide the reality of power in capitalist society, its more direct purpose, evading the real issues, has been to question and reject the people's aspiration for power to radically reconstruct their lives, if need be, by constructing socialism. In fact Acton's cliché, 'all power corrupts; and absolute power corrupts absolutely' has been repeated *ad nauseum* in this connection, as the most apt judgement upon such aspiration, all the more so in the wake of the Soviet collapse. When the long denied oppressed people aspire for freedom, and struggle for power to realise it, their aspiration and struggle are denied in the name of freedom itself. This is indeed how, for example, it happened in the 1960s, when, in the debates of the time, power was simply counterposed to freedom as its opposite, to become 'the commonsense' of bourgeois social theory on this subject. Power, we were informed, yet again, is a threat to freedom, thus bypassing the real problems of both power and freedom in contemporary societies, most of all those in the third world.

Such or similar bypassing of real problems remains a feature of current academic theorising on the subject of power in modern society. The latest intellectual fashion, post-modernism, is a good example. Drawing on the approach of Michel Foucault, who has argued that power is dispersed and does not by any means reside where people are accustomed to look for it, post-modernist discourse theorists have put forward explications of the workings of power almost totally within the realm of the subjective. Power is seen as something negotiated between individuals in the process of social interaction. Focus is on 'deconstruction' of individuals which, in effect, leaves them at the mercy of ruling class power as it really exists and functions in a capitalist society, even as it also directs people's attention away from any possibility of collective political action to win power for themselves. At the same time, it is interesting to note, such theorisation on power is accompanied by 'suspicion of power' which, a significant presence in it for long, has today again surfaced with renewed anxiety in bourgeois thought. It is in fact a central theme in post-modernism, underwriting much of the theory of Derrida and others. Once again power is necessarily corrupt, invariably tends to be authoritarian, is always a threat to freedom. It has an autonomous structure or logic of its own, and cannot be trusted, no matter who is 'in power'. Insofar as, once again, the real issues are evaded and no change in the existing structures of power is envisaged, the current discourse on power is, consciously or otherwise, supportive of these structures. 'Grand narratives are out', a Lyotard pronounces, which, in effect, endorses the 'grand narrative' of capitalism that is very much on, more 'grand' and oppressive today than ever before. There is deep scepticism about the possibility of any radical change in society and every such hope or project is cynically dismissed. The optimism of the left, in its aspiration for power in behalf of the alternative, socialist narrative can only be deserving of scorn by post-modernists. But, typically, this aspiration is also seen as dangerous and feared, for power, no matter who has it, is inherently authoritarian, a threat to freedom.

The counterposing of power and freedom, a regular feature of bourgeois discourse on power in recent times which has received a new fillip with the Soviet collapse, is an evasion of real issues, especially when looked at from the standpoint of the common people. For the common people, and even otherwise, the real issues are power and checks on power to win freedom and to ensure it.

The aspiration for power is central to people's struggle for freedom. Power is an essential key to social liberation of the poor and the oppressed. They need power to break up the existing structures of power embodying exploitation, oppression and unfreedom for them, and build up a life of freedom and justice for themselves. Hence the centrality of the question of people's power in the state. There are many, including quite a few involved in 'grass roots' activism or 'new social movements' as they are called, who in a legitimate disappointment with certain old or traditional emancipatory movements are also, most illegitimately, rather sceptical, even dismissive of the latter's concern with the question of political power or power in the state. Abandoning the perspective of struggle for state power as such they seek a straight path to people's salvation through the development, at best, of foci of local power. There are even socialists who, leaving aside the question of state power, for the time being at least, believe that a popular socialist movement can be built without any initial focus on the contest for state power. This is no genuine advance, only regression, often times an impotent pseudo-radical posture. All those who seek a genuinely radical or revolutionary transformation of society, including the best of those involved in 'grass roots' activism or 'new social movements' will do well to recognise the power, and class character of the power, of the existing state. The state remains central to the ruling class domination in society. It is the organiser of society in the interests of its class exploitative structures taken as a whole, 'the entire complex of practical and theoretical activities' with which, in Gramsci's words, 'the ruling class not only justifies and maintains its dominance, but manages to win the active consent of those over whom it rules' – and these 'activities' pre-eminently include those of its multiform, ever expanding, ever more sophisticated apparatuses of coercion. Those who would thus leave the state alone, would do well to remember that the state will not leave *them* alone. Anarcho-syndicalist IWW's slogan, 'leave the state alone, turn upon the masters' never worked. Abolished and banished by decree one morning by the anarchists in the town of Lille (in one of the episodes of

19th century revolutionary struggles in France), the state duly 'returned' by the evening to throw them out of power. Insofar as people's power remains central to the success of their struggle for freedom and better life, the question of this power cannot be decided outside of or apart from the state. It has to be people's power in the state, their 'political supremacy' in society. This remains a necessary condition for breaking up the established, exploitative and oppressive power structures and for initiating and carrying through pro-people transformation of society. 'To win the battle of democracy' is how Marx defined this primary political task in the *Communist Manifesto*.

It is precisely the centrality of the question of power, of people's power in the state, their 'political supremacy' in society, which, given especially the Soviet experience, accounts for the centrality of the question of checks on power. Abstraction for abstraction, as against Acton's 'all power corrupts; and absolute power corrupts absolutely', 'freedom *through* power' is any day more meaningful and certainly more relevant to the needs of the vast majority of men and women in the world today. For these men and women need not only freedom but also power, power to make their freedom come true. But once the abstraction 'freedom through power' is translated into such concrete questions as '*whose* power is it?', or, still better, '*whose* or *what* purposes does it serves?', it becomes a matter of checking and controlling power *in relation to* these purposes, which in the present context means so checking and controlling power that it serves only to give meaning and content to freedom. The issue thus turns into one of democracy, of effective democratic checks on power. And this is precisely the area of most grievous failure of the system in the Soviet Union and Eastern Europe.

With the experience of these communist regimes in mind, apropos 'the huge problems posed by the democratic exercise of power' in a post-revolutionary society, Ralph Miliband wrote:

> To tackle these problems requires that attention be paid to some quite ancient propositions. Of these, none is more important than the proposition that only power can check power. Such checking power has to occur both within the state, and also from the outside. Within the state, it involves mechanisms which Communist

regimes, to their immense detriment, have spurned: the checking of the executive and the administration by an effective legislature; the independence of the judiciary; the strict and independent control of police powers; the curbing and control of official discretion. Such devices could not properly operate in Communist systems, given the superior and supreme allegiance owed by all state organs to the Party and its leaders. In the light of this imperative requirement, it would have been idle to expect a legislative assembly to take seriously its formal constitutional powers. So too would it have been unreasonable to expect judges to make decisions that appeared to contradict what was wanted higher up.

This is not to imply that checks and balances are particularly effective in capitalist-democratic regimes, or even that they necessarily serve desirable purposes. It is only to argue that the checking of executive, administrative and police power – indeed all forms of power – is an intrinsic part of the politics of socialist democracy. Such politics can not entail the wholesale rejection of traditional liberal principles in the conduct of government, but rather their radical extension, far beyond anything that was ever dreamt of by liberal thinkers. This means a fostering of many centres of power outside the state, in a system of autonomous and independent associations, groupings, parties and lobbies of every kind and description, expressing a multitude of concerns and aspirations woven in the tissue of society. Such pluralism can only flower in a regime where 'bourgeois freedoms' are fully guaranteed and extended, and vigilantly defended by a free press and other media, and from many other sources as well. Socialist democracy, on this view, is a system of 'dual power', in which state power and popular power complement each other, but also check each other.

Here too, it is as well to acknowledge that all this constitutes a difficult and fraught enterprise. But the whole experience of Communist regimes suggests that, in socialist terms, there is no other way. There is always bound to be a tension between what are perceived to be the needs of government by those who are in charge of it, and the claims of democracy. The crucial lesson which Communist regimes teach is that the attempt to resolve that tension by sacrificing the claims of democracy to what are taken to be the needs of government is self-defeating. What one ends up with is bad government and no democracy. What is required is the maintenance of a balance between these conflicting claims – a difficult and precarious enterprise, but an essential one.

Miliband had added: 'There is also a very different dimension to socialist democracy, related to the previous one, but which is never given the requisite attention and concern: this is that socialism stands, or should by definition stand, for *humane rule*.'

XV

Before I return to the subject of democracy proper, a quick critical look at whatever little Marx and Engels wrote on the question of state and public power in socialist/communist society will not be out of place.

For Marx and Engels, as revolutionaries, the question of state was always above all a question of power. They saw the state as essentially a product of class antagonisms in society, spoke of state institutions as a system of organised and legalised class coercion, visualised the 'smashing' and transformation of the old 'state machine' as one of the key tasks of a socialist revolution, and postulated a post-revolutionary transitional state, the 'dictatorship of the proletariat', which was, however, yet not a state for them. Beyond these much-noticed specific concerns of their revolutionary politics, however, is the more basic fact that Marx and Engels always cnsidered he state as essentially antipathetic to human freedom. 'The existence of the state and the existence of slavery are inseparable', announced Marx in an early polemic. A little later he wrote that 'the working class in course of its development will substitute the old civil society by an association which will exclude classes and their antagonism, and there will no more be (any) political power properly speaking.' In the *Communist Manifesto*, Marx (and Engels) had argued that with 'production concentrated in the hands of the associated individuals, public power will lose its political character'. Marx praised the Parisian Communards for their 'revolution not against this or that state power... but against the *state* itself.' In his *Gothakritik*, he denounced the 'Lassallean sect's servile faith in the state', which Marx considers as 'remote from socialism'. And, finally, for Marx, after the demise of the proletarian political power along with the proletariat at the end of the revolutionary transformation period and the consequent disappearance of classes, the state too, even as 'dictatorship of the proletariat', will have no place in socialist/communist society. It will stand dissolved into public power that will look after the general interests of society as such, and not, not any longer, any particular class. Marx never seriously considered which social functions would remain in the communist society analogous to the present-day state functions. But the notion of public power in society for the performance of necessary social functions is a basic premise in Marx and Engels.

Marx and Engels did write of the 'withering away' of the state in a class-less society. But this is best understood as an ideal which is in one sense a logical projection from a view of the state where class coercion is the defining feature so that the state disappears with the disappearance of the classes, and in another the promise, in however long-term a perspective, of socialism: the possibility of a society where coercive power eventually ceases to be the organising principle of social life. This ideal of course constitutes an immense wager on the capacity of the human race to achieve unforced cooperation. But it is also indicative of Marx's awareness of the possibilities inhering in the human race, which lesser men, their humanity and vision blighted by centuries of existence in class-divided societies and now under capitalism, cannot even imagine and dismiss as 'utopianism'. The critics are only being presumptuous in thus foreclosing these possibilities of the future. Be that as it may, Marx and Engels' 'withering away' of the state did not mean disappearance of public power, rather it pointed, however implicitly, to its presence as non-coercive power that marks or should mark a truly democratic and humane society – something about which they were otherwise quite explicit. Note, for example, their proposition (in *Communist Manifesto*) that the 'public power will lose its political character'; or as Engels put it elsewhere, the state 'in the proper sense of the word' will disappear. In a still more pertinent observation, Engels wrote: 'public functions will lose their political character and be transformed into the simple administrative functions of watching over the true interests of society'. The implications are obvious: losing 'its political character' does not mean that public power will cease to be; rather, it will pose the problem of ensuring that it stays 'unpolitical', maintains its purely 'administrative' character and above all acts in only 'the true interests of society'. This, again obviously, will call for institutionalised measures to so check and control that it remains true to its purpose. What all this ultimately means is that a humane and 'unpolitical' public power may become possible in a socialist society, but it does not in any way become inevitable. There has to be a struggle, a conscious effort to secure it.

In Engels' account of origins of the state or Marx's discussion of the Asiatic mode of production and other pre-capitalist social formations, we have a clear hint of a possibility with public power which yields a similar conclusion. The suggestion is that in a class or even class-less situation public power may be and historically has often been itself a source of class differentiation, at its origins or later in society. In other words, public power, even as it performs, or is instituted to undertake socially necessary functions, it can have or come to have an explicitly 'political', class-exploitative character. These functions – warfare and public defence, necessary regulation of production and distribution, direction of communal labour, construction of vital public works, coping with natural or social disasters, and so on – have often been the original basis of the claims to and capacity for surplus appropriation, but ended up producing class divisions and the state in the narrow, class-coercive sense. If something like this could happen in the past, a parallel or similar transmutation of public power into something like class domination could not be ruled out in the future. This is indeed what can be said to have happened in the former Soviet Union, where the public or political power vested in those entrusted with the task of planned socialist development of society, ended up producing a historically specific class society with its own, equally specific, ruling class. Given this dangerous possibility, there is always the need for institutionalised protection against it, for constant democratic checks and control on public power.

This apart, we have in Marx the argument of a more positive nature on the subject. He saw the public power of the Paris Commune as consisting of officials who are 'responsible agents of society', but never 'superior to society'. In this connection, Engels explicitly warned against letting these 'servants' become 'masters' as had happened in previous revolutions. In his early writings Marx wrote of *absorption* of the state by society, but it never implied its dissolution per se. The problem of the state in socialist/communist society remained with him to find a more explicit answer in his later *Critique of the Gotha Programme*, where he postulated 'the subordination of the state to society'. He wrote: 'freedom consists in converting the state from an organ superimposed upon society into one completely subordinate to it, and today, too, the forms of state are more or less free to the extent that they restrict the "freedom of the state"'. However much Marx and Engels may have tended towards political utopianism, here is an explicit recognition of the persistence of the problem of the state in socialist/communist society. That, insofar as it continues to exist as public power, the state needs to be 'subordinated' to society, indicates the paramount importance of the allied problem of not merely democratically representative organisation throughout civil society, but more specifically, of conscious and institutionalised controls over public power, organised checks or restrictions on the state to prevent misappropriation or abuse of power, to secure what Marx described as the *subordination* of the state to society. And highly significant is the suggestion that the restrictions on state power instituted by the most 'liberal' of bourgeois societies may have something to teach on the score of dealing with that problem, to secure the maximum possible freedom. 'Freedom' in bourgeois society is, of course, something very different from the complete 'subordination of the state to society' which can occur only in a society without class domination. But whatever the transformations state may undergo in such a society, what its necessary or legitimate social functions, insofar as Marx recognises some kind of connection between freedom in the bourgeois state and the subordination of the state to society under socialism/communism, a connection that has something to do with the establishment of checks on state power, with the institutionalised restrictions on the 'freedom of the state', socialists who are followers of Marx have something to learn here from the tradition of bourgeois liberalism. Just as they also need to acquire clarity on the subject of democracy the way it has come up in our times as bourgeois democracy.

XVI

The critics' legitimate focus on its *bourgeois* aspect has often led sections of the radical left to an entirely illegitimate misunderstanding of bourgeois democracy, where it is not only bourgeois but only that, and democratic rights are 'so-called', merely bourgeois rights and nothing more. Bourgeois democracy is seen as something established or cleverly put up by the ruling classes to cheat the people and promote their own interests, and thus deserving to be rejected or boycotted. The conventional idealist interpretation of things, even as it rejects this view, yet lends it a vicarious credibility, for it tends to see modern democracy almost as a gift from the bourgeoisie, discovered or achieved by it over a long period of time, as per se 'the best form of government' that a society can have or aspire to. But nothing could be more misleading than such interpretations of the nature and development of democracy in modern times. There is indeed a connection between the evolution of modern democracy and the bourgeoisie's rise to power in the west. But the nature of such connection needs to be clearly understood, for, in many important ways, it has very little to do with democracy as it has developed in our times.

In the conventional writing on the subject which tends to identify milestones in the ascent of the propertied classes as the principal landmarks in history, modern democracy is often sought to be traced centuries back to some of these landmarks or developments, even of the late feudal period. In England, for example, these are Magna Carta, the 'so-called' glorious revolution of 1688, the establishment of constitutional principles whose real object was to safeguard feudal liberties, powers and privileges, and strengthen the hands of the propertied classes not only against monarchical power but against the common people, 'the multitude', as well. The Huguenot resistance tracts in France, in particular the *Vindicae Contra Tyrannos*, have been treated as classics of democratic political thought, when they more precisely represent the reassertion of feudal rights especially by lesser provincial nobles – those who benefited least from the favours of the court and from access to high state office – against an encroaching monarchy. Pointing this out Ellen Meiksins Wood has suggested that what such conventional accounts do is to conflate aristocratic 'constitutionalist' principles with democracy and present such advances in the power of the landed aristocracy as the pivotal moments in the evolution of democracy. This is obviously a mistaken reading of history. Such a definition of democracy would never have occurred to the major participants in the relevant historical events, for whom consolidating the power of the landed classes was, by definition, for good or for evil, *anti*-democratic. Theirs were backward-looking claims to a piece of the old parcellised sovereignty of feudalism, not a looking forward to a modern democratic political order claiming to represent and empower the people. The people were, in fact, still not 'people' as we now know them; they were the 'naturally inferior', only 'the multitude', at times 'the swinish multitude'.

In a sharp comment on the conventional view of origins of democracy, E.M. Wood has written: 'There were to be many long and arduous struggles before the "people" grew to encompass the labouring multitude, let alone women. It is a curious fact that in the dominant ideologies of Anglo–American political culture these struggles have not achieved the status of principal milestones in the history of democracy. In the canons of English-speaking liberalism, the main road to modern democracy runs through Rome, Magna Carta, the Petition of Rights and the Glorious Revolution, not Athens, the Levellers, Diggers and Chartism. Nor is it simply that the historical record belongs to the victors; for if 1688, not Levellers and Diggers represents the winners, should not history record that democracy was on the losing side?'

But if 'constitutionalism' has, historically, often been aristocratic, even feudal in its motivation, representing the assertion of independent *lordship* by European aristocracies against encroachment by centralising monarchies, and therefore should not be identified with 'democracy', it certainly made an important contribution to the development of 'limited' and 'responsible' government. It is this which the emerging bourgeoisie found useful when, after an uneasy, though not entirely unfruitful period with early absolutist monarchy, it sought a place for itself in a non-arbitrary, law-based state, which would provide for further and better development of the capitalist mode of production, governed by the laws of the market – Adam Smith's 'Providence' or 'unseen hand' – rather than by arbitrary feudal interventions. But having gained economic power, in the aftermath of the industrial revolution, the bourgeoisie also sought political ascendancy for itself – the limited, law-based state must also become *representative*, that is representative of the bourgeoisie. England is a good example; the 'rotten' and 'pocket' boroughs had to go. Thus began the struggle for suffrage. The bourgeoisie spoke in the name of general interests, as such classes always do, and in a sense it did at the time represent the interests of the society as a whole, though behind it all lurked its own class interests. The working classes rallied in support of its demands against the old order. They fought, the suffrage was won, but initially only for the bourgeoisie, who then called it a day. However, often brought in by the bourgeoisie itself, the working classes had entered the political arena, and the struggle continued. The struggle for democracy was waged and won by the working classes of England in the teeth of the opposition by the bourgeoisie.

In *Communist Manifesto*, speaking of 'collisions between the classes of the old society', Marx had written: 'The bourgeoisie finds itself involved in a constant battle. At first with the aristocracy; later on, with those portions of the bourgeoisie itself, whose interests have become antagonistic to the progress of industry; at all times, with the bourgeoisie of foreign countries. In all these battles it sees itself compelled to appeal to the proletariat to ask for its help and thus, to drag it into the political arena. The bourgeoisie itself, therefore, supplies the proletariat with its own elements of political and general education; in other words, it furnishes the proletariat with weapons for fighting the bourgeoisie...' This is how, entering the arena of political struggle, the working class won universal adult suffrage and associated freedoms of what is described as 'bourgeois liberalism'. The important point is that democracy and democratic rights – universal suffrage, right to individual liberty, freedom of assembly and association, of press and opinion, political pluralism – are neither a gift or achievement of the bourgeoisie, nor mere 'bourgeois' rights or institutions, but hard-won conquests of the labour movement and the working people.

Many struggles, often bloody had indeed to be waged before private property and other obstacles standing in the way of attaining electoral and other political rights were eliminated, or before workers achieved the legal possibility to strike and organise the unions and political parties, or before women became full-fledged citizens. While the democratic idea can be said to have evolved over the past two hundred years and more, and the American Revolution of 1776, the French Revolution of 1789, the revolutionary struggles of the 19th century in Europe and the great Reform Bill in England in 1832 can be treated as decisive events in the spread of this idea, democracy as we now know it is a rather recent affair. In England the universal adult suffrage was achieved only at the end of the 1920s. Parts of America and the whole of France were, from time to time, more democratic in the second half of the 19th century than Britain. But even there, fully democratic institutions at the centre, that is, representative government, only really got going in our own time. In the United States, the principle of 'one person, one vote' was extended to many black citizens only in the 1960s, and millions of migrant workers do not even have that right, though they pay taxes. Jean Ellenstein has calculated that from the beginning of the French Revolution, it took eighty years before universal suffrage was achieved, ninety-five years before the freedom of the press was instituted, and one hundred and twelve years before the right of association was acknowledged in France.

The long and hard struggle for democracy and democratic rights can indeed be viewed as a kind of class struggle because it has been waged and won by the working people against the bitter resistance of the ruling classes, who know that people is not only a majority, it is also a majority that is poor, and as Charles Beard once put it, democracy has 'a levelling tendency that ran in the direction of communism'. The Duke of Wellington expressly feared that democracy would declare war on property. The propertied ruling classes, fearing people and therefore fearful of democracy sought to oppose it, delay, check and limit it, as much and in as many ways as they possible could. Even as the struggle for suffrage began in England in early 19th century, opposing it George Canning thanked God that 'the House of Commons is not sufficiently identified with the people to catch their every nascent wish' and insisted: 'According to no principle of our Constitution was it ever meant to be so... it never pretended to be so, nor can ever pretend to be so without bringing ruin and misery upon the kingdom.' Decades later, in the 1960s, Lord Salisbury expressed the fear that democracy would 'place the employer at the mercy of the employed', and Robert Lowe, therefore, argued: 'If the House were placed on a more democratic basis, the English system of making the Executive directly responsible to the legislature would have to be abolished.' So it was in other areas of struggle for democratic rights. Whatever the variations or complexities of the struggle for democracy in England or other western capitalist countries, and these include the conflict of interests within the ruling classes, two facts stand out as unquestionable: it is the working classes and common people who struggled, pressed for and won democracy, and it is the ruling classes as a whole who always and everywhere opposed it.

This points to a contradiction lying at the very foundation of modern democracy as it came up in the west and elsewhere. The working people indeed won democracy but within a capitalist system, fully subject to its limitations; it has been a capitalist or bourgeois democracy, an encapsulation of two opposed principles or systems. As such it has carried an insoluble problem within itself. Ralph Miliband has written: 'on the one hand there is capitalism, a system of economic organization that demands the existence of a relatively small class of people who own and control the main means of industrial, commercial and financial activity, as well as a major part of the means of communication; these people thereby exercise a totally disproportionate amount of influence on politics and society both in their own countries and in lands far beyond their own borders. On the other hand there is democracy, which is based on the denial of such preponderance, and which requires a rough equality of conditions that capitalism repudiates by its very nature. Domination and exploitation are ugly words but they are at the very core of capitalist democracy, and are inextricably linked to it.' The contradiction is obvious and the problem involved was well expressed by the American Supreme Court Justice Louis Brandies a long time back: 'we can have a democratic society or we can have the concentration of great wealth in the hands of the few. We cannot have both'.

The contradiction between democracy and capitalism has meant that even as people from below seek to use and enlarge their democratic rights to contain the capitalist domination and promote their own interests in bourgeois democratic regimes, the capitalist classes and their political representatives are ever engaged in an effort from above to limit and erode such rights, to encroach upon and subvert democracy. They constantly seek, in the words of John Strachey, 'to manipulate and distort, and if necessary frustrate, the workings of ...democracy to (their) own advantage'. It has always been, as Laski once put it, an 'uneasy marriage between capitalism and democracy', which, when its interests so demanded, capitalism has never hesitated to dissolve in favour of its authoritarian, even fascist rule. The historical experience of the 20th century the world over, including the advanced capitalist countries, bears ample testimony to the fact that the threat to democracy has invariably come from the ruling classes, it is the people who have defended it, even if not successfully always.

That democracy is a hard-won gain of popular struggles and people need to defend it, seek to preserve and expand it, and that democracy has a tendency to run counter to capitalism so that capitalist classes constantly seek to contain and erode democracy and, when faced with the choice, abandon democracy altogether to opt for more direct authoritarian or fascist rule of capital, that, in short, there is a contradiction between capitalism and democracy – this is of course important to understand. But this is yet only a point of entry into understanding modern democracy.

The dialectics of the contradictory situation suggested by these two aspects is more complex and works out in many different ways. This demands that we take another, closer look at the relation between capitalism and democracy. This is all the more necessary because there are real dangers in failing to see the deeper structural connections here or mistaking their character. The accounts of western democracy as an autonomous development, independent of the historical process which produced capitalism, are quite common and these can be seriously limiting of not only our understanding of democracy and capitalism, or socialist democracy, but of socialism itself. It is indeed fashionable among certain well-meaning sections of the left today to see socialism as the gradual outgrowth of a socially progressive evolution of 'modern democracy' itself.

XVII

This closer look at the relation between capitalism and democracy can well begin by noticing a fact and the way its implications have found expression in contemporary bourgeois theorising on the subject of democracy. As we have noticed, the ruling classes feared and opposed democracy. In its original meaning democracy meant the power of the common people and was therefore seen as a threat to the interests of the rich and powerful in society. 'Democracy is born', a fearful Plato had written, 'when the poor win the day, killing some... banishing others, and sharing with the rest the rights of citizenship and of public offices, on terms of equality'. From the other end we have Engels' exultant cry of 1843: 'Democracy, nowadays that is communism'. More recently we had Charles Beard pointing to its 'levelling tendency that ran in the direction of communism', a fact that de Tocqueville had, in his own way, earlier noticed with his prediction that when the people is sovereign, it is rarely miserable. The ruling upper classes had reasons to be afraid of democracy. But as 'democracy of our times' arrived, they discovered they did not have to fear it, certainly not that much, that they could indeed not only accept it but also afford to declare themselves as committed to democracy. For, as the well-known British author, Walter Bagehot, writing in an earlier, more honest age, with obvious satisfaction, observed: 'democracy is the way to give the people the greatest illusion of power while allowing them the smallest amount in reality'. Apparently, the bourgeois context or capitalist limitations had effectively resulted in what Hobsbawm once described as 'taming of democracy'. Despite democracy, effective power in society had remained with the ruling classes. In addition it was discovered that over time this powerlessness of the people had bred large-scale apathy, indifference and depoliticisation among them.

These discoveries however have not been the cause of any worry or anxiety to bourgeois political theorists, persuading them to recover the original meaning of democracy as effective popular power in the affairs of society. On the contrary, this gulf between people and political power, the powerlessness of the people and their apathy and indifference in capitalist-democratic regimes, even as they are universally recognised, have been defended and actually celebrated as 'democracy' itself. As Robert Paul Wolff puts it, 'they have taken to stating in forthright terms that political apathy is a Good Thing!'. A Morris-Jones writes eloquently 'In Defence of Apathy', underlining 'the efficacy of apathy' on part of the people in sustaining democracy. Almond and Verba laud 'low-level', 'apathetic' citizenship and argue that democracy works well only if the people are 'relatively passive, uninvolved and deferential.' The belief that people can influence the behavour of their rulers, in part at least, is a myth; though, they add, insofar as rulers themselves share in this belief, it does act as a check on their exercise of power. Edelman agrees that the belief that people control their rulers in contemporary democracy is a 'myth', but regards it as a useful myth which provides the public with symbolic gratifications, and makes for the legitimacy of the 'democratic regime' by giving it an appearance of popular support. The 'illusion' of popular power or control almost becomes the criterion of a functioning democratic system. Absence of democracy comes to be the definitive feature of democracy, and popular involvement and participation in politics is seen as a threat to democracy. Thus, a Pulzer can write: 'High electoral participation, massive attendance at meetings, enthusiastic processions and heated discussions may... indicate fever, not robust good health.' The proponents of capital *uber alles*, like the economist Milton Friedman, who are explicit in their contempt for democracy, indeed equate markets with democracy, too find voter disinterest, apathy and cynicism highly desirable especially among those eligible voters who might have insufficient appreciation for the joys of class society and capitalist living. For an informed and active public sphere can only produce negative effects in that it might lead to government policies that interfere with profit maximisation. As C.B. Macpherson has written, depoliticisation of the masses is indeed the best way for the ruling classes to reconcile their inegalitarian economics with egalitarian politics of democracy. (Occasionally, worry is indeed expressed by ruling class politicians and ideologues over popular 'apathy', indifference or disinterest occurring on too large a scale but the reason is not any concern for democracy but fear, since it means the masses are beyond the reach of the control mechanisms of their 'democratic politics').

It is interesting to note that when in the 1960s and early 1970s, as a result of massive popular protests certain progressive domestic policies were adopted in the US, the business community had reacted with alarm and, according to the global neo-liberal group, the Trilateral Commission, the United States (indeed the world) was awash in a 'crisis of democracy' created by the fact that traditionally apathetic poor people – young people, women, and people of colour – were getting too involved in the political process! The implication is obvious: Democracy functions best and remains crisis-free if people somehow don't actively participate in it.

One is reminded of Aristotle who had discovered and said as much, far more honestly and intelligently more than two thousand years ago. More honestly because as against our modern theorists who profess to be democratic, Aristotle was frankly elitist in his politics (who rules) as well as ethics (good life); more intelligently because of the superiority of his analysis which, as against the modern empiricistic exercises, focussed on the deeper underlying social basis of democratic politics and the fact that the 'majority' we speak of in democracy is more importantly a majority that is poor. Aristotle accepted democracy as matter of practical or political necessity and not as anything desirable, and then sought to keep the people as much out of it as possible. He wrote of four forms of democracy, moving from the coastal city to the agrarian hinterland as its site, and opted in favour of a democracy of the agricultural people, because it has the least participation of the people – what with the people 'busily engaged' in farming and without 'time for attending the assembly', etc. – so that the better classes can rule without impediment from the lower classes. Ross, the well-known commentator on Aristotle wrote: 'What makes it in his eyes a good democracy is that it is hardly a democracy at all'!

With a slight exaggeration one could argue that the most important, if not the sole major discovery of modern political science, its ultimate wisdom on the subject is: if you want to have democracy, or to save it, keep the people away from it! The discovery however is not without its theoretical complement in the form of 'elite' or 'pluralist' theory of democracy which focuses on the importance of politically active elites with power to rule. Schumpeterian ideas which downsize the democratic promise to its formalistic or procedural arrangements take over and democracy itself stands reduced to a method solely aimed at the formation of a government, and occasional choice between competing sections of the elite provides all the political participation people require (or are deemed competent to provide). We are presented with a picture of ideal democracy where rulers are chosen by only a part of the citizens, many of whom are indifferent about their choice even as some of them are also at least partially deluded into believing that they can control their rulers if they wish, where rulers indeed exercise power effectively only if the masses are 'relatively passive, uninvolved and deferential'.

The 'elite' or 'pluralist' theory of democracy, with its under-pinning of Schumpeterian ideas is, obviously, a radical departure from the classical theory of democracy, above all, in depriving democracy of its essential ethical content. Political apathy, indifference or ignorance were vices for the founders of democratic theory and they had, for good citizenship as well as good governance, put highest possible value on popular participation in public affairs. In the context of his times, J.S. Mill had written: 'It has often been said, and requires to be repeated still oftener, that books and discourses alone are not education; that life is a problem, not a theorem; that action can only be learnt in action... The spirit of a commercial people will be, we are persuaded, essentially mean and slavish, wherever public spirit is not cultivated by an extensive participation of the people in the business of government in detail.' Now, vices have come to be reinterpreted as virtues, at least so long as they operate within the bourgeois framework, and popular involvement or participation in political process is seen as a threat to democracy.

This departure from the values of classical theory needs to be seen as part of a larger process of dilution as it were of the meaning and content of democracy in our times. Hence also the fact that the dilution of capitalist rulers' fear of democracy has been an important feature of the evolution of modern democracy. One has only to consider the difference between the horror with which the American 'Founding Fathers' regarded 'democracy' – and therefore carefully tailored the US Constitution in such a way that 'the people' were distanced from political control – and the overweening pride with which their successors have claimed the name of 'democracy' for the political order established by these founders and have pursued this 'ideal', its defence or establishment the world over, more recently in the countries of the former 'socialist world', and not only there. This, however, is not difficult to understand if we view the relation between capitalism and democracy as it came to be historically constituted.

XVIII

The idea of democracy has a long history, and in its original meaning it always had explicit class connotations. It was not merely majority rule, as the conventional theory has it, but the rule of a majority which was also poor. Democracy referred precisely to the dominance of the people as *plebs*, that is the most numerous poor. Thus, as Aristotle, for example, saw it: 'The proper application of the term "democracy" is to a constitution in which the free-born and poor control the government – being at the same time a majority' as distinct from oligarchy, in which 'the rich and better-born control the government – being at the same time a minority'. Overweighing the numerical criterion, it is the social criteria – poverty in one, wealth and high birth in the other – which are central to Aristotle's analysis of these phenomena. Recognising 'two cities within a city' and the class war between the rich and poor as the source of civil strife, Plato had written: 'And when the poor win, the result is a democracy'. In a situation where political and economic freedom are in a most important sense inseparable, 'the rights of citizenship' or political equality won by the common people, their direct political participation – in the assembly, in the courts, in the street – gave them substantial power to escape or limit economic exploitation and modify socio-economic inequality in society. For the British ruling classes when they opposed democracy or the American constitutional founders when they feared it, the word 'democracy' had the same meaning as for the Greeks: direct rule by the people, power in the hands of the *plebs*. Hence their fear, anxiety and opposition. But it is precisely this meaning that now gets diluted in modern democracy. One of the most significant aspects of the 'democratic revolution' of our times is that it marks the *dissociation* of democracy from its meaning as *popular power*, as rule by the *demos*. It is precisely for this reason, and not simply because of some general advance in democratic values, that 'democracy' ceased to be a dirty word among the dominant classes.

The dissociation of democracy from its meaning as popular power has been made possible and facilitated primarily by a certain historical specificity characterising the development of capitalism. Now, in a qualitative break from pre-capitalist social formations, not only does 'the economic sphere' so separate out from the rest of society as to constitute an autonomous domain governed by its own laws of motion, but with the complete separation of the producers from the means of production under capitalism, surplus extraction and appropriation no longer requires direct 'extra-economic' coercion or the producers' juridical or political dependence. Capitalists control the labour of others not by means of exclusive political rights but by means of their exclusive control over property. Although capital still needs the support of the state, workers are compelled to sell their labour power for purely 'economic' reasons. Since they do not own the means of production, the sale of labour power for a wage is the only way they can gain access to the conditions of subsistence, and even to the means of their own labour. Their exploitation now takes place by means of an apparently 'free' exchange between juridical 'equals', in a contract between capital and labour mediated by an 'impersonal' market. There is no immediate need for direct political coercion to make them work for capital. Thus a significant transformation of social power occurs wherein the market, separate from and autonomous of the state, becomes the locus of the social or class power of the now dominant capitalist class.

The bourgeoisie is now not a 'ruling' class in the literal sense; its class dominance does not depend on exclusive access to political rights or on a clear and legally defined division between capitalist rulers and proletarian subjects. In fact, once the economic power of the propertied classes no longer depended upon 'extra economic' status, on their judicial, political and military powers, as was the case under feudal lordship, a monopoly on politics was no longer indispensable to them. Under capitalism, therefore, democracy can well flourish in the political or judicial domain while the economy continues to be governed by its own essentially undemocratic principles of private property and the marketplace.

Capitalism's formal separation of 'political' and 'economic' spheres and the location of capitalist hegemony in the economic sphere, makes the universality of political rights possible in a way that no other form of class domination has ever been able to do. For the simple reason that this universality of political rights – in particular, universal suffrage – leaves property relations and the power of appropriation intact in a way that was never true before. Liberties that meant a great deal to early modern aristocracies and whose extension to the 'multitude' *then* would have completely transformed society, do not mean the same thing now because the economy has acquired a life of its own, completely outside the ambit of citizenship, political freedom, or democratic accountability. In the changed meaning of citizenship under capitalism, the equality of political rights has a minimal effect on inequalities or relations of domination and exploitation in other spheres of social life.

In other words, a specific feature of development of capitalism is its separation of the economic and political spheres and the location of the class power of the new propertied classes essentially in the economic sphere, which makes it possible to displace and confine democracy in the purely political sphere and thus devalue or dilute it. Democracy is now a 'formal' affair, having to do with political and legal principles and procedures rather than with the disposition of social or class power. This democracy, its freedoms and equality of rights have no directly radical implications for the autonomous realm of surplus appropriation and class exploitation in a capitalist society, unlike in pre-capitalist societies where appropriation and exploitation are inextricably bound up with juridical, political and military power, and where such freedoms or equality of rights would be impossible. Democracy thus diluted is quite compatible with capitalism. The capitalist rulers could well afford to accept and accommodate it. They have not only done so but also seen the advantage of effectively appropriating democracy by redefining it, assimilating its meaning to whatever political goods their particular interests could tolerate.

This redefinition became all the more necessary, ideologically, because of the pressure from below generated by the progress of 'mass democracy', of popular political mobilisation and mass electoral politics in the late 19th and early

20th centuries. Even as the ruling classes sought to limit mass democracy in practice, they also thought it necessary to place limits on it in theory. They recognised the obvious ideological advantages of redefining democracy to keep it safe for themselves against the growing popular pressure. In a clear dissociation of 'democracy' from the *demos*, the people, or at least a decisive shift away from popular power as the principal criterion of democratic values, democracy was defined in terms of liberal values, that is in terms of right to vote, civil liberties, freedom of speech, press and assembly, constitutional or juridical procedures to defend the individual or 'civil society' against the state, and so on. In a way, this was a throw back to pre-capitalist, feudal-era principles of constitutionalism, representation and civil liberties, political goods which *then* could not be shared with the people, but, as part of liberal democracy, could now be maximally expanded and extended to them, because they left untouched the prime sphere of capitalist exploitation and domination, the market. Class exploitative relations in society can survive even with juridical equality and universal suffrage. Democracy as it has come up in our times, presents no fundamental challenge to capitalism and its system of exploitation. It stands very much domesticated by capitalism on the one hand and modern liberalism on the other.

Democracy, in its original and literal meaning – the rule by the *demos* – has been very much on the losing side in our modern times. It is part of the current disorientation on the left that even democratic socialist movements that kept the original tradition alive have increasingly come to accept the capitalist-liberal domestication of democracy.

Let me conclude this argument by sharing two passages from Ellen Meiksins Wood who has written most perceptively on the subject of democracy in our times:

> Capitalism has been able to tolerate an unprecedented distribution of political goods, the rights and liberties of citizenship, because it has also for the first time made possible a form of citizenship, civil liberties and rights which can be abstracted from the distribution of social power. In this respect, it contrasts sharply

with the profound transformation of class power expressed by the original Greek conception of democracy as rule by the demos, which represented a specific distribution of class power summed up in Aristotle's definition of democracy as rule by the poor. Access to political rights in societies where surplus extraction occurs by 'extra-economic' means and the power of economic exploitation is inseparable from juridical and political status and privilege has a very different meaning from what it does in capitalism, with its expropriated direct producers and a form of appropriation not directly dependent on juridical or political standing. In other words, in Athens, where citizenship remained a critical determinant in relations of exploitation, there could be no such thing as purely 'formal' political rights or purely 'formal' equality. It was capitalism which for the first time made possible a purely 'formal' political sphere, with purely 'political' rights and liberties.

That historical transformation laid the foundation for a redefinition of the word 'democracy'. If capitalism made this reconceptualization possible, political developments in a sense made it necessary. As it became more difficult for dominant classes simply to denounce democracy, with the intrusion of the 'masses' into the political sphere, the concept of democracy began to lose its social connotations, in favour of essentially procedural or 'formal' criteria. The concept was, in other words, domesticated, made acceptable to dominant classes who could now claim commitment to 'democratic' principles without fundamentally endangering their own dominance. Now, the purely 'formal' principles of liberalism have come to be *identified* with democracy. In other words, these formal principles are treated not simply as good in themselves, nor even as necessary conditions for democracy in the literal sense of popular rule, but as synonymous with it or as its outer limit.

Again:

Capitalism makes universal citizenship possible but at the same time makes it less important. In precapitalist societies, possessing political rights had very direct and immediate economic implications. In capitalism, it just doesn't. A capitalist doesn't need direct political and military powers to exploit workers the way, for instance, a feudal lord needed them to exploit peasants. And having rights of citizenship doesn't prevent workers from having to sell their labour power for a wage. Feudalism, by definition, was inconceivable with universal citizenship rights. Try to imagine feudalism with universal adult suffrage. But capitalism can live with some kind of democracy. The world isn't divided any more between rulers who appropriate the surplus and subjects who produce it. Capitalists and workers are equally citizens. But that's because so much of our life under capitalism goes on in spheres outside the reach of democratic accountability. Capitalist exploitation goes on, and the imperatives of capital accumulation continue to operate, however much democracy there may be in some other, separate political sphere. So capitalism has changed the whole meaning of citizenship and democracy. If we want to achieve a truly democratic society now, it isn't for the most part a matter of extending political rights to people who didn't have them before. It's a question of replacing so-called economic imperatives – not just the direct class power of capital but the coercions of the market – with democratic power.

XIX

Two aspects of capitalism's acceptance or accommodation of democracy, though implicit in our account so far, still need to be specifically taken note of. Democracy has been 'domesticated', and 'made acceptable' to dominant classes, but not entirely. It must not be forgotten that people have struggled to win democracy and that original meaning of democracy as popular power has persisted throughout this long and hard struggle. As the people have struggled for it, the ruling classes have seen democracy as a threat to their class rule and it has been a major battle on their part in societies across the world to oppose democracy, to limit and dilute it in every possible manner. Capitalism has indeed domesticated democracy by confining it to the political sphere while retaining autonomy for its interests in the economic sphere. But however much its capitalist context may have diluted or domesticated democracy, using their political rights and associated democratic freedoms people have sought to curb the coercive, exploitative logic of capitalism, the logic of its economic sphere, the market. They have put constant pressure and made their own demands on the system. An important aspect of capitalism's acceptance of democracy has been its ability to accommodate such pressure or demands – an ability made possible by capitalism's remarkable productive achievements, its expansion on a capitalist-imperialist basis, a world polarisation to the benefit of its advanced industrial centres. Hence the gains of the working people in the west collectively referred to as the 'welfare state'; which gains however remain reversible when the capitalist economy flags and the logic of its profit-governed accumulation can no longer afford them. It may be noted here that such accommodation of popular pressure or demands is highly problematic, if not impossible, for the belated, peripheral or semi-peripheral capitalisms of the post-colonial third world, and that capitalism's long drawn out downturn since the mid-1970s has been accompanied by a retreat or dismantling of the welfare state even in the advanced capitalist countries of the first world.

This only underlines that its contradiction with capitalism has been and remains a basic feature of democracy in our times. Implications are obvious. It is a contradiction that sooner or later demands to be resolved one way or the other. And capitalist classes have had no compunction in resolving it in favour of their authoritarian, even fascist rule. Which means that while in certain historical conditions capitalism is conducive to or compatible with democracy as we have known it in our times, it can, when it deems necessary, easily do without it – as it has done more than once in recent history. Which also implies that for democracy to survive or be truly democratic, it perforce needs to do without capitalism.

Issues of acceptance, accommodation or compatibility apart, a most important associated aspect of the matter is that democracy, such as it is, has been most useful to capitalism in so many ways. Class domination in any 'actually existing' capitalist society is of a non-monolithic nature, where, almost invariably, what we have is an alliance or a coalition of ruling classes with real, even if non-antagonistic, internal conflict of interests. 'Formal democracy', its 'democratic politics', provides these ruling classes with an impersonal, non-arbitrary device for articulating and resolving their inevitable conflict of interests even as the democratic state aggregates and promotes these interests as a whole. Again, as we have already noticed with

Edelman, this democracy may be a myth, but it is useful in providing the public with symbolic gratifications and serves to legitimise the system by giving it an appearance of poplar support. Referring to elections in colonial America, Edmund Morgan has recently noted that participation in politics that these elections involved, was 'a safety valve, an interlude when the humble could feel a power otherwise denied them, a power that was only half illusory. And it was also a legitimizing ritual, a rite by which the populace renewed their consent to an oligarchical power structure'. This describes perfectly the same process two hundred years later in capitalist-democratic regimes. The elective principle is indeed the dominant form of legitimation in these societies. It furnishes the ruling classes with the most precious elements of legitimation and stability for their class domination. Yet again, it is not to be dismissive about the importance of democratic or parliamentary procedures, even under capitalist conditions, to notice, even emphasise, that these procedures, under such conditions are also a means of containing popular pressures from below. They bring the masses within the reach of the control-mechanisms of bourgeois democratic, pluralist politics and help channelise popular anger or protest into safe 'democratic' channels, that is, contain and deradicalise it. Accompanied as it is by the sustained effort of bourgeois political ideologies to depoliticise the world outside the legislative assemblies and delegitimise 'extra-parliamentary' politics, such containment or deradicalisation is an essential part of class politics from above in societies of bourgeois democracy.

Most important by far are the hegemonic functions that bourgeois democracy performs as an ideology legitimising the capitalist class domination and social order. Embodied or expressed in a wide array of legal and political forms, procedures and institutions, 'democracy' has today come to be the most potent ideological force available to the capitalist class – in some respects even more powerful than the material advances achieved under the auspices of capitalism. A particular class ideology, whatever its class origins or purpose, in order to be hegemonic in society needs to have not only the appearance of universality but a plausible claim to it, for which it must contain an important element of truth. Only thus does it win, to a greater or lesser extent, the allegiance of other classes. To speak of an ideology as 'hegemonic' is to say both that it serves the particular interests of a class and that its claims to universality have an element of truth. This is indeed the case with bourgeois democracy which is both a class ideology of the capitalist class and a plausible claimant to universality to the extent that it has captured the allegiance of other classes not simply by deceit or mystification but also by bringing them real benefits. The seduction of working class movements by bourgeois democratic political forms cannot be lightly dismissed as a failure of class consciousness or a betrayal of the revolution. The attractions of democracy have been very real for them. Outcome of long and painful popular struggles 'bourgeois democracy' has conferred genuine benefits on subordinate classes, given them real strengths, new possibilities of organisation and resistance which cannot be either dismissed or abandoned to the enemy as mere sham. It is indeed such benefits as these which account for the hegemonic reach of 'democracy' as a bourgeois ideology.

It is not only that 'democracy' has come to serve capitalism as a hegemonic ideology. With 'democracy' as its political form, the bourgeois state itself, and not simply the ideological or cultural apparatuses that sustain it, becomes ideologically persuasive and hegemonic. As Perry Anderson has argued, what gives this political form its peculiar hegemonic power is that the consent it commands from the dominated classes does not simply rest on their submission to an acknowledged ruling class and their acceptance of its right to rule, as was the case in pre-capitalist times. The bourgeois democratic state is a unique form of class rule – 'the best form of rule for the bourgeoisie', it has been called – because on the one hand it casts doubt on the very existence of a ruling class, and on the other, the coercive power on which capitalist property ultimately rests, itself appears in the form of a 'neutral' and 'autonomous' state. It is thus that the ruling classes rule and exploit the people with their own willing consent. In its appearance of class neutrality, the capitalist state stands perfected as a *class* state. What more can an ideology do for a ruling class and its state power.

I may add that capitalism's use of 'democracy' as a bourgeois ideology has been duly facilitated by the fact that obscuring the class character of bourgeois democracy has long been a major concern of the mainstream scholarship on the subject. A good example here is the upsurge of neo-liberal theorising over political developments in Latin America in recent decades. Scholars writing on the emergence of civilian regimes in different countries there, have even sought to promote the notion of 'democracy without adjectives'. The argument is based on typically empiricistic studies which narrow the discussion to changes at the level of government or political regimes resulting from electoral procedures without examining either the larger historical-structural configuration within which these changes take place or the role of political structures as apparatuses of bourgeois domination. Identifying democracy with multiparty elections, etc., the focus is on electoral procedures and their outcome, on individual political choices or calculations. Ignored altogether are the non-electoral power centres that set the parameters and determine the substantive outcome of electoral systems under capitalism. Class interests or class conflicts simply disappear in these studies of Latin American politics together with any consideration of deeper-lying economic structures or class-institutional interests that shape the direction and substance of political change. James Petras has most aptly observed: 'Cutting off "political analysis" from its long-standing and deeply entrenched power matrix, the neo-liberal theorists focused on the epiphenomena of narrow electoral interests, personalities and partisan party concerns – the stuff of North American political science vintage 1950 (passed off as the latest up-to-date post-Marxist intellectual innovations).'

When electoral processes produced the civilian (as against military) regimes in some Latin American countries, a political change almost totally divorced from any profound changes in the totality of society, this has been described as 'a democratisation process' which has produced 'democratic states'. When the plain fact is that the prevalence of democratic forms in Latin America has all too often only signalled the powerlessness of the people and retreat of the national state before the power of global capitalism. 'Democratisation' to be really so has to be a process in which regime or governmental changes are accompanied by radical changes in the state apparatus and the economy breaks with the capitalist accumulation model to make possible a pro-people economic development. And this is true of not only Latin America.

XX

Modern-day liberal or 'representative' democracy, as we shall specifically argue later, has a valuable dimension to it. Even so there are good reasons to describe it as bourgeois or capitalist democracy. As Adam Przeworski has observed, 'to discuss democracy without considering the economy in which this democracy is to function is an operation worthy of an ostrich'. The economy in question in the present case is capitalism, and the capitalist context of modern democracy certainly defines and leaves it crippled in many important ways. Confined to a separate political sphere, this democracy leaves large areas of human life outside the reach of democracy. The major decisions that shape people's lives are taken outside the framework of democratic decision-making, in a separate sphere called 'the economy'. A kind of democracy may prevail in the political sphere, but people in capitalist societies spend most of their waking lives in activities and relationships where there is no democratic accountability at all. Being a 'citizen' does not protect the modern worker from being sacked, from speed up at work, from low wages and long hours, from the direct control of others in the workplace, etc. Life in general remains subject to the essentially undemocratic imperatives of 'the market' – 'the market', it may be repeated, is not so much a sphere of opportunity, freedom and choice that its ideologues make it out to be, as of coercions of capitalism capable of subjecting all human activities and relationships to its requirements. Far from being a system of government that empowers people to self-govern themselves, bourgeois democracy gives people no power to challenge the principles of class exploitation on which a capitalist society is based. Its political equality poses no threat to the incorrigible structural inequality of capitalism. By the very fact that it is based on a deep and insurmountable class division, bourgeois democracy remains powerless to effectively question the property, power and privileged position of the people at the top of the social pyramid, the ruling classes. Rather, its main task is to sustain and defend their profoundly inequitable class and exploitation-based social order. Its democratic features are, for all their importance, hardly anything more than political modifiers of the underlying undemocratic structures of a capitalist society. Insofar as the rule of capital is rooted as much in the capacity to gain the consent of the governed – to obtain their collaboration in their own marginalisation and exploitation – as it is in the actual material means of control, bourgeois democracy provides capitalist rulers the necessary means or channels to secure this consent. Several recent studies have even suggested that 'the present-day elites are interested in democracy only as a means for legitimizing their power'. Containing, manipulating and corrupting democratic forms for this purpose is certainly an essential part of 'democratic politics' as it is practised in capitalist societies.

Unrelated to the official and social context proper to democracy and indifferent to the implications that deep-seated social contradictions and class inequalities have for the political process, democracy has now been 'depoliticised' to become a system of formal rules and procedures that only pose 'technical' problems, and politics, or the political – the highest form of social life for the ancient Greeks – has been reduced to a dirty business of lies, bribery and chicanery. With democracy almost identified with voting, technical speciality of electoral tactics and manipulation has come centre-stage in 'democratic politics'. Within political parties, power, taken away from their mass membership, has passed into the hands of small groups of professional politicians – 'people who make a business of politics' – and their market-savvy, media-oriented advisors and spokespersons. The leaders, as E.H. Carr pointed out long ago, are concerned 'no longer primarily with the reflection of opinion, but with the moulding and manipulation of opinion'. With its legal form regularly frustrated by economic power, in the oligarchy or plutocracy that bourgeois democracy is turning out to be, elections, free discussion and the struggle between parties are now increasingly only a 'democratic facade'. 'The US', William Pfaff, a mainstream journalist, has recently written (in *The International Herald Tribune*), 'has become a plutocracy, in the dictionary definition of that word, governed by wealth – mainly corporate wealth...anyone with money can have a shot influencing government. It's merely that the rest of the people are left out, and there now seems little hope of changing the way the country is run'.

Wealth indeed means privileged access to power in bourgeois or capitalist democracy. Use of money power and corruption that goes with it, is today a distinctive feature of democratic politics in capitalist societies. Opinion manufacturing has grown into a massive 'opinion business' in support of the capitalist system. Mass capitalist control of books and periodicals, news gathering and distribution, radio, cinema and television, helps capitalist class and their ideologues to monopolise public discussion and wage a constant ideological war to limit the capacity of working class and oppressed people to act in their own interests or, as historian Alex Carey has put it, 'to take the risk out of democracy'. Politics becomes a matter of public relations and democracy itself a marketable commodity, to be inevitably accompanied by trivialisation of elections and nullifying the significance of associated democratic procedures. Adlai Stevenson, twice a victim of it all during his presidential election campaign in the US, had once sorely remarked: 'The idea that you can merchandise candidate for high office like breakfast cereal... is the ultimate indignity to the democratic process'.

Bourgeois democracy, with its multi-party system is supposed to offer people choices in politics. Whatever the occasional validity of such claims, now or in the past, genuine political choices have been generally absent in bourgeois democratic politics. Even according to mainstream scholars, a properly functioning modern democracy needs to have 'agreement on fundamentals' between the contending political parties. Democracy works best, they say, on the basis of 'consensus politics'. That is how it happens that the 'adversarial politics' between rival contenders for power is often fake and people's freedom of choice stands reduced to using their ballot every few years to choose between Tweedledee and Tweedledum. Long ago (in 1955), in his *British Political Parties,* R.T. McKenzie had written: 'After he had examined the Conservative and Liberal Party organizations almost half a century ago, A.L. Lowell wrote: "Both are shams, but with this difference, that the Conservative organisation is a transparent, and the Liberal an opaqu sham." It can be argued that if the word "Labour" is substituted for "Liberal" there is a sense in which Lowell's remark is equally appropriate today.' Nearly half a century later (in 2001) we have the notoriously conservative *The Times* backing the Labour Party for elections with the argument that it is best capable of carrying out the Thatcherite conservative agenda! Across the Atlantic, in the US, Big Money is King as H.L. Mencken labelled it in 1920 and remains a king no matter which political party is in power. The Republicans are traditionally considerd the party of 'Big Money,' but this is how Robert Reich, the Harvard economist and Clinton's former labour secretary, has written of the Democrats recently in power (in *The FinancialTimes*): 'No administration in modern history has been as good for American capitalism as the Clinton–Gore team... None has been as solicitous of the concerns of corporate leaders. None has generated as much profit for business, and none has presided over as buoyant a stock market or as huge an increase in corporate executive pay'. Replacing them in power, this is how the Republican George W. Bush has seen it: 'Whether we be Democrats or Republicans, our goals are the same. The differences between us are minor.' As for these 'minor differences' Ralph Nader, the well-known American radical, has sarcastically observed: 'what differentiates them is the speed with which their knees hit the floor when Big Capital summons them.' A very similar situation obtains in Japan, especially after the liquidation of the former Social Democratic Party and the split in the LDP, there is hardly any real line of principle separating the main contenders for power. In Europe, with the disintegration of Social Democracy in the face of globalisation, even the old choices *within* the system are fast disappearing. And it is not much different in the third world. In India, for example, with most political parties adopting similar economic programmes and swearing by 'reforms' (a euphemism for the economic agenda of global capitalism), the people stand denied of any *real* choice within the framework of current democratic elections.

The question of 'choices' apart, it needs to be particularly noticed that in the third world, whatever other benefits it may have brought them, democracy as we now know it, has not empowered people to defend and promote their interests, nowhere have the people been able to carry out the fundamental socio-economic transformation they need. Writing of India, 'the largest democracy in the world', Gunnar Myrdal has observed: 'Democracy has not enabled the majority of poor people to grasp, and organise themselves for utilising political power to advance their own interests.' V.K.R.V. Rao has emphatically stated that so far as 'the poor and deprived sections of the people' are concerned 'parliamentary democracy has not been able to meet the challenge'. Mahbub-ul-Haq of Pakistan has noted: 'in many South Asian states, democracy is fast turning into an empty ritual; elections are often the only bridge between the state and society. People continually feel excluded from the larger political process through which decisions that directly affect their livelihoods are made.' Far away on another continent, Hugo Chavez has pointed out that while the usual political advice calls for 'a little more patience' until the elections scheduled a few months ahead, 'every minute hundreds of children are born in Venezuela whose health is endangered for lack of food and medicine, while billions are stolen from the national wealth, and in the end what remains of the country is bled dry'. He goes on to add: 'With the appearance of the populist parties the suffrage was converted into a tool for putting to sleep in order to enslave the Venezuelan people in the name of democracy. For decades the populist parties based their discourse on innumerable paternalistic promises devised to melt away popular consciousness. The alienating political lies painted the "promised land" to be reached via a rose garden.

The only thing the Venezuelans had to do was to go to the electoral urns, and hope that everything will be solved without the minimal popular effort... Thus the act of vote was transformed into the beginning and the end of democracy.' That backed by their extra-electoral sanctions, Chavez-led common people of Venezuela are trying to get something out of it does not invalidate this summing up of the situation, and not in Venezuela alone. Democracy, as bourgeois democracy, is fast losing its meaning and purpose for the vast masses of common people in the third world.

This democracy, however, has been quite compatible with the new class-exploitative systems built in India and other countries of the post-colonial third world, and profitable for American imperialism to export abroad, when its interests so demand. And now, as the ruling classes or elites in the third world play out this US-sanctioned voting game, it is the whims of international financial agencies rather than the demands of the local population which are becoming the prime determinant not just of economic policy, but of the entire gamut of policies. (These agencies in any case are ever ready to intervene to ensure that elections do not get in the way of the interests of global capitalism. Within a few short weeks in November-December 1997 the IMF extracted public undertakings from all the leading candidates in the South Korean Presidential election *before* the poll that they would abide by the liberalising conditions of an IMF loan – without which an economic disaster was categorically promised). This erosion of sovereignty can only mean attenuation of whatever democracy there is in the third world countries. Policies conforming to the demands of global capitalism and contrary to the interests of the people can be pursued only if democracy is effectively curtailed.

As an integral part of the deepening structural crisis of the global capitalist system, there is a crisis of politics all over the world which often assumes the form of understandable bitterness and a resigned withdrawal from political activity by the popular masses. Bourgeois democratic politics fully shares in this global crisis of politics. The experience with bourgeois democracy, its overall failure to deliver, especially the social deterioration that has occurred in the course of the last couple of decades within the framework of bourgeois democratic institutions, has seriously undermined people's trust in these institutions. The legitimacy and prestige of electoral system or bourgeois parliamentarianism has radically declined. In the established democracies opinion polls show that representative party politics have never been more despised. There is growing apathy or indifference towards participation in electoral politics. The percentage of voting-age people not voting is rising steadily. In most electoral contests, the percentage of those who actually vote is less than a majority of potentially eligible voters. In many parts of Latin America as much as 90 per cent of the population is known to have demonstrated its 'rebellion against the absurdity of the vote through its electoral abstention'. Bourgeois democracy is indeed in a real crisis. But unlike the case of Europe in the 1920s or in Latin America during the 1970s, it is leading not to a rapid collapse of bourgeois democratic institutions but their slow degeneration and dying out. They are increasingly by-passed not only by economic decision-making, but even by the political process itself. The lack of alternatives is leading to democratic political establishment itself turning to populist authoritarianism, the rise of extreme right-wing organisations and a rebirth of fascism, each an important symptom of the current crisis of bourgeois democracy. Disillusionment has also overtaken the much-touted globalisation of 'liberal democracy', celebrated by Fukuyama as heralding the 'end of history', and the so-called 'third wave' democratisation announced by Huntington and other apologists for neo-liberalism in the aftermath of the collapse of the Soviet-style socialism in the East. As often as not it has ended up as a reminder of what Marx said of 1875 Germany – 'a military despotism and a police state, bureaucratically carpentered, embellished with parliamentary forms', Marx had said. We have Perry Anderson's apt summing up of the situation: 'Democracy is indeed now more widespread than ever. But it is also thinner – as if the more universally available it becomes, the less active meaning it retains.'

XXI

'Democracy' still remains an important ideological weapon in the armoury of bourgeois ideologues in their struggle against socialism. Efforts continue to be made to idealise 'liberal democracy' and obscure its bourgeois dimension, to 'declass' bourgeois democracy as it were into just democracy, 'democracy without adjectives'. Let me therefore conclude this part of my argument by taking another pointed look at the bourgeois dimension of present-day democracy, go beyond its formal or political aspect to draw specific attention to capitalism's structures of economic, ideological and political power which underlie it, which even as they effectively condition its working and outcome, equally effectively lie outside its democratic reach, and which it can seek to reach only at the risk of inviting its own abrogation. It is these structures of capitalist power which, with or without democracy, sustain and defend the bourgeois social order.

At the core of these structures is the private ownership and control of the main industrial, financial, commercial and communication resources of capitalist societies. This means gross economic inequality in society and represents an extraordinary concentration of power in the hands of a relatively small number of people, in a systemically favourable situation to act as collective actors in society. With economic inequality go social inequalities – and even according to the most-talked of recent celebrant of capitalist liberalism, Fukuyama, 'major social inequalities will remain even in the most perfect of liberal societies'. This only reinforces the economic power of the few, the holders of corporate power who, it should be remembered, are linked in a difficult but very real partnership with the holders of state power, and whose degree of freedom from any kind of democratic control is the most flagrant denial of the democratic pretensions of the present-day capitalist-democratic regimes. For all the talk about the transformation of capitalism, this remains a basic fact about it. To this we may add the all-pervasive, coercive economic power that capitalist market represents, a power inherent in the very economic structures of capitalism. Democratic procedures in capitalist regimes are a simulacrum of democracy, utterly vitiated by the context in which they function.

An important fact about the complexity of class power in bourgeois democratic states, in contrast to more openly coercive or dictatorial regimes, is that in addition to its somewhat obscured but still tangible reality in economic and political spheres, it is almost invisibly diffused throughout society and its ideological and socio-cultural practices. It was to the credit of Gramsci to have drawn pointed attention to this aspect of class power in modern capitalist-democratic societies. Of course, Gramsci's appropriation of the concept of 'civil society' for this purpose was part of his revolutionary project, it was to mark out, more clearly and with better emphasis than ever before, a most important but relatively neglected terrain of struggle against capitalism; capitalism has to be fought not only on economic or directly political plane but also to its ideological and cultural roots in everyday life. Quite a few who today speak in the name of Gramsci, have grossly distorted his teaching to justify their own reformist practices or 'cultural' politics. But this is not a subject I want to pursue here. Immediately important is to recognise the massive reality of bourgeois hegemony in society, the ideological and cultural class power of the bourgeoisie that seeks to reach out to every nook and corner of capitalist society to sustain and protect its class domination. Necessary for ruling classes in all class-divided societies, the need for it is all the more paramount in a capitalist society which is also 'democratic'. Capitalist democracy, even as it features a considerable and regular use of force against the subordinate classes, also provides them with formal rights of free expression, association and participation. The availability of channels of expression and association increases the importance of what people think and believe, and therefore also of their ideological control, which comes to play a more central role in maintaining the order and stability of a capitalist-democratic society. In capitalist democracy, in the final analysis, the real enemy of the ruling classes, their 'ultimate target', is the human mind itself. The preservation of its inequalities and unjust advantages requires regular thought control, the deliberate 'manufacture of consent', as Walter Lippman phrased it way back in early 1930s.

The ideological class power of the bourgeoisie is purveyed through 'ideological state apparatuses', as Althusser called them, through any number of public and private ideological and cultural institutions and channels. In capitalist democratic regimes, if democratic procedures are regularly manipulated by the ruling classes in many ways, the communications media that they control do no less, all the time advancing ideas that conform to their interests, including a torrent of obfuscations, half-truths, and plain lies. Libertarian principles notwithstanding, the debate, even on problems deemed important, proceeds within very narrow limits in these societies. More specifically, the range of positions featured in the mass media, the issues that receive emphasis, the timing of stories, the sources that are treated as respectable, and the interpretation of the role of the media itself, are all 'highly functional' for established power and responsive to the needs of the government and the dominant groups and classes. Dissidence, to a greater or lesser degree, is no doubt always there, and it even lends a certain legitimacy to the system, but the ideological, artistic and cultural activity as a whole tends to reinforce bourgeois hegemony in capitalist society, of course each in its own way. This is apart from the more direct 'hitting below the belt', and 'corruption of consciousness' that is taking place all the time. It only needs to be added that senior journalists and the 'secular priesthood' (Chomsky's term) of primarily academic experts and social scientists too make their contribution. Members of this class typically attain their positions by propagating views that serve the dominant class interests, or at least don't seriously question them, or are distractive of real issues and strictly harmless and thus useful in their own way. It is a different matter that displaying the normal human intolerance of conscious deception, including self-deception, they commonly come to believe and feel comfortable with what they say.

Above and beyond capitalism's economic and ideological power structures, or its electoral democratic politics, stands the capitalist state, the final arbiter on issues of struggle and dominance in society, the coercive power on which the regime of capital ultimately rests. Here it is imperative to notice a conceptual confusion current in conventional writing on the state, which fails to make the necessary distinction between the state and the government or political regime in power at a particular point of time. 'The state', as James Petras has clarified, refers to the *permanent* institutions of *government* and the concomitant *ensemble of class relations* which have been embedded in these same institutions. The permanent institutions include those which exercise a *monopoly over the means of coercion* (army, police, judiciary), as well as those that control the *economic levers* of the accumulation process. The 'government' refers to those political officials that occupy the *executive* and *legislative* positions and are subject to renewal or replacement. Consequently, changes at the level of government or political regime do not in the least change the nature of the state. The military, police and juridical officials in the overwhelming majority of cases remain in place, with the same power or control and with the same values and ideologies as before. 'Moreover', as Petras points out, 'the same class linkages that defined the state before the political changes continue under the new regime. The continuities of the basic *state structures* define the essential nature of the new political system: the boundaries and instrumentalities of social action. The new political regime exercises its prerogatives, executive and legislative initiatives within the framework established by pre-existing configuration of power.' It is the state, thus understood, which stands guard over the capitalist society. Regardless of the outcome of electoral politics or changes in government, it protects this society, relatively peacefully and when necessary violently, against threats from within and without. It ensures that whatever the vagaries of the marketplace, the rules and necessities, the conditions of capitalist production and reproduction are maintained, at times even in opposition to sections of usually short-sighted capitalists themselves, as has indeed happened in the history of modern capitalism, especially when it runs into crisis which it does regularly. The state remains the overall organiser of capitalist society and a defender of the long-term interests of its ruling classes as a whole.

It is fashionable these days to disparage 'determinism' of any kind and speak of the 'uncertain' 'contingent', 'accidental', 'unpredictable' or 'indeterminate' nature of political or historical processes, even of 'autonomy of the state'. But there has never been anything uncertain or indeterminate or autonomous about this relationship of the capitalist democratic state to capitalism or the interest of its ruling classes, at home or abroad. The 'democracy' involved has certainly allowed for reforms, a certain curbing of the exploitative structural logic of capitalism, but it has never allowed or made possible a radical challenge to capitalism, the existing system of power and privilege. On the contrary, whenever such a challenge arose, or was perceived or suspected to be there, democracy itself or democratic rights have been, fully or partially, the first casualty in almost every capitalist democratic country in the west. Abroad, every such effort to seek radical change through democratic procedures has been seen as too dangerous to be allowed to proceed. It was thwarted and finally destroyed with the help and encouragement of the leaders of the same 'capitalist-democratic' west. One has only to recall the overthrow of Mohammad Mossadegh in Iran in 1953, of Arbenz in Guatemala in 1954, of Joao Goulart in Brazil in 1964, of Juan Bosch in the Dominican Republic in 1965, of George Papandreou in Greece in 1967, of Salvador Allende in Chile in 1973, and so on, right up to the current efforts to overthrow Hugo Chavez in Venezuela – all of them constitutional democratic regimes.

It may be noted that such overthrow of constitutional democratic regimes has often been demanded, justified and defended in the name of democracy. The invulnerability of the separated and enclosed economic sphere that lies at the very base of bourgeois democracy makes it easily possible to invoke democracy *against* any incursion of democratic power in this sphere and thus use it *in defence* of the old established regimes of private property and class exploitation.

There is certainly much validity in the commonly held view that was once thus expressed by Horkheimer: 'With all its faults, suspect democracy is always better than dictatorship, which its collapse would bring into being.' But there is still greater validity in Marcuse's response. He had written: 'Can the Horkheimer of the 1930s really write so undialectically, so untheoretically today? The sentence appears to me to be just a version of the platitude about the "lesser evil". But is it even that? "Democracy" is isolated, sealed off from its real content: the form of domination of late capitalism. This isolation permits repression of the question: "better" *for whom*? For Vietnam? Biafra? The enslaved people in South America, in the ghettos? The system is global, and it is its democracy, which, with all its faults, also carries out, pays for, and arms neo-colonialism and neo-fascism, and it obstructs liberation. Double isolation: neo-fascism and this democracy are not alternatives; *this* democracy, as a capitalist one, drives, in line with its inherent dynamic, towards a regime of force.' We will also readily concede that bourgeois democracy has often checked or corrected particular abuses of capitalism, made the struggle against its exploitation less painful, sometimes ratified victories that occurred elsewhere. But it needs to be even more firmly stated and recognised that it has never yet led to the liberation of the oppressed classes.

XXII

'Bourgeois', then, is a meaningful adjective for democracy as it has come to exist under capitalism, and reason enough to justify its criticism by Marxists. The class context in which it originated and functions vitiates it all through. Capitalism's structural power is beyond its reach, its decision-making sites are well protected against any exercise of democratic power, its institutions are amenable to capitalist dilution and neutralisation in the interests of the established order. The status of its 'civil liberties' is at best ambiguous; they not only obscure class oppositions of capitalist society with a false equality but are more often than not turned into instruments of capitalists' class power and domination. Its electoral process, amenable to manipulation in diverse ways, supports and sustains this domination, not the least by disorganising people into isolated citizens through their reconstitution as individual voters so much so that, as Rosa Luxemburg noted, even 'the active, class-conscious sector of the proletariat' gets dissolved 'in the amorphous mass of an "electorate"'. The corrupting power of money and market so inform this process that it loses whatever democratic meaning it may have to the point of being reduced to a shameful commercial exercise where votes are bought and sold and 'candidates for high office' come to be merchandised 'like breakfast cereal'. Ways are found to actually disenfranchise people without taking away the right to vote from them; which includes offering them only sham choices in the electoral arena. People are put through a process of deconstruction through manipulation of the media, reshaping of politics as spectacle, and promotion of supposedly 'charismatic' leaders – people are not just 'used' or cheated or suppressed but lobotomised. The politics of bourgeois democracy, appropriated by professional politicians, easily degenerates into *politique politicienne* ('politicians' politics'), as Andre Malraux called it, which has little to do with people's interests and is only parasitic on them, and where squabbling politicians violate even the rules of their own game in a fight for power and pelf in the state. As a report says, 'steadily falling rates of electoral participation, increasing financial corruption, deadening mediatization.... not democratic aspiration from below, but the asphyxiation of public debate and political difference by capital above' are today the recognised features of democracy in their original capitalist homelands. More than all this – its essentially undemocratic institutions and functioning, or the hollowing of democracy itself that has occurred over time – bourgeois democracy is bourgeois in sustaining capitalist relation of production and the position of the dominant classes in many ways, most importantly through its *hegemonic* functions which obscure the class character of the bourgeois-democratic state, its active participation in the class struggle on behalf of the capitalist class and its allies. And it is bourgeois in that, as is well-established by the historical experience of our times, nowhere has bourgeois-democracy given real power to the oppressed and exploited, or allowed for a radical (or socialist) transformation of society by its democratic means.

As with bourgeois democracy, Marxists are also right in criticising and rejecting what has come to be described as 'social-democratic revisionism', which has tended to accept bourgeois democracy as being synonymous with democracy as such, if not in theory always, certainly in practice, even to the point of social democratic parties meekly integrating themselves into its parliamentary framework, accepting its anti-labour constraints and progressively abandoning their original emancipatory strategies. It has shown little awareness of either this democracy's structural relationship with capitalism, both in its origins and development, or its class-determined role in capitalist society and thus not unoften ended up delivering the working classes and people in general as so much *electoral fodder* for the spurious legitimation of the established capitalist order under the pretext of an 'open' and 'fully democratic' electoral process. That bourgeois democracy is in principle class-less has been the fundamental premise of social democratic programmes. There is the accompanying assumption that its 'freedom' and 'equality' are somehow antithetical to capitalist domination and inequality, and therefore the maintenance of (bourgeois) juridical and political institutions will not only win concessions from capitalism but would also produce a tension between freedom and equality at this level and unfreedom and inequality at economic and other levels of society, which would progressively erode capitalism and in a sense replace class struggle as a motor of social transformation, making for a slow and peaceful transition to a more just post-capitalist society, which social democracy was once willing to describe as socialism, but does so no longer. Social democratic is a grievously mistaken view of bourgeois democracy and there is nothing in history to justify the hopes social democracy places in it from a strictly socialist point of view. The fact that even its aspirations have today got reduced from socialism to 'capitalism with a human face' is damning enough of the theory and practice of social democracy, here as elsewhere.

Though penned more than half a century back, it will not be out of place here to quote two relevant passages from Rosa Luxemburg. She had underlined that 'only by an insight into all the fearful seriousness, all the complexity of the tasks involved, only as a result of a capacity for critical judgement on the part of the masses, which capacity was systematically killed by the Social Democracy for decades under various pretexts, only thus can the genuine capacity for historical action be born in the German proletariat... As bred-in-the-bone disciples of parliamentary cretinism, these German Social Democrats have sought to apply to revolution the home-made wisdom of the parliamentary nursery: in order to carry anything, you must first have a majority. The same, they say, applies to revolution: first let's become a "majority". The true dialectic of revolutions, however, stands this wisdom of parliamentary moles on its head: not through a majority to revolutionary tactics, but through revolutionary tactics to a majority – that is the way the road runs.' Again, and almost prophetically, she had written: 'parliamentarism is the breeding place of all the opportunist tendencies now existing in the Western Social Democracy.... [it] provides the soil for such illusions of current opportunism as overvaluation of social reforms, class and party collaboration, the hope of pacific development towards socialism, etc... With the growth of the labour movement, parliamentarism becomes a springboard for political careerists. That is why so many ambitious failures from the bourgeoisie flock to the banners of the socialist parties.'

This observation of Rosa Luxemburg is suggestive of another highly significant aspect of bourgeois democracy. Its other corruptions apart, bourgeois democracy and its politics have a way of coopting or deradicalising revolutionaries, 'civilising' them as it were, and turning them into harmless parliamentarians. There is a certain 'repressive tolerance' about it all so that if you want to work and progress through the established bourgeois democratic institutions, the further you go, the broader sectors of society you address, the more concessions and compromises you make and at the end when you come closer to power you make so many concessions that you are not dangerous, not radical anymore, or you are radical but with a very limited sphere of political freedom to act according to whatever radical views you are still left with. In fact what is far more likely is that as an expert in rules and procedures of parliamentary institutions and their dedicated practitioner, you end up being hailed, even officially honoured, as a 'great parliamentarian'. We have Istvan Meszaros' scathing comment:

> When the title of 'great parliamentarian' is conferred upon representatives of the Left, it is used by the conservative system as a way of congratulating and patting itself on the back. Such political figures are supposed to be 'great parliamentarians' because, as the legend goes, they have 'learned to master the rules of parliamentary procedure' and with their help 'continue to raise uncomfortable issues'. However, the truly uncomfortable truth is that the issues thus raised are invariably ignored, or ruled 'out of order' in parliament itself. In this way the apologists of the substantively anti-socialist parliamentary system can demonstrate to 'democratic public opinion' that there can be no other way of dealing with the problems of society than submission to the rules of the parliamentary game and the strict observance of its procedures which produce 'great parliamentarians' also on the political Left. *Futility* and *political marginalization* are the criteria for being promoted to the exalted rank of 'great parliamentarians' on the Left. Thus a few of them are allowed into the hall of fame in the interest of putting the system of parliamentary democracy beyond and above all conceivable 'legitimate criticism'.
>
> In truth, given the political marginalisation inseparable from the acceptance of parliamentary constraints as the only legitimate framework of political action, conformity to the internalized rules of the parliamentary game – even if it is practised with radical intent – can only produce the *parliamentary self-imprisonment* of the Left...

XXIII

There is much in the historical experience and facts of the contemporary situation, therefore, to justify Marxist or socialist skepticism towards bourgeois democracy and its 'democratic politics'. The revolutionary Left's suspicion of political strategies that put exclusive emphasis on electoral politics or privilege electoral strategies over all else, is well grounded. Given our experience with it, no condemnation of vacuous parliamentary politics can be considered too sharp. Very little indeed can be expected by common people from the democratic institutions as they are articulated today, especially in view of the onset of the long-term structural crisis of capitalism. It is also that the importance of a radical critique of bourgeois democracy has never been greater; for the question of working people's emancipation through it apart, we are not only faced with capitalism's self-legitimising appropriation and use of democracy, but democracy is being touted as, and by many even believed to be, a substitute for socialism. Nevertheless, however legitimate such skepticism and suspicion, criticism or condemnation, it yet does not justify dismissal of bourgeois democracy as only bourgeois, or rejection of electoral politics as inherently corrupt and useless, only a waste of valuable time and resources. In rejecting the liberal and social democratic misunderstanding and mystification of bourgeois democracy, we must not opt for the opposite error of regarding it as wholly a deception, a mystification and nothing more. Such, it may be noted, is roughly the position of various ultra-left revolutionary groups or formations. Bourgeois democratic institutions and forms are treated as if they 'reflect' or 'correspond' to capitalism so completely and exclusively that they can be dismissed as useless to socialists in their struggle to transform society, and of no use either after the overthrow of capitalism. They are even seen to be antithetical or inimical to socialism and therefore deserve to be destroyed as a precondition to its realisation. Bourgeois democracy, in this view, is not substantially different from authoritarian and even fascist forms of capitalism.

This view is not altogether without a basis in history, or in the tradition of revolutionary socialism. For example, although qualified or underpinned by a certain 'historical' understanding – whose merits do not concern us here – this view found a typical expression in a resolution of the Comintern in August 1920, entitled 'The Communist Party and Parliament': 'In the preceding historical epoch parliament was an instrument of the developing capitalist system, and as such played a role that was in a certain sense progressive. In the modern conditions of unbridled imperialism, parliament has become a weapon of falsehood, deception and violence, a place of enervating chatter.

In the face of the devastation, embezzlement, robbery and destruction committed by imperialism, parliamentary reforms which are wholly lacking in consistency, durability and order lose all practical significance for the working masses.' The resolution warned: 'At the present time parliament cannot be used by the Communists as the arena in which to struggle for reforms and improvements in working class living standards as was the case at certain times during the past epoch. The focal point of political life has shifted fully and finally beyond the boundaries of parliament.' In its approval of the insurrectionary path, the Comintern advised the working class to have its 'reconnaissance units in the parliamentary institutions of the bourgeoisie in order to hasten their destruction'.

Nuances or specificities of particular historical situations apart, I would like to state that like the liberal or social democratic view, the ultra-left view of bourgeois democracy too is a grievously mistaken one. If the liberal or the social democrat needs to be told that the democracy he lauds is yet bourgeois, the Marxist must always remember that though bourgeois, it is yet democracy in the sense that if it is important not to fall into the mystifications that sustain bourgeois democratic hegemony, it is no less important to avoid dismissing bourgeois democracy as nothing more than a mystification. In fact, as we have suggested earlier, bourgeois democracy is able to perform effective hegemonic functions for capitalism precisely because it has its 'elements of truth', the benefits which even as bourgeois democracy it brings the people. These benefits are real and cannot be overlooked. If bourgeois democracy cannot and must not be separated from the principles of capitalist exploitation, nor can it be simply reduced to those principles. Not to see the connections of democracy with capitalism, or to mistake their character, certainly limits our understanding of both democracy and capitalism. But a Marxist view of the connections between formal or political democracy and capitalism does not involve rejecting the one with the other. We can recognise the historical and structural connections involved without denying the value of political freedoms and civil liberties. A Marxist understanding of these connections does not in any way compel us to devalue these freedoms or liberties. We may not, very rightly, accept the *identification* of democracy with, or its confinement to, the formal freedoms and safeguards of bourgeois democracy, but its legal and political forms normally do guarantee a certain degree of free space for 'civil society'. Our view must consider both the foundations of bourgeois democracy in capitalist relations of production and its historic role in checking the excesses of capitalism and providing the working classes with means, however lame or poor, to resist and struggle against it. It must take account of the degree to which political and legal forms of bourgeois democracy are the legacy of historical struggles by the subordinate classes, winning them the rights to organise and resist, and the value these forms have had for their exercise of these rights in pursuit of their own interests. Our understanding of bourgeois democracy must not fall into what may be described as an essentialist idealist trap. Forms have a reality of their own and contradictions exist between the formal and essential aspects of bourgeois democracy as well as within the latter. Within the *essence* or content of bourgeois democracy is contained the opposition between its universal human dimension that democracy as popular power implies and the particular class domination of the bourgeoisie which constitutes its basic inner limitation. Possibilities, however limited, inhere in this contradiction of bourgeois democracy for the subordinate people or classes to struggle for their interests. Again, the role of bourgeois democracy in civilising capitalist exploitation and oppression, or making the struggle against it less painful must be acknowledged. Yet again, it is important to differentiate among various forms of capitalist regimes, ranging as they do from the plain bourgeois democratic to the plain fascist, to be at all able to work out appropriate tactics of revolutionary struggle in each case, both nationally and internationally. The failure to distinguish between dictatorial and democratic capitalism during the 1930s had disastrous consequences throughout the entire world. At the very least, we must recognise that institutional protections of the kind that bourgeois democracy provides are *necessary* conditions of any democracy worth the name. With the Soviet experience behind us, surely there is much to learn from the intellectual traditions and practices of bourgeois-democratic liberalism, its civil and political liberties, rule of law and freedom from arbitrary arrest and imprisonment, its diverse modalities of 'bourgeois legalism' and ways of dealing with political authorities, its checks on arbitrary exercise of power and restrictions on the 'freedom of the state', and so on, even if we believe that such protections or modalities against abuse of power will have to take different institutional forms in democracy under socialism.

XXIV

That democracy, though formal or liberal-bourgeois, is yet of undoubted value for the working people calls for a brief comment on two related issues of immediate political importance, namely, its defence against the threat posed by 'globalisation' *and* revolutionary left's participation in its electoral or parliamentary politics.

We have repeatedly noticed capitalism's ever present tendency to limit and erode democracy, and it indeed stands much limited and eroded today. Much of the erosion of recent years is due to contemporary capitalist globalisation which, even as it needs and uses the state as its agent, has been steadily undermining the decision-making powers of whatever democratic institutions it has. The issue here is more than just transfer of these powers to international institutions, multinationals, the centres of private finance, etc. that has taken place. It is not merely that the sphere of economic power in capitalism has today expanded far beyond the capacities of 'democracy' to cope with; liberal democracy, in any case, whether as a set of institutions or a system of ideas, is not designed to extend its reach into that domain. It is that for capitalism caught in a structural crisis, the old mode of assuring electoral consent – through 'welfare state', etc. – has become too costly. The 'normal' cohabitation of hegemony-as-coercion and hegemony-as-consent has become problematic. In order to assert its grip on the economy and society capitalism now needs to accentuate still further the oligarchic and repressive character of its political power. Hence a renewed crisis of democracy in the old established capitalist democracies of the first world. It is no different in the third world where democratic structures appeared more recently together with decolonisation and the formation of a state based on class alliances led by the bourgeoisie. As, succumbing to 'globalisation', this state turns even more neo-colonial than before, as the post-colonial bourgeoisie seeks to become a junior partner of metropolitan capital, this transformation occurs through a jettisoning or attenuation of democratic structures. As Prabhat Patnaik has put it: 'Such jettisoning or attenuation is more than a mere temporary phenomenon, since a neo-liberal or neo-colonial economy contributes neither to economic prosperity nor to economic stability. Imperialist interests (or the interests of the bourgeoisie seeking to become a junior partner of imperialism) are served therefore not through the maintenance of democratic structures but precisely by the opposite course of smothering such structures.' As for the newly implanted 'democracies' of the former second world, global capitalism's autocratic grip over them has shown no signs of slackening. Democracy in Russia remains as far away as ever. The upshot of it all is that despite the noise over the 'spread of democracy', and 'rolling back the boundaries of the state', what we are witnessing all over the world is ever greater impositions of 'regressive political determinations' over the everyday life of the popular masses. With capitalism thus posing a renewed threat to democracy throughout the globalised world, defence of democracy has today emerged as a key task for the left and popular masses everywhere.

This key task, however, is also a great opportunity for the left provided it is taken seriously and the battle to defend democracy is fought as part of the larger battle against capitalism, that is as part of an agenda for socialism. It is essential to attack not only the explicit forms of authoritarianism of the capitalist state but also the internal corporate regimes and international institutions of global capitalism as well as the de facto centres of capitalist power such as education and information apparatuses. Fought in the midst of society, in every arena and day-to-day struggle, it has to be a battle for real democracy, a battle that goes beyond the traditional institutions of formal democracy, capital's actually existing and feasible parliamentary democracies, to restore democracy in its literal meaning as popular power – popular power that encompasses not only political but economic domain as well and both demands and makes possible a socialist transformation of society.

Our view of the struggle in defence of democracy also points to the right perspective for revolutionary Left's participation in electoral or parliamentary politics – an issue to which, given its importance, I shall be returning later in these notes. There is no denying that this politics has built-in pressures towards reformism. But this by itself is not and cannot be an argument against participation in such politics, against the use of electoral or parliamentary politics as part of the revolutionary struggle against capitalism. What is important here is the meaning you put into it, the ideology or political consciousness that informs such use, or for that matter the struggle against capitalism as a whole. Every form of political activity or struggle is potentially 'reformist' if it is conducted in ideological and organisational isolation from the broader struggle where capitalist system is the enemy to confront, if the immediate struggle is not linked to the ultimate or strategic object of a socialist transformation of society. Reform, a contest with the ruling class where you are, or within the existing institutions, is where you begin the revolution, – and you cannot begin it otherwise, elsewhere. But it is a beginning, a part of revolutionary process only if it is suffused with the revolutionary consciousness of a socialist. What is really involved here is the relation between reform and revolution where its mistaken understanding has often seen it as an either or question and thus counterposed one against the other. A proper understanding, as Marx, the active revolutionary, himself emphasised, says 'yes' to both but insists that in revolutionary politics reform needs to be subordinated to revolution. A revolutionary struggle against capitalism, therefore, does not in any way rule out the exercise of the rights of bourgeois democracy or the use of its institutions as futile.

On the contrary, and very rightly too, revolutionary socialist politics enjoins such exercise and use whenever, wherever and to the degree possible. And this, in principle, includes participation in electoral or parliamentary politics. To argue for such participation is not to deny or overlook either the ultimately violent nature of the bourgeois democratic state or the subordination of the electoral-parliamentary regimes to the rules established by this state. It is to suggest that notwithstanding its problems and pitfalls, or 'civilising' influence on the revolutionaries, electoral or parliamentary politics can be and needs to be treated as another arena of class struggle, where openings are available for ideological-political struggle against the capitalist social order, where we can carry our own agenda to a vast potential constituency of ours, where we can educate and organise people for non-electoral, extra-parliamentary revolutionary socialist politics. What is ruled out is primary reliance on electoral strategies or anything else that would encourage the illusion of a primarily electoral or parliamentary route to socialism.

Participation in electoral or parliamentary politics is essentially a tactical and not a strategic question which, therefore, always admits of exceptions. But wherever possible or opted for, it has to be subordinated to extra-parliamentary class and mass politics, including the larger counter-hegemonic struggle against capitalism. People's power grows primarily out of such politics, out of their own activity, organisation and struggle, as these come to be suffused with revolutionary consciousness. Following Lenin, Gramsci is a good guide here. For him, participation in electoral or parliamentary politics is a tactical issue contingent on the strategic struggles centred on the class and mass organisations challenging the ruling class state. This relationship between strategic extra-parliamentary and tactical electoral politics must not be inverted. Nor the notion of revolutionary praxis is to be divorced from the self-organised and autonomous class struggle of the working masses in the name of 'flexible tactics', 'realism' and 'possibilism', or by raising the bogey of 'sectarianism', 'adventurism' or 'political immaturity' – formulas and phrases which social-democratic reformism has used over the years, all over the world, to rationalise class collaboration and justify or condone any and every kind of pragmatism, even opportunism on the terrain of bourgeois democratic politics.

It is necessary to recognise the decisive importance of extra-parliamentary class and mass politics for any renewed struggle for socialism, or, for that matter, any significantly radical pro-people change in society today. This is particularly necessary in view of the dismal failure of parliamentary politics in recent decades and globalisation's continued undermining of parliamentary-democratic institutions. It is not only that capital, which is 'by definition, and very effectively in its mode of acting and functioning, an extra-parliamentary force,' is powerful over society by virtue of its dominance in the economy, its power is further reinforced by capitalist classes' ideology and personnel-wise domination of the various apparatuses of the state. This truly massive extra-parliamentary power of capitalism can only be matched by working people's extra-parliamentary force and modes of action, their articulation in forms which are capable of offensive action against capitalism. It is significant that important economic or political 'gains' of the working people have almost invariably been the result of their reliance on 'extra-parliamentary' forms of struggle and organisation, whether in unions, protest movements, militant actions, or elsewhere, through the extra-electoral pressure they exercised on different institutions of the state. Indeed, to be at all effective, parliamentary politics itself has needed and today even more badly needs the radicalising pressure and support of extra-parliamentary politics. Beyond that, if the aim be socialism, it is unthinkable that struggle for socialism can today at all advance without a radical reconstitution of the socialist movement as a strategically oriented and sustained extra-parliamentary mass movement capable of mounting an effective challenge to the capitalist powers that be.

Our emphasis on the importance of active extra-parliamentary politics does not imply any kind of lawlessness, nor, as we have already clarified, an aprioristic rejection of electoral or parliamentary politics. But it does demand freeing of working people's movement from the crippling constraints which the parliamentary 'rules of the game' one-sidedly impose on it in the name of 'democratic politics'. It certainly rejects delusions of successful struggle against capitalism through parliamentary means. But it does not in any way pre-empt the issue of peaceful transition to socialism. Socialism, as we had insisted earlier, is not a matter of resorting to violence or picking up arms, which are purely tactical questions, though not to be dismissed on abstract moral grounds. Socialism is about a fundamental change in social production relations which a real, not merely juridical or formal, social ownership of the means of production makes possible. And here, properly interpreted, Marx still remains the guide: 'peaceful if possible, with arms if necessary'. That is, it all depends on historical conditions and possibilities of the objective situation. A peaceful transition is of course the desirable thing. But the issue involved – peaceful or otherwise, or how peaceful – is really one for the ruling classes to respond to: are they willing to accept people's peaceful, democratic verdict for socialism? As it is, these ruling classes have not even remotely shown this willingness so far. Instead they have invariably used their enormous economic and political power, often across countries, to thwart changes far, far less radical in nature than socialism. For the people, therefore, if or when they decide to travel the peaceful road, the principle is clear. This is how, in his times, Cromwell, forced to make a revolution, put it: 'Trust in God, and keep your powder dry?' How people 'keep their powder dry' is not my concern at the moment. Only do it they must. What is involved is forging adequate extra-parliamentary sanctions to defend and enforce their democratic verdict, which includes preparedness to counter the inevitable 'slave-holders rebellion', as Marx had called it. Failure to do so will cost them dear, as it did the Chilean people in 1973. They failed to develop own armed counterweight to defend their democratic verdict against the military coup which soon defied and overturned it, and eventuated in a most brutal counter-revolution, massacre of virtually the entire Chilean left including the democratically elected President Allende himself and the setting up of the notorious Pinochet dictatorship, all aided and abetted by the forces of international capital headed by the well-known defender of democracy in the world, the United States. I don't have to detail the lessons.

XXV

The tragedy in Chile certainly underlines the fragility of bourgeois democracy in any real or perceived confrontation with capitalism. Bourgeois democracy came up in close association with capitalism and has been useful to it in many ways, but it has been a troublous association, 'an uneasy marriage' as Laski called it. The powers that be have had no compunction in dispensing with it, whenever they had no use for it or it was perceived to be a threat to their interests. This, however, does not justify viewing bourgeois democracy as just a convenience to capitalism. A historically more valid understanding would see this as pointing to the need of transcending the bourgeois limitations of this democracy. This understanding has been implicit in our argument about the relations between modern democracy and capitalism. It bears being stated in explicit and definitive terms, if only as a summing up of our views on the subject.

It is no doubt true that democracy of our times has come up in close structural relationship with capitalism. Bound up with the social development of the times, it is a characteristic product of the epoch of capitalism. But it would be wrong, for this reason, to treat and dismiss it as only and exclusively a capitalist phenomenon. That is too simplistic, indeed a most vulgar form of economic determinism. Analogically, but only very strictly analogically, one recalls what Marx once wrote of the Greek art and epos: 'But the difficulty is not in grasping the idea that Greek art and epos are bound up with certain forms of social development. It rather lies in understanding why they still constitute with us a source of aesthetic enjoyment and in certain respects prevail as the standard and model beyond attainment... why should the social childhood of mankind, where it had obtained its most beautiful development, not exert an eternal charm as an age that will never return.' The implication is that as an ideological-political product of the bourgeois epoch in *human* history, 'one of the truly great achievements of the capitalist revolution' as it has even been rather ineptly called, the class context and content of contemporary democracy do not exhaust all its meaning, or entirely prevent its being a significant *human* achievement too; however partially, a permanent gain for any humane arrangement of organised social life. Freedoms of speech, assembly, organisation and so on are no less freedoms because they were originally bourgeois. Genuine socialists, Marx onwards, were never against these basic freedoms because they were originally bourgeois. No doubt, they have always, in the words of Rosa Luxemburg, 'revealed the hard kernel of social inequality and lack of freedom hidden under the sweet shell of formal equality and freedom', but they have done so not to abolish this democracy or to foreclose the issue of its usefulness – of course without liberal or social democratic illusions – in the struggle for socialism or the construction of a socialist society. The revolutionary Marxist critique of bourgeois democracy always carried with it the demand not to reject it but fill it with the social content it lacks, to *transcend* it in a socialist democracy.

XXVI

The *transcendence* that socialist democracy represents must be clearly understood. Especially now, when the hollowness of the 'socialist' forms in the ex-Soviet Union and elsewhere has made capitalist liberalism seem attractive, and quite a few even among socialists are talking about democracy in the abstract, without adjectives, or advocating particular democratic forms as if they were equivalent to democracy or even hoping to build socialism on the foundations of liberal democracy by pushing it much further in democratic direction, etc. etc. The difference between socialist and bourgeois views of democracy remains valid and of crucial importance primarily because of the latter's essential incompatibility with socialism.

Socialist democracy must not be understood in merely quantitative terms, a matter of extension or expansion of liberal or bourgeois democracy. It is not as if capitalist democracy is incomplete, one stage is an unambiguously progressive development which must be perfected by socialism and advanced beyond its limitations of being a 'formal democracy', as if the transition from capitalism to socialism itself is nothing more than an extension and completion of the democratic forms inaugurated and nurtured by or under capitalism. Nor is it correct to detach and *abstract* bourgeois democracy out of its capitalist class context, emptying it of its specific social and historical content, reducing it to more or less formal propositions of more or less universal application, which can then be reconstituted for articulation with a new set of socio-historical interests, in the present case proletarian or socialist. This is a tempting option in these days of 'crisis of socialism', for it encounters no class barriers, rules out all questions of class struggle. But it is wrong to thus bridge the gap between bourgeois and socialist democracy, to conceptualise away the radical break between them.

This break is very real because there is a chasm between the forms of democracy that are compatible with capitalism and those that represent a fundamental challenge to it, making for a gap in the continuum of 'democratisation' corresponding to the opposition of class interests involved. In the final analysis the differences between meanings of democracy, bourgeois or socialist, and the struggle over them, are expressive of different class interests and antagonisms. Although there are aspects of liberal democracy that may have a general value, the two diverge irreconcilably at the point where they express the conflicting interests of two opposing classes. There is a qualitative difference between democracy conceived in formal-juridical terms and democracy conceived, for example, as entailing the self-organisation of freely associated producers that socialism postulates. The fact that some institutions of the former may not be in principle antagonistic to the latter does not mean that all social interests compatible with the one are also compatible with the other. As represented by capitalism and socialism they are not. We must not obscure the fact that while bourgeois democracy can be compatible with capitalism precisely because it leaves production relations of capitalism intact, socialist democracy by definition entails the transformation of these production relations. Hence, while we do not dismiss bourgeois democratic forms as mere sham or mystification, and recognising their class specificity yet acknowledge their value and even the plausibility of their claim to a certain generality or universality, we need to also acknowledge the break between liberal democracy and socialist democracy. This break has even been described as the 'river of fire' between them. The expression may appear a trifle too strong but the difficulty of proceeding from one to the other, sans class barriers or class struggle, is obvious.

This, let me emphasise, does not mean any denial or disparagement of the heritage of bourgeois democracy which, as I have insisted earlier, is a permanent gain for any humane arrangement of organised social life. The liberal values it enjoins, indispensable for any democracy, remain indispensable for democracy under socialism. So long as there is state, for example, there will be a need to check its power. In fact, any kind of social power needs to be hedged around with protections for freedom of association, communication, diversity of opinion, an inviolable private sphere, and so on. The bourgeois democratic forms providing for such checks and protections would be used and extended in a socialist democracy. Its institutional arrangements would embody many of the features of bourgeois democracy, including frequent elections and representative assemblies, the separation of powers, accountable executives, the rule of law, constitutionally enshrined civil and political rights, political pluralism and a vibrant civil society, and so on. But functional in a socialist society, all these would be effective and meaningful in a way very different from that in a capitalist, class-divided society. An *extension* of bourgeois democracy, it would at the same time mean a *break* with it, a transcendence in the classical Marxist sense, where socialist democracy incorporates within itself the best features of bourgeois democracy, of course transformed by their socialist context and content.

What is involved in this transcendence will be better understood by returning to Ellen Meiksins Wood on the subject of bourgeois democracy's historical and structural relationship with capitalism. As she has argued, in the pre-capitalist modes of production, the exploitative force of property depends upon a unity of political and economic power, so that political rights must necessarily remain class exclusive, a monopoly of the dominant class. Any kind of popular power in society, 'rule by the *demos*', or their share in political power, is ruled out. It is different under capitalism. Here the exploitative power does not depend directly on the exclusive possession of political force but on absolute ownership of private property and the exclusion of producers from it. It is possible therefore to extend political rights more or less universally. (Though this is not necessary and capitalist mode of production does not of itself require such rights or democracy.) As development of capitalism makes for a formal separation of economic and political spheres in society, and therefore of economic and political power, and as the appropriative or exploitative powers of capital, essentially located in the economic sphere, do not rest on direct possession of 'extra-economic' force, there is a structurally separate political sphere in which 'rule by the *demos*' – or rather by their elected representatives – can exist without directly affecting the exploitative relations between capital and labour. And such a rule does come to exist in the shape of bourgeois democracy. Here indeed lie the foundations of modern democracy, which entails a separation of political rights and powers from economic and social ones and a definition of democracy itself in essentially formal terms. This is not just a flaw in the system, to be removed or overcome by further extension of democracy, as conventional left criticism has it, but the very essence of bourgeois democracy. In other words, what is involved is a particular delineation, definition and isolation of spheres of power which delimits the political sphere as one where democratic principles, political equality or popular power may be allowed to operate, without in any way endangering private property and its power in society, located in the economic sphere, with the additional advantage of being able to hide, even deny the relations of inequality, of domination and subordination on which the capitalist power rests. This is how bourgeois democracy, however progressive it may be in some respects, and however much subordinate classes may have appropriated it and even helped to create it by means of their own struggles, serves the class interests of capital; and this is also why it comes to be an ideal acceptable to the dominant classes.

Bourgeois democracy is certainly an improvement on regimes lacking the principle of representation, the rule of law, civil liberties or political freedom in general. But given its formal character or effective dissociation from economic power, it is also, equally and at the same time, a *subtraction* from the substance of the democratic idea. The association of capitalism with bourgeois democracy represents a contradictory unity of advance and retreat, both an enhancement and devaluation of democracy. The socialist democracy is a resolution of this contradiction in favour of the people by overcoming the 'subtraction' and devaluation of democracy inherent in bourgeois democracy.

This resolution, in essence demands the abolition of the power of capital in the economic sphere, which is ultimately the source of its overall dominance in society. Insofar as a rigid separation between political and economic spheres is a structural characteristic of capitalism on which the power of capital depends, it means reuniting these spheres in favour of the people, that is, an end of capitalist relations of production and the forms of democracy compatible with them. Compatible with socialist relations of production, socialist democracy will be an expression of popular power in both political and economic spheres, of self-rule that encompasses a classless administration of social production. It will be a restoration of democracy to its original meaning, which once reflected the interests of the *demos* as against those of the propertied classes in ancient Greece, and now in its modern socialist form, that is at a much higher level, expresses the interests of the working people against the propertied classes of the present-day capitalist social order, a recovery of the true meaning of popular power extended to the classless organisation of social production as well. It is obvious that such an effort to unite economic and political spheres, and powers, will entail all the antagonisms and struggles which attend battles between exploiting and exploited classes. No socialist strategy can be taken seriously that ignores or obscures the class barriers beyond which the extension of democracy becomes a challenge to capitalism. We must not conceptualise away such struggles or barriers, the contradiction between capitalism and socialism, by transforming the revolutionary transition into an unbroken continuity between one form of democracy and another.

XXVII

Democracy belongs to the very essence of socialism. There ought to be no dispute about it. Classical Marxist vision of socialism is a society of self-emancipated working people directly participating in making and carrying out the decisions affecting their lives as members of a caring and sharing society. This vision of a fully participatory democracy that socialism enjoins is as far beyond democracy under capitalism as the latter is beyond the constitutional representationism of the feudal era. It extends democratic control to the very foundations of social organisation encompassing both the individual workplace and the whole mechanism of economic life, which, under bourgeois democracy, remain subject to 'despotism of capital', as Marx called it. Socialist democracy means empowerment of the people in every sphere of life, 'the sovereign people transforming itself into the object *and the subject* of power', as Hugo Chavez of Venezuela recently put it. And we would, with Chavez add: 'This option is not negotiable for revolutionaries.'

It is part of the tragedy of socialism in our time that, after an early start, this option soon disappeared in the Soviet Union. The so-called 'Soviet democracy' had nothing of the socialist commitment to democracy about it. As Ralph Miliband has written: 'socialist democracy has nothing to do with the "model", or rather the anti-model, represented by Soviet Communism. Socialist democracy involves neither all-embracing and imperative central planning, nor a command economy under bureaucratic state ownership, nor the monopoly of power by the leaders of a single party, nor total control of society by the party and the state, nor the cult of personality.

All this has nothing to do with socialism, or for that matter with Marx's Marxism.' With the damage done by the Soviet experience, it is in fact a major task of the socialist movement today to recapture the terrain of democracy and democratic struggle which now, more than ever before, stands ceded to 'liberal' or bourgeois politics. This however is not a subject I want to pursue beyond what I have already written. I shall conclude with a few additional observations on the subject of socialist democracy or democracy in a socialist society.

Democracy, to be at all socialist requires as an absolute, though not sufficient condition, the dissolution of the existing structures of economic and political power that is capitalism and the transfer of the main means of economic activity into one form or another of public ownership, so that this activity can be carried out in a planned manner to fulfil human needs. Nothing less will do, if what is wanted is a truly democratic society. The public ownership of course has to be really and not merely juridically so. Otherwise, as the Soviet experience has shown, this too can go into the making of a system of exploitation. Such exploitation, however, is not inherent in public ownership, it is a *deformation*. A system based on public ownership does not necessarily rest on or require exploitation; under democratic control, it, and it alone, provides the basis for free and cooperative association of the producers, unlike the system of private capitalist ownership where exploitation, profit-making through appropriation of others' labour, is the whole purpose of economic activity. This system indeed makes no sense if it is not to result in the private enrichment (whatever other purpose this may serve) of the owners and controllers of the means of economic activity.

It is true that conditions of democratic control in a socialist economy have long remained unrecognised as a problem in Marxist theory. As we have seen, what little Marx and Engels had to say on the subject was not entirely unambiguous or very helpful. But by the very nature of socialism, the problem is a most crucial one. he socialist aspiration is a planned economy in which working people themselves decide what needs to be produced and how, as against the present set-up where capitalist profitability is the key criterion of what is produced and distributed. In other words, under socialism, by definition, it is politics which commands economy and not the other way round as under capitalism. And to be socialist, this politics has to be democratic. To put the argument a little differently, public ownership does not by itself take care of the necessity of the allocation of social labour which, as Marx said, is the central organisational problem of *all* societies. Capitalism, in principle, allocates social labour (as well as material resources) via the market, its mechanisms of commodity exchange. The corrections, when necessary, also come via the market. In a socialist society with its planned economy this is essentially a political and not economic question. It is politics, via planning, which decides and corrections too can come only via politics. And this politics, in a socialist society, has to be democratic. This apart, planning immediately poses a substantial organisational problem, the administration not only of things but people as well – and this raises issues of *representation, authority,* even subordination of some people to others. These issues obviously involve the exercise of power and therefore also carry with them the possibilities of its misappropriation and abuse. Ensuring a genuinely democratic exercise of power thus, again, becomes a matter of major concern in a socialist democracy; it has to be a part of the democratic politics of a socialist society.

Democracy in a socialist society is posed a problem by the very nature of a socialist transition, a rather difficult enterprise which has been well described as 'steering between Scylla and Charybdis, the Scylla being excessive state power and the danger of an all-too strong state, and the Charybdis being an excess of popular power, or rather a fragmentation which gets out of hand'. A socialist revolution is, by definition, an assertion of popular power which demands its continued assertion and dominance in society. But whether it is called the 'dictatorship of the proletariat' or by some other name, there is always also a need for the state, however transitional, to break the rule or power of the old exploiting classes. It may furthe be necesary to strengthen this state in order to defend the revolution, achieve the necessary change in the old order and build, or initiate the building of a new society. This state cannot, by self-definition , claim to be Marx's transitional state – a most advanced form of democracy (*a la* Paris Commune) on the road to ultimately 'wither away'. Therefore, unless immediate steps are taken to institutionalise socialist democracy, the danger is always there that this 'revolutionary state' may itself assume undemocratic features and escape accountability to the people, as has indeed happened in our time. This is not to deny that there are circumstances where a socialist regime seriously concerned to advance the socialist process, may well have to dispense with some of its democracy – for instance, to defend itself against violent or conspiratorial opposition from within and without. But any such erosion of democracy represents a grievous *loss*, and should be clearly understood to be such, a departure from socialist principles to be ended as soon as possible.

It is not for me to offer any detailed sketch, blueprint or model of a functioning socialist democracy. That would be a utopian, essentially un-Marxian exercise, composing 'music of the future', that Marx always disavowed. Once the centrality of the question of democracy in the construction of socialism is recognised, this is the concern of those called upon to carry out the historical task of such construction. Abolition of capitalism, the economic, political and social transformation and the shift of class power in society this implies, will create unprecedented new possibilities for the flowering of popular democracy, but the realisation of such possibilities is and will always be the responsibility of those involved in the actual construction of a socialist society, it is they who have to find concrete answers to the concrete problems of building a socialist democracy. Even so while this remains the principled position, the way the historical changes of our times have brought the question of democracy centre stage in contemporary politics, some at least of the 'music of the future' here has to be composed; it cannot be condemned or dismissed as a diversion from real tasks, as Marx could in his time. Immediately I would only suggest that resources for it are not entirely lacking.

There is of course the historical experience of the ex-Soviet Union which no serious concern with the problematic of socialist democracy can bypass, if not for what should be done, certainly for what should not be done. This apart, failure of democracy in the former 'socialist' world and its deep crisis in the advanced capitalist countries has given rise to a most useful and relevant corpus of writing dealing with such issues as participatory democracy, combining direct and indirect forms of democratic decision-making and centralisation and decentralisation, decentralisation of power and ways of reducing and weakening bureaucracy, reforms in deliberative democratic procedures, various kinds of monitoring, reporting and accountability, different forms of democratic management, 'socialised' information systems and institutions, and so on. Self-administration is no longer seen as an abstract utopia. Alternatives both to bureaucratic despotism and the rule of the reified market are sought in a *qualitative* extension of democracy. Attempts are being made to develop, in greater or lesser detail, the outlines of a viable model of participatory democracy. Socialist democracy, even as it incorporates the values of liberalism, can draw upon the insights of this vast and growing body of literature. Again, there is a rich legacy of genuinely democratic theory and of practical experience, from the Paris Commune, through the Soviets in Russia and the Italian Council Communism to the 'social movement' organisations and experiments (east and west, south and north) of our own times, that is waiting to be assimilated into a viable theory of socialist democracy. The legacy of classical Marxism – especially of Marx and Engels, Lenin, Luxemburg and Gramsci – and the bequests of other currents within the socialist movement have their own resources to offer. Particularly important are the democratic traditions of the revolutionary and working class movements that theory and practice of socialist democracy can draw upon.

More specifically, revolutions of our times have certainly taught us a great deal about what 'people's power' should be like, if we may allow this much-abused expression to take on its literal meaning. What Marx said apropos the working class, applies no less to the actions and organisations of other sections of the popular masses in different revolutionary situations. A revolutionary class, Marx wrote, 'finds the content and material for its own revolutionary activity directly in its own situation: foes to be laid low, measures dictated by the needs of the struggles to be taken; the consequences of its own deeds drive it on. It makes no theoretical inquiries into its own task.' That is how every major revolutionary process – for example, in 1905 and 1917 in Russia, in Germany in 1919-23, in the Finnish Revolution of 1918, in Bela Kun's Hungary in 1918-19, in Spain in 1936, in Chile in 1972-73, in Portugal in 1975-76 – witnessed the emergence in some form – embryonic, infant or adolescent – of organs of direct democracy and rule of the working people. Time after time during periods of revolutionary struggle or upheaval throughout the world, including major strike actions and peasant revolts, workers and peasants have produced and reproduced their own Soviets, peasant and worker committees, factory movements, councils and communes, often without theoretical rationale, as democratic structures of popular power and control, which despite his animadversions against 'ideals', are Marx's ideals. As suggested above, socialists can certainly return to Marx's own suggested example, the Paris Commune in 1871, or to the Soviets which followed upon it in Russia in 1905, and later in 1917 as structures of workers and peasants democracy on which the Russian Revolution was based, however briefly. Revolutions in China, Vietnam and Cuba, Republican Spain in 1936-39, the not so-successful revolutions in Algeria and elsewhere, the peasant struggles in India – the Telengana and Tebhaga movements — provide many examples of such popular democratic initiatives. *Ordine Nuovo* movement of northern Italy in 1919, the workers' committees of the general strikes in Seattle in 1918 and San Francisco in 1934, or the British general strike of 1926, the workers' councils of Hungary 1956, Czechoslovakia 1968, the Solidarnosc of 1979-81 in Poland, and the Soviet miners' committees of 1989, are a few random examples from within the working class movement itself.

On historical record, these were most of the time spontaneous strivings, much too insufficient and shortlived to provide any kind of firm basis for socialist democracy. Even in the Russian Revolution, where Lenin wanted 'every cook to learn to govern', the Soviets never became effectively institutionalised to continue as organs of people's power, and disappeared rather fast, except in name. Obviously what was required was a more pointed awareness of the centrality of democracy in socialism and accordingly a more conscious organisation and leadership. The immediately important point however is that these strivings were expressive of the principle and possibilities of a direct democracy of the working people. They are rich with lessons, negative and positive, in the theory and practice of socialist democracy.

Socialist democracy requires democratic life at all levels of society, at work and everywhere else, with a vigorous and pervasive direct, grass roots democracy. But this direct democracy, its different forms, institutions and mechanisms – referendum, right to recall of elected representatives, workplace democracy and other possible forms of direct self-government – need to be effectively institutionalised. Even so, these are no substitutes (as the Comintern sanctioned orthodoxy once believed them to be) for democratic mechanisms in the internal organisation of political or public power in society, the indirect democracy of 'universal suffrage institutions' as Ernest Mandel has called them, coming to us from the other, much better theorised and practised, democratic tradition of our times, that of western liberalism and bourgeois democracy which we have already explored at some length. This democracy, with its associated set of forms and institutions – representative parliaments, accountable executives, separation of powers in the state, rule of law, constitutionally enshrined civil and political rights, independent judiciary, a plurality of parties, voluntary associations of civil society, etc. – has not only ensured a certain degree of democratically controlled and accountable exercise of power and freedom of the individual, it has come to receive a deep commitment and endorsement of the working masses the world over, particularly in view of their experience with all sorts of dictatorial regimes. As Ernest Mandel has noted: 'After the traumatic shocks of fascist, military and Stalinist dictatorships, the working masses throughout the world are deeply committed to free democratic elections to parliament type bodies. It would be suicidal for socialists to set themselves against that commitment'. Its capitalist limitations transcended, the heritage of this liberal or bourgeois democratic tradition has to be an inalienable part of socialist democracy. Viewing forms or institutions of direct and indirect democracy as complementary, what socialist democracy requires is their articulation in a manner that mobilises the creative and critical intelligence and knowledge of the whole people on behalf of a common enterprise that is the construction of a socialist society, solving its problems and correcting errors, and gives the notion of citizenship a far truer and larger meaning than it could ever have in a class-divided capitalist society.

There can be no illusions, however, about either the difficulties standing in the way of achieving socialist democracy or the new contradictions it will naturally harbour within itself, demanding ever new resolutions on the part of the people. For this reason, it must be viewed not as a destination but as a never-ending historical process involving constant struggle and ever greater democracy. Unlike Fukuyama's liberal democracy, socialist democracy is not 'the end of history'.

APPENDIX: COUNTERPOSING FREEDOM TO POWER*

This approach to the problem of freedom in contemporary society is quite common with western political theorists of liberal-conservative persuasion today. Lipset, for example, has told us in a typical argument... that these theorists are agreed 'that an increase in overall state power', whatever 'economic problems' it may claim to solve, carries with it serious 'dangers to freedom'. Popper has gone so far as to suggest that it was Plato who by asking the question: 'Who should rule?' created a lasting confusion in political theory. For this, according to him, put the question of unchecked political power or sovereignty at the centre of political theory, whereas the really fundamental question – in the interests of freedom and democracy among other things – is that of controlling and checking political power, of how 'rulers can be prevented from doing too much damage'....

This manner of argument is really part of a much wider contemporary phenomenon, of what Kettle has called 'this twentieth-century suspicion of power'. Today, as Cobban too has pointed out, 'men increasingly see power as a force they did not create, do not understand and cannot control, as something outside of them which masses them, the individual atoms, together, hurls them about and even disintegrates them'. This profoundly pessimist fear and dislike of power together with the sense of man's essential helplessness in face of it, which today pervades so much of the liberal consciousness, is not to be understood merely as a reaction against widespread abuse of power in our time. Its roots lie deeper in the loneliness inherent in the bourgeois-liberal outlook, which always sees man *primarily* as an isolated, atomistic individual, and only secondarily as member of a social group, a loneliness intensified, perhaps, by a sense of living at the end of an epoch. 'Power is bad', we are told, the true villain of political and perhaps every other piece – a view which is expressive of so many fears and prejudices of the intellectual in capitalist society. But if this suspicion of power thus becomes articulate in the intellectuals,

* An extract from the author's *Reason, Revolution and Political Theory* (1967).

it quite often evokes a very sympathetic response from the common people also in whose awareness power, economic as well as political, has for so long been the prerogative of the exploiting classes and therefore associated 'predominantly with ruthlessness, self-seeking and chicanery and scarcely at all with principle and responsibility'; who, given the undemocratic *practice* of even the most democratic capitalist society, 'have comparatively little sense of the possibilities of a responsible use of power', of being able to so participate in its exercise as to control their own destiny; who, in other words, have the knowledge and the feeling that ultimately it is *They* who have the power and who rule. Power is seen as *Their* power and therefore felt to be bad....

These general considerations apart, it seems to me that the poser freedom *versus* power, in whose terms so many western social and political thinkers discuss the question of freedom today, is not only highly abstract but arbitrary also. Within the broad ideological context mentioned above, this approach stems, in part, from the false atomistic view of man and society and the collateral laisse faire view of government and political authority, which lie at the base of much of social and political thought of these thinkers. In part it also reflects the refusal of these thinkers to understand what Cole pointed out when he wrote that 'there are more kinds of tyranny and oppression than the political, and more kinds of freedom than the liberal-democratic freedoms that are rightly valued in the countries of the West'. And on the whole the most that can be said for this approach, in theory at least, is that it may be relevant to the situation of men and societies that are comfortable and affluent. But then universally comfortable and affluent societies simply do not exist, not yet. Therefore, in practice, and particularly in relation to the situation of underprivileged men and societies, this approach is largely meaningless. A more meaningful approach, and one particularly relevant to the needs of men and societies now emerging into history, will not only restore such question as '*whose* power is it?' and '*what* purposes does it serve?' to their rightful place in political theory, but also recognise that Popper's two supposedly different and even mutually exclusive questions are really parts of a single fundamental question: Men need to have power, often great power, for they have to achieve great human purposes which alone can give meaning and content to their freedom, *and* men also need to check and control this power *in relation to* these purposes, so that it serves only to give meaning and content to their freedom. Viewed from this angle, the repetition of such well-worn assertions as Acton's 'all power corrupts; and absolute power corrupts absolutely' is not very meaningful or illuminating. At any rate the truth of the latter part of this assertion must not blind us to the absolute pointlessness of the former, which is really tantamount to saying that all action or doing, and therefore living itself, corrupts. You cannot live by the principle 'all power corrupts' unless you have decided to do nothing and therefore have nothing, no freedom either. To regret power or to condemn it, to try to avoid it or to seek its absence or destruction is therefore both meaningless and futile, and all this certainly does not mean freedom. In other words, it is wrong to treat freedom and power as mutually exclusive entities. Besides, one must always remember that there are more dimensions to human freedom than the liberal-democratic or the conservative thinker generally shows himself to be aware of. And even with regard to 'the liberal-democratic freedoms', there was Laski who argued that 'liberty has no meaning save in the context of equality' and that 'equality, also, has no meaning unless the instruments of production are socially owned' – an argument which has the clear implication that the road to freedom lies *through* power which can establish this socialist ownership.

All this is only to suggest that the problem of freedom in contemporary society is far too complex and concrete to be comprehended and settled in terms of the poser 'freedom *versus* power', and that we need to build a concept of freedom which is based not on escaping from power as the liberal-conservative thinker is often asking us to do, but on making a wise, responsible and effective use of power. Abstraction for abstraction, 'freedom *through* power' is any day more meaningful, and certainly more relevant to the needs of the vast majority of men and societies in the world today. For these men and societies need not only freedom but *also* power, power to make their freedom come true.

2

The Single Most Important Wrong Conclusion: 'Triumph of Capitalism'

It is most necessary to draw the right lessons from the failure of 'actually existing socialism' in the Soviet Union and Eastern Europe. And the single most important right lesson is that a society to be really socialist has to be fully democratic. It is not merely that democracy, as a value or ideal, is integral to socialism, whose absence was a most grievous deformation in what was built as socialism in the Soviet Union. Democracy is also a matter of economic necessity for socialism, whose absence in the Soviet Union was ultimately disastrous for its socialism. Under socialism it is politics which commands the economy, and this politics of necessity needs to be democratic. For, as against capitalism, where 'market' commands the economy providing it with necessary indications and correctives, under socialism the necessary guidance or correctives can only come from the people. Ultimately, as Lenin very rightly pointed out, 'people's experience' alone can be the guide in the construction of a socialist society. Hence the sheer economic necessity for socialism to be democratic, and the right lesson emerging from its failure in the Soviet Union. But if it is necessary to draw the right lessons, it is equally necessary to not draw any wrong lessons or conclusions from the failure in the Soviet Union. And the single most important wrong conclusion is the one according to which the failure of 'actually existing socialism' signifies a triumph of capitalism over socialism.

Such a conclusion has indeed been explicitly drawn in the capitalist west and not only the ever-compliant social democrats but many others on the demoralised left have come to share it. 'Western capitalism defeated Soviet communism', proclaimed *The Sunday Times* at the end of 1989. Since then phrases like 'the collapse of Communism', 'the death of Marxism', 'the failure of socialism' have been used as interchangeable, and, repeated *ad nauseam*, have attained the status of self-evident axioms. People have been encouraged to abandon history as a criterion for judgement and the notion of 'victory' substituting for facts or explanation, the recharged image-makers of the Right, in Washington and London, Tokyo, Paris and Bonn, with the new hopefuls of the third world in tow, have been labouriously busy articulating, drumming up and celebrating 'a triumph of capitalism' they had always yearned for but never expected to occur in this manner.

This articulation and celebration found an early, blatantly ideological expression in Francis Fukuyama of the US State Department who declared that the upshot of what has happened is nothing less than the 'end of history'. In the 1950s, the western philosophy had an understandably desperate 'apocalyptic tone' about it, what with its eschatological themes of the 'end of history', the 'end of philosophy', the 'end of man', the 'last man', etc. etc. With the unexpected 'fall of the enemy', there has been a discernible return of confidence; with Fukuyama it is the 'end of history' *in favour of capitalism*. Fukuyama of course prefers to speak of 'liberal democracy', and not capitalist democracy or capitalism. In fact capitalism and liberal democracy are explicitly equated by him. According to him the main challenge to what he calls 'liberal democracy' in this century was Soviet-style Communism, which has now revealed itself to be a definite failure. Other possible alternatives – fascism, various forms of rightist authoritarianism, or Iranian-style theocracy – are infinitely less satisfactory and not viable. To Fukuyama 'The triumph of the West, of the Western *idea*, is evident first of all in the total exhaustion of viable systemic alternatives to Western liberalism'. The *idea* is 'liberal democracy', and with its triumph, in this happy condition, 'all prior contradictions are resolved, and all human needs are satisfied'. The march of history has indeed reached its splendid final end. In other words, the post-war 'American way of life' should be accepted as the ideal society for which humanity has been long aspiring. This is how Fukuyama proclaimed it all in the summer of 1989: 'What we may be witnessing is not just the end of the Cold War, or the passing of a particular period of postwar history, but the end of history as such: that is, the end point of mankind's ideological evolution and the universalisation of Western liberal democracy as the final form of human government.' Many others echoed in a more or less sophisticated manner what Fukuyama, 'the poor man's Hegel', said in his notoriously bold manner. It was repeatedly, though variously, argued that after the collapse of 'Soviet socialism,' in the emerging new world order humankind has no viable alternative to global capitalism. Upon this foundation and within its clearly established limits, humankind may aspire, at most, to be ruled according to the tenets of liberal democracy along the lines practised today by the leading capitalist states: this is the furthest point humanity may justly and rationally seek to reach.

Of course the euphoria of those early post-collapse years is long over. Fukuyama himself has beaten a cautious retreat. Capitalism and democracy do not naturally go together, and he has been compelled to recognise that 'authoritarian regimes are in principle better able to follow truly liberal economic policies undistorted by redistributive goals that constrain growth'. It is also clear that the early predictable pronouncements about the end of both socialism and history are proving to be (equally predictably) premature at best. While the prospects for the left as an internationally significant political force continue to be pretty dim, a large measure of disenchantment with free market capitalist realities is undeniably being registered – through electoral verdicts or otherwise – in a number of places, not the least in Russia and Eastern Europe where the condition of the people has gone from bad to worse. In advanced capitalist societies, capitalism's legitimation in terms of its ability to maintain relatively affluent living standards for a majority of the labour force is no longer assured. Global capitalism, in it structural crisis, is confronting these societies with an unpalatable choice between permanently higher levels of unemployment or permanently lower levels of real wages and social benefits – and increasingly even this choice is disappearing in favour of higher permanent unemployment and poorer living conditions for the working people. The rest of the world gets what it has always gotten from capitalism – misery and exploitation on a vast scale. The 'new world order', dominated as it is by global capitalism is turning out to be an immense disorder, with which capitalist powers are unable to cope. Country and region-wise economic crises regularly shock the global economy and scores of wars and conflicts are going on among and within the states. The threat of nuclear annihilation by war between the 'super-powers' has gone but nuclear proliferation makes a 'local' war more rather than less likely in the years ahead. To this may be added the possibilities of an ecological disaster which capitalism's accumulative logic now portends. Far from being in the least attenuated, the woes of the world have only grown more pronounced and painful with the renewed capitalist domination of the world. The end of the cold war, far from representing a triumph of capitalism, has only revealed the ugly reality of capitalism at home and abroad that anti-communist demagogy had earlier helped to mask or obscure.

The euphoria may have disappeared and the complacent and self-congratulatory politics of the Right may no longer be in upswing as before, but its ideological gains, well-consolidated, are very much still there, expressed above all in the ideological hegemony of the capitalist gospel, masquerading as 'the end of ideology'. Fukuyama himself may have been 'first argued with, then laughed at and finally forgotten', but his argument was not about economic or political successes of capitalism. It was essentially about the success or victory of an ideology, about the ability of the world ruling class to destroy, to suffocate, corrupt, or discredit, any constructive alternative to itself. The belief is thus still widespread that not only have the specific 20th century socialist movements and regimes run their course, but even the idea of socialism, of a future transcending capitalism, is one whose time allegedly has passed. It continues to be maintained that it was a contest in which socialism has finally lost out to capitalism. Capitalism has indeed triumphed over socialism.

These are rather dubious propositions. I don't need to examine the utterly reductionist and adversarial, and obviously questionable logic which equating what was built in the Soviet Union with socialism as such, conflates its failure with a victory for capitalism. I would only suggest that even the proposition that this 'actually existing socialism' has lost out in a contest with 'actually existing capitalism' is to say the least ambiguous and ultimately unsustainable.

II

What contest does capitalist triumphalism has in mind? If the contest was military, the history of our times, from Churchill in 1917 to Reagan in 1987, and Hitler in between, is witness to the total failure of capitalism, despite repeated efforts, to destroy socialism as it existed in the Soviet Union or any other socialist state by force of arms. The Soviet Union established this fact in a most authoritative manner by its decisive victory over fascism in the second world war.

In the economic sphere what was ultimately built in the Soviet Union was a very much deformed socialism – deformed partly at least by its 'productivist' push to 'catch up' with capitalism rather than build up *socialist* relations in the economy. The failures of central planning under the 'actually existing socialism,' especially during its last decades, are now universally understood – chief among these failures being the way in which the lack of democracy engendered an all-powerful stifling bureaucracy so that the central premises of socialism were, time and again, debauched. Yet it bears repeating that flawed in planning or deformed otherwise, socialist economy in the Soviet Union had great and in some cases truly astonishing achievements to its credit, without parallel in the history of capitalist development anywhere in the world – all the more significant because of the surrounding circumstances, particularly the starting point of extreme backwardness, made worse by the ruination of the first world war and a civil war, and later, having to begin from scratch again after the second world war, along with a totally hostile international environment, globally dominant capitalism's constant pressure of hot and cold war, throughout its troubled history. During the early phase of central planning, in the period of the first two five-year plans, from 1928 to 1937, the Soviet Union recorded unprecedently rapid, indeed stunning economic growth, which in a single decade transformed a semi-agrarian backward country into the world's second industrial power, capable of withstanding and finally defeating the Nazi onslaught of 1941. While the West was suffering its worst depression, a world economic crisis which brought even the strongest of capitalist economies to its knees, the Soviet Union not only remained immune to this crisis but advanced rapidly, its industrial growth as measured by conservative Western analysts averaged more than 12 per cent. There was an equally remarkable self-reliant recovery and reconstruction after the massive destruction of the second world war when even CIA estimates placed industrial growth at an average of 9.3 per cent during the 1950s, more than twice the rate in the United States during the period, making the Soviet Union an indisputable other super-power in the world. Even Friedrich von Hayek, the renowned free-market economist and arch-enemy of central planning acknowledged 'the conspicuous successes which the Russians have achieved in certain areas'. For socialists, conspicuous in the Soviet economic construction and reconstruction were the epic feats of creativity of the Soviet people and communists, their idealism, heroism and self-sacrifice for a cause, witnessed among other things, in mass mobilisations on a gigantic scale to create major capital assets, *socialist* assets in the economy. It was not an empty boast to those who heard it in 1956, when Khruschev said: 'Whether or not you like it, history is on our side; we will bury you'. With its economic successes beginning with the five-year plans, triumph over Hitlerism, rapidity of post-war recovery, steady improvement of the Soviet standard of living, and aid it could give to other socialist countries and friendly post-colonial states, socialism, whatever its deficiencies in the Soviet Union, was increasingly seen in large parts of the world as a successful challenge and alternative to capitalism.

Incidentally, in view of the persistent talk about the 'planned economies' having failed to keep up with the west in the sphere of scientific or technological progress, it should be remembered that the Soviet period saw the creation of a mighty scientific and technological potential in a backward, underdeveloped country under extremely adverse conditions. Overcoming the devastation caused by the Second World War, the number of people with more than a secondary education rose from twelve million in 1960 to over forty million by 1985, and the number of trained scientists exceeded those in Western Europe and Japan together. Soviet education not only produced a new scientific and technological intelligentsia out of its worker and peasant population, its successes here jolted the western education, prompting the writing of such books as *What Ivan Knows That Johnny Doesn't*. Soviet record of growth and innovation in areas like defence, space research and nuclear science, calling for the most sophisticated of the latest technologies, more than matched that of the west. Intelligence agencies of the western capitalist countries had indeed known it for long, even though for cold war propaganda purposes, they often found it expedient to depict Soviet Union as scientifically backward. It is not without reason that the post-collapse period has witnessed a fierce competition between the US and other western countries to buy up, grab and if necessary destroy Russian scientific and technological potential in areas in which Soviet Union had been ahead of even the most highly advanced capitalist countries of the west and which the present economically prostrate Russia has been trying, without much success thanks to its comprador leadership, to turn into hard cash.

If the 'contest' is seen as social or cultural, in terms of quality of life in general, of how economy affects the everyday life and well being of the common man, the issue is at best debatable when it is not entirely favourable to socialism as it existed in the Soviet Union and Eastern Europe. Socialism promised full employment and secure jobs, a modest scale of income and consumption for all even if it lacked west's consumerist affluence. It guaranteed cradle to grave social security with health care, education, housing or transport within every one's easy reach. Socialism ensured stable prices throughout its seventy-odd years of existence. Supply of housing, offered at unbelievably low rates may have lagged behind demand, but there were no extensive shanty towns in the Soviet Union. Nor did one ever see an old person begging in its streets. The Soviet Union had by far the highest ratio of doctors (and hospital beds) to population of any large or even medium-sized capitalist country. It had the best infant and child care in the world. Socialism indeed took care, in fact loving care, of old men and women and children. Even in the remotest villages and most backward republics of the Soviet Union, socialism connoted universal literacy and health care and a greatly enhanced status for women. Women, throughout the Soviet Union won levels of participation not seen before. They mass advanced into the professions earlier than any other country and remained statistically far ahead of the west. To the already noticed educational achievement of socialism we may add widespread promotion of sports. It used to happen almost as a matter of course that two-thirds of the Olympic medals came to be won by young men and women from the socialist world. Socialism also meant huge subsidisation of literature, music and arts, and the diffusion of classical world culture on a mass-scale unprecedented in any major country of the world, including the US, Germany and Japan, symbolised by the selling of hundreds of millions of copies of Shakespeare, Tolstoy, Pushkin, Gorki and Tagore and discs of Beethoven and Bach at throwaway prices or distribution of Bolshoi Ballet tickets among the workers. To which may be added across-the-board resuscitation of people's art, music and dance forms in the vast stretches of central Asian republics, quite apart from the pinnacles of achievement the Bolshoi and Kirov Ballet groups attained with direct encouragement from the Soviet authorities. Even if we choose to ignore the significance of the exceedingly short time within which all this was accomplished or the fact that it was accomplished while achieving a balance in military strength with the world's most powerful nation, the United States, socialism as it existed in the Soviet Union represents a social and cultural achievement that is unparalleled anywhere in the advanced capitalist world.

Origins of social security and welfare in the west may be traceable in Sweden, Germany or England long before the October Revolution, but it really arrived only decades after it was fully implanted in the Soviet Union and later in Eastern Europe. And the reach or thoroughness of western social security systems would be unthinkable without the example or threat of, or shall we say, contest with the socialism of the Soviet Union. Even so, they compare unfavourably with the social security and welfare that had been achieved in the Soviet Union and Eastern Europe and has now been lost with the advent of capitalism.

So far as the common people are concerned, in terms of employment which is the very basis of dignity and hope in society, in terms of nutrition, health care, education, housing, etc., items that consume 60 to 80 per cent of a family's budget in most capitalist societies, socialism of Soviet Union had done decidedly better than capitalism has. And socialism in Cuba still does – life expectancy in Cuba is already higher than in the United States. Far more important is the fact that capitalism and the free market have failed to tackle successfully the problems of unemployment and income distribution in the Western countries. Along with the ever increasing economic and social inequality, there is chronic unemployment for a sizeable segment of the working class who are forced to live on dole. The situation, social welfare and employment wise, is particularly bad for those who may be described as 'third world peoples' within the advanced capitalist societies, the nation's poor and the old, or others like the Blacks and Hispanics in the United States. They remain permanently disadvantaged. About the vulgar and degenerate consumerist culture of contemporary capitalism, less said the better. The vacuity in social mores induced by poverty-prosperity polarisation inherent in capitalism only pushes people, those at the bottom more than others, into a culture of racial discrimination, of crime and violence and drugs.

It is interesting to note that the celebratory claims of having won the 'contest' with socialism have been made at a time when, overtaken by a deep structural crisis, capitalism is finding it difficult to afford even the limited gains people had won from it in the past. Always reversible, 1980s onwards, they are being reversed. Beginning with Reagan and Bush in the US, and Margaret Thatcher in England, these gains have been under attack all over the advanced capitalist world, the 'welfare state' is being, more or less successfully, dismantled. Far from winning any contest, capitalism today is failing to deliver the goods more dramatically than at any time since the Great Depression. So far as the contest with socialism in the matter of social security and welfare is concerned, it can now be seen to have gone against capitalism more than ever before.

If we turn from the first to the third world, the balance sheet of the so-called 'contest' between capitalism and socialism is, if anything, even more in favour of socialism. The outcome of the Korean war, or the war in Vietnam, or America's continuous aggressive posture against Cuba, or of capitalism's armed counter revolutionary interventions in the third world leaves the military issue, at the very least, open and debatable. In the economic sphere, that of land reform and economic development, the record of third-world post-revolutionary regimes, opting for socialism, is impressive and any day better than that of countries which have remained a part of the global capitalist system, apart from a few exceptional cases. China started with a far more backward industrial base and infrastructural development than India, but its subsequent performance during 'the Mao period' was incomparably superior both in terms of aggregate accumulation and in the material security of the vast majority of its people. Cuban performance has likewise been better than that of comparable countries in the Caribbean and Central America – all this with no imperialist loot, no Marshall Plans, and under conditions of extreme duress. Particularly significant and decisive is the comparison in terms of living standards or quality of life of common people. Appropriate comparisons of countries with roughly similar level of development of forces of production to begin with, but opting for socialism or staying with capitalism – for example, Cuba with its peers in Latin America, including Mexico, Brazil and Argentina, its three largest economies, or China with India when the former was still struggling to build socialism, or Asiatic republics of the Soviet Union with comparable countries on their borders, etc. – would easily reveal that the former have been far ahead of the latter in dealing effectively with some very basic problems affecting the lives of the masses – problems of employment, education, health care (including infant mortality and life expectancy), social welfare, and so on. From death at an early age to a life expectancy approaching the attainable span of the human organism, from semi-starvation to enough to eat, from chronic illness to reasonable health, from illiteracy to the ability to read and write, from grinding insecurity to the peace of mind of a steady job and a pension in old age and access to a cultured life, in short from a subhuman to at least the beginnings of a human existence – this is what socialism brought to many peoples in the third world as against capitalism which has almost invariably meant the perpetuation and growth of poverty, deprivation and destitution in its peripheries. On historical evidence, it is socialism rather than capitalism which has proved to be the form of organisation of production and distribution of goods and social services that better improves the quality of life of the large majority of people living in the underdeveloped world. It is not at all surprising that the example of the post-revolutionary societies, which represented socialism as against capitalism, has had a great appeal for the masses in the third world. And, it may be added, if reports from Russia and everywhere east of the Oder-Neisse line are to be believed, now that they are at last face to face with capitalism, the people are discovering, *ex post*, the virtues of socialism they had scorned and so thoughtlessly abandoned for it in the name of democracy.

(Incidentally, in their efforts to denigrate socialism, ideologues of capitalism make much about the millions who died as a result of Stalin's policies. Now, socialism in the Soviet

Union – 'actually existing socialism' as it has been called – was indeed most grievously deformed. Socialists, including communists, particularly need to undeservedly condemn the excesses and crimes, the Terror and the gulags of the Stalin era. But the anti-left critics of Soviet socialism must not forget that the record of 'actually existing capitalism' here is far worse. Their assessment of things needs to take account of the human costs of European colonialism, South African apartheid, imperialist wars, fascism, and the US armed and unarmed interventions, including the war against communism in Central and South America. They could well do a body count of the numbers who have died in recent years because of the policies of American Presidents from Truman to Bush and Clinton and Bush again. One may particularly mention China where the United States backed the nationalists and prolonged the civil war, the Korean and Vietnam wars, the Angolan civil war created and prolonged by the US, the messy intervention in Afghanistan, America supervised 'ethnic cleansing' in the Balkans and the more recent wars on Iraq and Afghanistan; or more generally point to diverse US military actions (including the use of atomic, napalm and fragmentation bombs on civilian populations), US-sponsored coups and limited wars, American economic boycotts, sanctions and austerity policies imposed on Third World governments, or CIA-financed assassinations, destablisation campaigns, and dirty wars. The total of all these activities, even when the count is confined to the post-Second World War era, would surely be staggering – far surpassing anything that critics can blame on the Soviet Union. This is not to even remotely defend or justify what happened in the Soviet Union, the wrong done in the name of socialism; it is only to make a point that anti-left critics involved in the controversy over capitalism or socialism, or plain defenders of capitalism, need to be aware of).

Socialism of our times had its flaws, economic and political deformations, grievous departures from its original vision in classical Marxism. There was also the constant hostility and pressure of global capitalism. But, ultimately, it did not fail the way it did for any of these reasons. Nor did it lose out in any 'contest' with capitalism. As we have already seen, thanks to the long-time and many-sided corruption and bankruptcy of its leadership which turned treacherous towards the end, this socialism had simply self-destructed. Capitalism seems to have 'won' more by default than by any of its supposed superiority over socialism. In a fundamental sense the contest between capitalism and socialism still remains very much an open one. I would however like to return to this issue, 'the triumph of capitalism', to make a different and more basic point, which has come up, more sharply than ever before, consequent upon the now finally established failure of the Soviet Union to build socialism.

III

The collapse in Eastern Europe and the Soviet Union has led any number of scholars, journalists and politicians, ideologues and writers of all sorts, to play zero sum games. If socialism has lost, then its antagonist, capitalism, must have won. If planned socialist economies have broken down, then their binary opposite, free-market capitalism must have triumphed. Such an assessment of the situation found an early and very representative expression in an article by the noted economist, Robert Heilbronner. Towards the end of the 1980s, as the communist regimes collapsed in Eastern Europe, Heilbronner wrote his much noticed piece in *The New Yorker* entitled 'The Triumph of Capitalism'. The very first sentence summed it all up. It read: 'Less than seventy-five years after it officially began, the contest between capitalism and socialism is over: capitalism has won.'

In the years that followed Heilbronner has been somewhat more cautious in his assessment and in expressing himself on the subject, particularly with regard to capitalism and its future. He has since pointed out that 'it is not ignorance but amnesia that has blocked out the problems of unemployment, maldistribution, and other market disorders that were a prime cause of socialism in the first place'. He does not think that 'a thoroughgoing decommerciali-sation of life or a far reaching democratisation of the workplace or an equitable reorganisation of the world economic system is likely to be a realizable goal under the aegis of even the most advanced capitalism.' Aware of the impending ecological disaster – 'the closing window of environmental tolerance' – he notes that coping with or averting it will demand control and containing of the basic institutions of capitalism, including markets and private ownership of production, to a degree that a society doing so in order to save the environment will be difficult to describe as capitalism. To him capitalism is 'a civilisation whose historical thrust has been in just the opposite direction'. Even if 'socialism has been a great tragedy this century', he very much doubts 'whether socialism has now disappeared from history'. He even hopes for his grandchildren to live in a society approximating one that is enshrined in the original vision of socialism.

Be that as it may, Heilbronner's original article received wide currency and endorsement at the time, and over the years the supposedly self-evident character of its widely shared opening proposition has continued to be relied upon to proclaim the victory or success of capitalism. It is worth our while therefore to take another look at the matter to point out the logical flaw underlying the 'self-evidence' of such zero-sum propositions and, more importantly, make a basic point about the condition in which the world really finds itself after the failure of socialism in our times, in the Soviet Union or elsewhere. And we shall do so with the help of Heilbronner himself.

Heilbronner has never been a great admirer of capitalism. On the contrary, over a very long period of time, since he wrote *The Worldly Philosophers* in 1953 till the mid-1980s and even afterwards, he has been, if anything, a very perceptive critic of capitalism. Writing in 1967 ('The Future of Capitalism') this is how he had argued about capitalism: 'The essential idea of a society built on scientific engineering is to impose human will on the social universe; that of capitalism is to allow the social universe to unfold as if it were beyond human interference. Before the activist philosophy of science as a social instrument, this inherent social passivity of capitalism becomes archaic, and eventually intolerable. The "self-regulating" economy that is its highest social achievement stands condemned by its absence of meaning and intelligence, and each small step taken to correct its deficiencies only advertises the inhibitions placed on the potential exercise of purposeful thought and action by its remaining barriers of ideology and privilege. In the end, capitalism is weighed in the scale of science and found wanting, not only as a system but as a philosophy.' (Here it may be remembered that socialism is precisely the possibility for human beings to organise their economic system intelligently so as to make it work for the benefit of humankind, as against capitalism which leaves human beings victims of market forces beyond their control). Nearly two decades later, in 1985, (*The Nature and Logic of Capitalism*) this is how Heilbronner saw the historical perspective on capitalism: 'Finally, all the great scenarios (of Smith, Mill, Marx, Keynes and Schumpeter) envisage the (capitalist) regime as having a bounded future. Its span of life cannot be precisely predicted, but its eventual demise or supersession by another social order is universally foreseen'.

One wonders how what has happened in Eastern Europe or Soviet Union or elsewhere, invalidates Heilbronner's earlier, better considered argument or perspective. How the 'failure' of socialism such as it was becomes an argument for the 'triumph of capitalism'. Logically it is a *non-sequitor*. One simply does not follow from the other. Besides, the assumption which gives the argument a deceptive plausibility – all the more deceptive because of its gratuitous equation of 'actually existing socialism' with socialism as such – namely that capitalism or the deformed Soviet version of socialism are the only two possibilities in the world today, is simply false. The only proposition that can be asserted with any logical validity is that about the failure, however qualified, of 'actually existing socialism'. It is illogical to conclude from this failure the success or triumph of capitalism. On the other hand, if taken seriously as they were meant to be, Heilbronner's argument and perspective on capitalism clearly suggest that capitalism has not been much of a success either and is destined to be superseded by a new and better social order. This being so, the only logically valid proposition Heilbronner is entitled to advance is that both capitalism and the attempt to build 'another social order', namely socialism, have failed in our time. I would like to suggest that this is indeed the case with the world today. That is, logic apart, the argument for triumph of capitalism is false on empirical grounds as well. In other words, if there is no denying the failure of 'actually existing socialism' which came into the world with the October Revolution in 1917, a careful look at the reality of our world, that goes beyond the current confusion or euphoria, will reveal that 'actually existing capitalism', existing for nearly four to five hundred years, has been in most ways a worse failure.

That both capitalism and the effort to build socialism in our time have failed has important short- and long-term implications for the future of humankind. But before we explore them, the fact of failure of capitalism must be clearly recognised. This is necessary because, given the renewed global domination of capitalism, its ideologues and any number of hangers on in the academy and the media are busy not only obscuring its failure or, most illogically, suggesting that the removal of the ugly face of 'actually existing socialism', necessarily removes the ugliness from the face of 'actually existing capitalism', but painting it a success, if not the system beautiful itself.

IV

Particularly Marx onwards, there is a vast corpus of critical literature, Marxist and non-Marxist, on what can be legitimately described as failure or failures of capitalism as an economic system and as a social order. (Incidentally, the dominant capitalist ideology is now persuading us to ignore or forget this literature as the product of an era that has passed). Most noteworthy, indeed prophetic, here is the work of Marx himself whose analysis or critique of capitalism we have already noticed. He had lauded the extraordinary productive achievements of capitalism and even spoken of 'the great civilising influence of capital', emphasising – with a critical edge to it that we shall be noting in the next chapter – that through it 'for the first time, nature becomes purely an object for humankind, purely a matter of utility; ceases to be recognised as a power for itself; and the theoretical discovery of its autonomous laws appears merely as a ruse so as to subjugate it under human needs, whether as an object of consumption or as a means of production. In accord with this tendency, capital drives beyond national barriers and prejudices as much as beyond nature worship, as well as all traditional, confined, complacent, encrusted satisfactions of present needs, and reproductions of old ways of life'. But Marx had also underlined capitalism's 'shameless, direct brutal exploitation', its accumulative logic that has no other objective than capital's own self-reproduction to which everything else must be absolutely subordinated, from nature to all human needs and aspirations. Marx had pointed to the *essential* irrationality and inhumanity of capitalism as a market and profit-based economic-social order, and written: 'There must be something rotten in the very core of a social system which increases its wealth without diminishing its misery, and increases in crimes even more rapidly than in numbers'. Today every aspect of our life, every sphere of activity or set of human relations carries the mark of capitalism's essential irrationality and inhumanity and bears witness to the ultimate failure of capitalism as a necessary or desirable form of economic or social organisation.

Here, it may be pointed out, it is not only a question of capitalism failing to approximate to the notion of a good society that humankind has dreamt of through the ages, one of material well-being for all and rich in its moral, cultural-aesthetic and spiritual social life. Capitalism has failed in its own promise, and in terms of the potentialities it has created done much worse. Its theory of 'social welfare', then and now, always had it that each individual's free and selfish pursuit of gain in a competitive market will be transformed into a socially optimal result. This will happen, Adam Smith said, 'as if by an invisible hand'. But Adam Smith's 'invisible hand' never became visible in behalf of human welfare. Production may have increased and profits for the few maximised but most of whatever else it produced had little to do with 'socially optimal' in any meaningful, humane sense. GDP or growth rates alone are no indication of social welfare. 'The economy is doing fine, the people are not', as a president of Brazil once reported it to his patrons in Washington, this was and remains the essential reality of capitalism as an economic system. This apart, for well over two hundred years liberal capitalism has been promising 'liberty, equality and fraternity' for all, but has instead delivered a world in which these ideals are systematically subverted by its own operations. The 'liberty' of capitalists to accumulate wealth undermines the freedom of just about everyone else; 'equality' is not only subdued and restricted by the overarching powers of capital but, as George Monbiot of *The Guardian* has recently pointed out, inequalities have steadily increased since the French Revolution, and 'now, just as then, the desperation of the poor counterpoises the obscene consumption of the rich'; and 'fraternity' literally loses out daily in the capitalist market. (Incidentally, as Monbiot also says, 'now, just as then, the sages employed by the global aristocrats – in the universities, the think-tanks, the newspapers and magazines – contrive to prove that we possess the best of all possible systems in the best of all possible worlds'.) Capitalism encouraged innovation and enterprise, indeed awakened the 'miracles that slumbered in the lap of social labour' and created unheard of productive capacity, which as Marx had pointed out could be the material basis, lacking hitherto in human history, for a more humane social order in which every person can live in reasonable comfort and with plenty of leisure for the pursuit of intellectual, spiritual, artistic or cultural activities of one's own choice, that is live a 'truly rich human life'. But far from realising this possibility, capitalism has not been able to ensure even a remotely equitable distribution of what it manages to produce with the aid of its science and technology. Instead, it has only served the interests, even egotistic caprices and consumerist appetites, of a small minority in the developed and underdeveloped countries of capitalism, though some more have also been able to extract limited social benefits for themselves in the advanced capitalist countries. Apart from the worldwide cruelty and inhumanity of its origins and early evolution in the west, capitalism in its centuries-long existence has only brought misery and suffering for the overwhelming majority of humankind. And the failure here is all the more glaring in view of the possibilities that scientific and technological revolutions of our time have now opened up for humankind but which remain blighted because of capitalism.

V

Even as East Europe collapsed and the West was busy wallowing in the 'failure of socialism' and celebrating not merely the 'triumph of capitalism' but capitalism as 'the end of history' itself, Ellen Meiksins Wood 'put things into perspective', and wrote:

> In the 'richest country in the world', the capital city is riddled with poverty and crime, as sleek civil servants cohabit with beggars. In the first half of 1989, the infant mortality rate in Washington D.C. apparently rose by 40% over the previous year, in large part because of the spread of crack-cocaine addiction. At 32.3 deaths per 1000 births, this mortality rate exceeds, among others, those of China, Chile, Jamaica, Mauritius, Panama, and Uruguay, according to World Bank statistics. One end of the country is dominated by a city, New York, the heartland of the nation's wealth, where unparalleled luxury coexists with the most abject squalor, poverty, crime, drug addiction and homelessness. At the other end, in Los Angeles, the city's core is being eaten away by drugs and gang-warfare, while privileged whites increasingly retreat into fortified enclaves where every manicured lawn sports a notice that its owner is protected by one of many and multiplying security services, with the menacing announcement: 'Armed Response'. In many places, the school system is a shambles, producing illiterate graduates; and millions of Americans cannot afford health care. It is estimated that 20 million workers in the US take illegal drugs (not to mention many more with alcohol problems), and that drug and alcohol abuse is costing US companies more than $100 billion a year (*Guardian*, November 17, 1989). In Britain, the birthplace of capitalism, under a government more implacably committed than any other to the values of 'free enterprise', the infrastructure crumbles, mass unemployment persists, public services decline, education even at the primary level becomes less accessible, and squalor deepens, while the poor and homeless multiply. The much vaunted 'economic miracle' in Italy has spawned a large and growing population of near-slaves in the form of Third World immigrants, many of them illegal, who have become the objects of yet another lucrative trade for the Mafia. In Japan, the well-spring of

> consumerism, ordinary citizens typically work longer hours than in any other developed country, live in postage-stamp-size flats, and take no holidays. As I write, here in prosperous Toronto, the richest city in Canada, one of the city's two major newspapers is conducting a food drive to feed the hungry – not in Ethiopia, but in Metropolitan Toronto, where property developers are making a killing while people go hungry because 70 per cent of their income goes to pay impossibly high rents. The Daily Bread Food Bank, representing 175 emergency food programmes, today helpfully supplied paper bags with every newspaper, inscribed with the following information: '217,000 people a year (84,000 a month, according to the Toronto *Star*) in Metro need food help (out of a population of about 3.4 million). Half of them have gone without food for a day or more. One Metro (Metropolitan Toronto) child in seven belongs to a family who needed food help last year. Daily Bread now distributes as much food in a week as it did in all 1984.'
>
> And that is just in the prosperous corners of capitalism. If these are the successes of capitalism, what standards should we use in comparing its failures to those of the communist world? Would it be an exaggeration to say that more people live in abject poverty and degradation within the ambit of capitalism than in the Soviet Union or Eastern Europe?

Wood's was a reposite, but she was not alone in thus pointing to the failure of capitalism even in its most advanced centres, including the United States where 'the other America' as Michael Harrington called it, has been and remains a stubborn fact of American life. Early in 1990, Michael Prowse, in an article (in the American *Financial Times*) entitled 'The not so great society' said: 'figures suggest the US is steadily becoming a harsher and meaner society'. He pointed out that whereas in the late 1970s 24.5 million Americans were below the official poverty line ($6,000 for a single person), this figure in 1988 had arisen to 32 million, that is, about 13 per cent of the population. Many more families are classified as 'near poor', as the average pre-tax income of the bottom fifth of US families is only 84 per cent of the official poverty threshold. Michael Prowse continued: 'Nearly a third of all Blacks and more than a quarter of Hispanics are below the poverty line. Children suffer disproportionately. Among Blacks and Hispanics, child poverty is running at 44.2 per cent and 37.9 per cent respectively. Nearly a fifth of ALL American children are officially classified as poor.' Prowse concluded: 'The US thus faces chronic problems across the whole spectrum of social policy. It does not matter whether you look at poverty, inequality, housing, crime, drugs, health care or education, the US is either losing grounds or treading water.'

This is how John Cassidy, writing about the same time in the *Sunday Times*, portrayed the scene in New York, the major city of the US: 'The city that swaggered through the 1980s portraying itself as a new imperial Rome is now worried it might be turning into a Calcutta: an urban nightmare racked by crack, crime, AIDs, homelessness, racism, economic recession, a crumbling infrastructure and pollution... (some) areas are now so dangerous that even local priests carry guns.' He added 'About 25 per cent of New Yorkers remain below the poverty line and life expectancy among black males in Harlem is lower than in Bangladesh. Infant mortality rates in New York's ghettos are nearly as high as those in tropical Africa. The first thing that strikes visitors to New York is the number of homeless, even in the richest areas. About 250,000 live on the streets and subways. A recent survey suggested that more than 40 per cent of them suffer from tuberculosis.'

A few months later, speaking of 'American malaise', Tom Wicker, a columnist of *New York Times* reported: 'While the economy deteriorates at home, our children go begging and shooting, the schools educate poorly if at all, millions neither have nor can afford medical care, and bridges fall down on the homeless sleeping beneath them'. Somewhat later the well-known social scientist, Johan Galtung wrote: 'Perhaps the basic point about the new world order is not that the Soviet Union has disappeared but that the United States is becoming a Third World country. While it is certain that the US still has many rich people and possesses awesome military power, the unyielding unemployment, the 24 million Americans on food stamps and the one child in five that is raised in poverty outstrips the gloomy realities of many Third World countries. Other indicators of this tendency are the grave insufficiencies in health insurance and the extent of functional illiteracy.' Capitalist triumphalism notwithstanding, the public mood in the United States was gloomy and uncertain. The 'victorious' Bush lost the elections, MIT economist Paul Krugman was soon speaking of the 1990s as America's 'Age of Diminished Expectations' and writing *The Return of Depression Economics* and *New York Times* carried stories headlined 'America's Treadmill Economy' in which people are 'Going Nowhere Fast'.

VI

Capitalism's failure is today evident both in the developed or advanced capitalist countries and the underdeveloped or backward ones located in the semi-periphery and periphery of the global capitalist system, including the newly converted-to-capitalism ex-socialist countries. There is evidence enough in our discussion of capitalism so far, particularly in chapters on the first and third worlds. A brief supplementing account would suffice to further establish the point before we return to the basic issue which the failure of both capitalism and the attempt to build socialism in our time has raised.

The failure of capitalism is, perhaps, nowhere more evident than in its leading countries, with their rising levels of open or disguised unemployment and poverty, increasing inequalities and deteriorating conditions of life and work of the common people that we have noticed earlier (in the previous volume). In the United States around thirty million are reported to be unemployed. According to Staughton Lynd, 'American capitalism no longer has any use for, let's say, 40 per cent of the population. These are the descendants of folks who were brought over here in one way or another during the period of capital accumulation. They are now superfluous human beings. They're nothing but a problem for the people who run the society.' Those who are still employed live in a chronic state of anxiety, all the time worried about getting a pink slip. Wages and incomes are under attack. Wage cuts are accepted to save jobs, the situation made worse for both men and women workers because of the lower wage rate for women which is two-thirds that of men. For two-thirds of workers, average incomes are below the late 1970s. (Incidentally, a currency speculator living in New York earns in a few weeks what it would take an American in a minimum wage job 150 thousand years!) As wages go down, support systems decline and working conditions deteriorate, working hours have gone way up – Americans apparently work about a month per year more than they did twenty-five years ago. Naturally enough, the levels of poverty have been rising. By government's own estimate, 36 million Americans, roughly one in eight, lived in poverty in 1995 – and they have continued to live in poverty. Around 20 per cent of children are reported to be living below the poverty line. One out of two black children and one out of three Latino children are poor and the US infant mortality rate is higher than at least 19 other countries. Life expectancy for Blacks is lower than in many 'underdeveloped' countries. As reported in *Guardian Weekly*, towards the end of 1999, 'more than 40 million Americans have no health insurance. According to a US census report about 44.3 million Americans – one-sixth of the population – cannot afford high-priced private health care. This is a 4.3 million increase since President Bill Clinton took office in 1993.' Inadequate public education has produced 20 to 30 million functionally illiterate adults. Hunger is widespread and increasing. According to Second Harvest, the largest US Food Bank, in the early 1990s, roughly one in 10 Americans, or an estimated 26 million people, relied on charitable food agencies to eat. According to Congressional testimony, the hungry increased from 20 million in 1985 to 30 million in 1995. Most of these are desperate families driven into the ranks of the destitute, the hungry and the homeless by joblessness. Over 3 million Americans are homeless of whom one-third suffer severe mental problems. As an accumulated outcome of all this, major American cities are fast becoming so many disaster zones.

The existence of mass poverty in the United States, as in other advanced capitalist countries, is a pointer to the inequality inherent in the structural logic of capitalism. While mass living standards have stagnated or deteriorated since the mid-1970s and the number of poor and marginalised has grown, those in the upper income brackets have prospered, and those at the very top have benefited both absolutely and relatively more than, perhaps, in any previous period of American history. The emergence of the American underclass over the past couple of decades has accompanied a tremendous economic boom for the rich and the upper middle class, reminiscent of the roaring 1920s (that were, incidentally, soon followed by the Great Depression). The top one per cent of American families are reported to have increased their post-tax incomes by 102 per cent over the 1980s and the number of billionaires in the US increased sevenfold from 1985 to 1990. Three fourths of income gains during the 1980s went to the top 20 per cent of the families. It was thus also a period of growing disparity between the nation's rich and its poor, the gap between them becoming the widest since the Second World War. In the middle of the 1970s, the income gap between the very rich and the very poor was relatively narrow: one per cent of the population controlled 18 percent of private wealth. Now, the richest one per cent of the population controls 40 per cent of nation's wealth – twice as much as the figure in Britain, which has the most unequal society in Western Europe. The top 10 per cent of the American population own approximately 65 per cent of all wealth in the US and the super-rich, the top 0.5 per cent own a quarter of all individual wealth. According to the Budget Office of the US Congress, the income of the top 1 per cent is equivalent to that of the bottom one hundred million people, i.e., nearly 40 per cent of the population. Twenty years ago it was 'only' 1 per cent against forty-nine million, i.e., less than twenty per cent of the US population. According to another estimate, 94 per cent of all financial wealth in the US is owned by the top 20 per cent of the population (48 per cent by the top 1 per cent), leaving only 6 per cent for the bottom 80 per cent. Some 15–20 trillion dollars is possessed by the wealthiest 10 per cent of families, roughly half of it in the top 1 per cent, and the bottom 90 per cent have about the same as the top 10 per cent. At the very bottom, large numbers live in abject poverty. The per capita income of the poorest in the US is less than a fourth of the country's average per capita income. Not only have the ranks of the poor multiplied, the poorest decile of Americans is poorer today than at any other time in recent US history.

While noise continues to be made over 'equalisation' and the 'merging of the classes' into a happy 'middle class', social polarisation is today greater in the US than ever before. And this polarisation is growing with the growth of an underclass in America: people concentrated in the slums of great cities; on deprived farms; as rural migrant labour; as more diffused poor of the old south; and as members of minority groups, Blacks or people of Hispanic origin. The Harvard economist Robert Reich sees a split in US society between an elite twenty per cent and a downwardly mobile, or already marginalised, eighty per cent. He has also spoken of 'the secession of the successful' from those who have failed to make it in the capitalist marketplace. The economist Richard Freeman has recently suggested in the *Harvard Business Review* that the United States may be moving towards an 'apartheid economy' in which 'the rich live aloof in their exclusive suburbs and expensive apartments with little connection to the working poor in their slums'. Another US analyst, Charles A. Murrey, Bradley Fellow at the American Enterprise Institute, who describes himself as a believer in 'classic conservative principles', characterises this phenomenon as 'an American caste system, with the implications of utter social separation', the underclass postulating a separate, parallel state system too. Kevin Phillips, recognised as a conservative *guru*, so to speak, in his *The Politics of Rich and Poor*, has written of a possible political confrontation that pitts the rich against middle to low income Americans. Maybe, the possibility cannot be discounted. But given the overall dominance of manifold capitalist ideology which persuades the underclass into accepting their fate peacefully, if not gladly, what exists at the moment is something different as pointed out by Galbraith. The poor are no longer just social disgrace, as he characterised in his earlier book *The Affluent Society*. Now, inner city and rural backwater inhabitants serve a basic economic function in the US society. They are a semi-permanent 'functional underclass' which, Galbraith says, 'does the dirty work no one else wants to do'. The underclass is now integrally a part of larger economic classes and serves the living standards and the comforts of the more favoured sections of the community. This class is needed so that the more fortunate may be relieved of distasteful, disagreeable and low-paid jobs. The underclass may occasionally protest as they did in the Los Angeles riots some years back. But this does not much disturb the upper class, reassured as they are by the hiring of personal security guards, escape to the safe suburbs, more extensive enforcement of laws of detention against rioters or rebels, armed repression by the police and then, if need be, by the military. Their 'culture of contentment' as it has been called, even 'causes people like (the then Vice-President) Dan Quale to say, as Galbraith has sarcastically pointed out, 'the riots were the fault of the poor'!

Capitalism as a system based on private property and competition-driven money-making in the marketplace, even as it has produced unemployment, inequality and poverty, also brought in all sorts of other maladies in its train which today blot and disfigure the life and culture of the United States. Its inner cities, decaying over a long time are now raging infernos of poverty, crime and drugs, where life in the streets has become a grubby crime-ridden survival of the fittest. The US has the largest prison population anywhere. Two million Americans are behind bars on any given day; obviously the number of persons in jail or prison over the course of a year would be several times larger. Among them the proportion of black Americans is six to seven times as high as whites. According to a recent study 40 per cent of young black men in California are either in prison, on probation or on parole, and two-thirds of the state's black and Latino men between the ages of 18 and 20 had been arrested at least once. The largest free market in the world has not only criminalised vast sections of society but also institutionalised crime along racial or class lines. There is increasing social disorganisation, rising levels of violence, growing culture of gun and drugs and multiplying teenage slaughters. Money-making in the marketplace (or GDP) makes no distinction between benevolent or murderous economic activity – there is highly profitable drug trafficking, flesh trade, exploitation of child labour and business that is organised crime. There is racism and religious bigotry, unbelievable corruption in politics and wasteful and desensitising consumerism. Family structure is in crisis with broken homes where elderly are neglected and children, if they escape suffering from malnutrition or hunger, as in much of the world, are yet tyrannised by child-abuse, the decay of moral values, and the dehumanisation of society around them. There is an all-pervasive alienation in human relationships, a society stricken with loneliness and isolation, massified neurosis and mental illnesses. The situation, if anything, was better a couple of decades back. Even so, we had Irving Kristol, one of America's leading intellectuals with known conservative sympathies complaining, in his own mixed sort of way: 'economic progress has been accompanied by an unforeseen tidal wave of social disintegration and moral disorientation... Whoever expected that the successful creation of a welfare state in an affluent economy would be accompanied by an incredible increase in criminality, so that our streets would be blanketed with fear? A sharp increase in teenage pregnancies? In drug addiction? In the creation of a dependent, self-destruct underclass?... fatal venereal disease called AIDS?... two million abortions a year?...' The complaint is typical in what it saw and what it failed to see. This is how a more to the point recent assessment of the situation has it: 'drastic social polarization and immiseration, the destruction of the middle classes, large-scale structural unemployment without any welfare safety net, one of the highest incarceration rates in the world, devastated cities, disintegrating families – such are the prospects of any society lured towards an absolute free market'.

VII

The failure of capitalism is no less evident in the advanced capitalist countries of Western Europe. Once again, capitalism, driven by an inner compulsion to accumulate has necessarily generated, through the behaviour of the market system itself, unequal distribution of income and wealth which indeed has reached new extremes in these countries in the post-Second World War period – wealth at one end creating and continuously refreshing and replenishing the sources of poverty on the other. Poverty is often considered a blot on national pride, and several of these countries refuse to give poverty figures or discuss the problem, even taking shelter under the plea that poverty is a 'local problem for which local solutions should be found'. Yet public statements of leaders and occasional economic surveys are noticeable for their expression of fear and anxiety over the present situation. And any number of scholars have written about it with equal fear and anxiety. 'For a long time we believed that poverty in Europe was a residual phenomenon which would disappear with development. We were wrong, for new pockets of poverty have appeared even during periods of sustained growth,' says sociologist, Evelyn Sullerot, 'Moreover, the new poor are no longer old people like in the past. Most of them are young, functionally illiterate (unable to read or write despite eight years of compulsory schooling), unemployed and often single parents. They constitute 15 per cent of the EC population, they can no longer be considered a marginal phenomenon.' Economist Francoise Euvard has warned: 'Unless the community takes urgent measures to stop the problem dead in its tracks, the situation is going to get worse very quickly... Money is not the only problem. Many of the new poor suffer terribly because they are of no use to society, because society no longer approves of them. There is a new "poverty culture" that is growing in Europe – violence, delinquence, social marginalisation.'

The evidence of failure of capitalism in these countries has indeed been piling up during the last two or three decades. Today, along with poverty and mass unemployment or underemployment, destitution, houselessness, racism and violent crime, and abnormally large number of people in jails, seem to have become permanent fixtures in these world's richest and most developed countries. The situation is getting steadily worse as a result of the continuing crisis in the global capitalist economy and the consequent globalisation-ordained 'restructuring' – jobs and wages, and social security systems conceived in the earlier, easier boom days of the 1950s and 1960s are all being cut down to keep costs low in order to retain the competitive edge in the shrinking European and world markets. According to UNDP Human Development reports poverty has long passed any tolerable level in Western Europe. Figures for the early 1990s show Ireland, Spain, the Netherlands, the UK, France, Belgium and Germany, all having over 12 per cent of the population below the poverty line, defined as an income per person of below $14.40 a day. New poor are being added to the old ones and the number of poor in West European countries has grown from 38.5 million in 1975 to over 50 million during the next two decades. According to European Commission, 57 million people, roughly one out of six Europeans is now poor, including 13 million children who live below the poverty line. Child poverty in Britain trebled in the two decades after 1975 and according to 1997 UNDP report 'one in six children in the UK is income poor'. According to another report more than 100 million people in OECD countries live below the national poverty lines. About 36 million are unemployed and more than five million are homeless. In the European Union structural unemployment rate runs around 12 per cent. There is no commitment any longer, even on the part of social democratic parties, to a policy of full employment. A permanent 'industrial reserve army' has come to exist, the huge numbers of unemployed workers condemned to rot, under techno-bureaucratic supervision, on the dole queues of Europe's advanced capitalism. As in the US, those with jobs are having to work harder and more hours and what have come to be called 'bad jobs' – low-wage, low-status, part-time jobs that are insecure and offer few benefits – are proliferating. One conservative estimate predicts that 80 per cent of new jobs in the so-called post-industrial society of the future will be bad jobs.

Again, while the rich have grown richer within these countries, at the other end thousands more have been pushed into the ranks of the poor, and the gap between the bottom third of the population and the top ten or twenty per cent has been widening. In Britain, for example, the richest 20 per cent earn 10 times more than the poorest 20 per cent. While the richest 1 per cent of the population owns 18 per cent of the nation's wealth, half of the population lives in households that receive means-tested benefits. Basing himself on the data from Government's Family Expenditure Survey, Istvan Meszaros has pointed out: 'The gap between rich and poor has widened (in Britain) under Conservative rule with a record one in three living in what Brussels defines as poverty, according to new government figures. The income of the poorest 10 per cent of the population dropped 17 per cent between 1979 and 1991, while the income of the wealthiest 10 per cent rose 62 per cent... The figures, in the latest *Households Below Average Income* report, show that the number of the people living below the European poverty line, that is with an income less than half of the average, rose from 5 million in 1979 to 13.9 million in 1991-92. Another 400,000 people had gone below the poverty line since the last report, 200,000 of them children. In 1979, 1.4 million children lived below the poverty line, rising to 3.9 million in 1990-91 and 4.1 million a year later... In cash terms, the average income of the poorest 10 per cent of the population was down from 74 pounds to 61 pounds (i.e. 91 dollars) a week...' The situation has continued to be aggravated under the 'New Labour' government.

Already, by the 1980s, Western Europe had come to be described as 'one third-two third' society where a third of the population prospered, another third gained little and the rest, comprising the remaining one-third of the population, was progressively excluded from the benefits of material progress, doomed to become an underclass or a decaying segment of modern society, unable to be 'reconverted' or reinstated in the formal labour markets of advanced capitalism, though still useful to its prosperous classes at the top for doing the necessary 'dirty work no one else wants to do'. It has since moved to become an 'iceberg society', as it has been called, where an eighth does well and the rest face an uncertain future or simply go under. This mass deprivation of people is now hideously visible everywhere in Western Europe. In London and Paris, as in New York, there are people living on the pavements and feeding from soup kitchens, when not scrounging from the dustbins. The beggars, as in New York City, are omnipresent and the marginalised are to be found in all the major and minor cities of Europe. As the social welfare regime built up in the post-Second World War era is being gradually but steadily dismantled in Western Europe, instead of the promised or hoped for 'capitalism with a human face', we are witnessing the journey back to capitalism with a Dickensian face.

Scholars have written of 'Americanisation of Europe'. This is not merely Europe's return to American-style 'normal' capitalism with massive inequalities in the distribution of wealth and 'the welfare state' reduced to a rudimentary safety net, the prevalence of market-oriented instruments for the distribution of all resources – including health and education. It is also Europe experiencing a 'peripherialisation of the centre' akin to the United States, latter's 'Latin-Americanisation' as the scholars have called it. The cliché about 'east is east and west is west and never the twain shall meet' notwithstanding, the twain are already meeting on the territory of the wealthiest capitalist societies. The massive and persistent poverty, mass unemployment, underemployment and lumpen-classes, the homelessness and squalid slums, illiteracy and lack of basic health care, destitutes floating around in the streets, sleeping on the pavements or scrounging around for a meal, the ultimate humiliation and degradation of human beings, which were once considered the exclusive blight of poor 'third world' countries have all made their appearance in the rich societies of the first world, on the streets and slums of New York, Paris or London.

VIII

Indicative of capitalism's failure is the material, moral and cultural damage it inflicts on human beings (to say nothing of its destruction of natural environment that we shall later touch upon). Much of this damage of capitalism is direct, obviously visible. But far more damaging is the essential inhumanity of the extraordinary invisible power that market in advanced capitalist societies (and not in these alone) has come to exercise over men and women, both rich and poor, in these societies. We have earlier noticed Marx's critique of capitalism on ethical or aesthetic moral grounds. Everything he said about consumerism and the damage that capitalism as a market-governed system does to the essential humanity of man has come to pass with a vengeance in the countries of advanced capitalism, making his *Economic and Philosophic Manuscripts of 1844* one of the most discussed books of recent times. In its consumerist thrust, duly backed by a reinvented, extraordinarily powerful advertisement industry, market has today tightened its grip over men and women of capitalist societies as never before. It has penetrated their heart, the spirit and the imagination in the supreme interest of selling them something more so that more profits can be made. 'Create More Desire', as an advertisement in the *New York Times* had it, is its motivating principle. In its endless pursuit of profit it goes on to invent ever new wants and desires, and therefore new commodities, services and products to satisfy them, to sell and make profit. In the process it has not only laid waste the environment but also made the men and women of advanced capitalist societies ever more dependent on itself, indeed captives of the market and therefore powerless to shape either their own lives or the society around them. This moral impotence is just part of the hidden cost, the unseen price they have to pay for the deep penetration of their lives by market values which supplant human values. The market has simply alienated these men and women from themselves, their essential species being, the potentiality for free and conscious, creative activity.

For capital, nothing is sacred, not even the bones of the saints, Marx had said. Here everything is reduced to mere cash nexus. 'The *divine* power of money', he had written, overturns and confounds 'all human and natural qualities' in the marketplace, and the very things which were once 'communicated, but never exchanged; given, but never sold; acquired, but never bought – virtue, love, conviction, knowledge, conscience etc.' become marketable and pass 'into commerce'. Marx's prognosis has come literally true in societies of advanced capitalism. As it has grown and expanded, market has invaded all areas of human activity. It has commodified every human value and set a price on it. Commodity relations have penetrated everywhere, turning all aspects of existence, every other thing into a matter of investment for profit in the marketplace. Kidneys are for sale and wombs are for rent. Pollution rights can be leased and living things patented. Everything, including education and health, is subject to cost–benefit analysis. Even the most personal is a dependency of the market. Today in advanced capitalist societies, millions of desperate, lonely and lost, alienated and other directed individuals seek to buy in friendship, care, tenderness, consideration or consolation, all the precious free gifts of humanity, in the marketplace, paying large sums of money to experts, to counsellors, therapists and advisors of all sorts, even newspaper columnists and radio and TV chat shows anchorpersons to learn how to make themselves more desirable, more successful, to find out what has gone wrong with their relationships, their marriages, why they have been abandoned or deserted, neglected or abused, in short, to be told how to lead their own lives! To those in need of it, 'spirituality', 'Supreme Bliss' itself is sold, by all sorts of more or less sophisticated charlatans, as yet another commodity.

The situation is made worse by competitive or 'possessive' individualism, the central motivating principle of the capitalist market society, so that the wants of men in societies of advanced capitalism, determined by aggressively individualist and competitive drives, are directed towards the attainment of private privileges, and the exploitation of others, who are primarily seen as actual or potential rivals or objects of exploitation in the market. This competition makes any kind of genuinely cooperative living, which a good society must be, impossible. It has only enhanced the high degree of stress and insecurity, a widespread exhaustion and a scarcely hidden clinical depression that making a living in capitalist society ordinarily involves – even for better placed workers and professionals with a job in hand, what with the furious acceleration in the need of skills, the lengthening of the workday through extended commuting and two-income families, the growing fears about career choices and financial security, and the increasing remoteness of any life outside the cities or the suburbs, etc. If Marx had written of 'greed and the war between the greedy – competition', Keynes had counted competition among 'the pseudo-moral principles which have hag-ridden us for 200 years (and) by which we have exalted some of the most distasteful of human qualities into the position of the highest virtues'. Competitive individualism has only accentuated the alienation born of the corrupting and destructive logic of pervasive commercialisation and passive consumerism in the western capitalist societies. In fact, beyond unemployment, inequality and poverty engendered by it, the damaging outcome of capitalism, indeed the deep moral and cultural crisis of contemporary capitalist civilisation, is nowhere more manifest than in the emergence of 'alienation' as a major and ever-worsening social phenomenon in the societies of modern capitalism. This phenomenon finds expression in man's growing sense of anomie and estrangement, of isolation, loneliness and homelessness, of hostility and frustration; it has resulted in a society really sick with these and a hundred other social and psychic ailments born of the essential irrationality of capitalism, sick with apathy and boredom, with 'other directedness', conformism and self-abasement, with insanity and crime and widespread dehumanisation. Alienation under capitalism as a system of private property, competition and exploitation is today far more pronounced, far more inclusive and monstrous, than when Marx first wrote about it more than a hundred and fifty years ago. The evidence is written large in the sociological and socio-psychological literature of contemporary capitalist societies in the West.

I may digress a little here to point out that the all-pervasive alienation in society is an important reason for the present and continued popular acquiescence in and acceptance of capitalism, despite all its injustices and cruelties, its crises, mass unemployment and widespread poverty, its homelessness, drug-addictions and crime, its starved public or social services, and the basic inhumanity which goes with it as a society whose social relations are dominated by the market. Among other things, it has helped prevent people from relating their personal situation to the systemic nature of the society in which they are living, something even otherwise difficult for those engaged in the all too often harassing daily business of life in a capitalist society. Of course, there are other more or less important reasons too, including the extraordinary resilience and innovative power which capitalism has continued to display and the fact of the welfare state which, its inadequacies notwithstanding, has certainly served to prevent any great demand for radical change.

The standard bourgeois state too has been and is always there to protect and support capitalism. If need be, since pure capitalism is always desperately vulnerable, there can also be and often is the added appeal of imperialism, or fascism, or racism, or religion or nationalism, of social demagogy of some sort or the other. This issue however is not my concern at the moment. Immediately I only want to underline the alienation-related reason for people's acquiescence in or acceptance of capitalism: the alienated and isolated individual of capitalist society is today exceptionally vulnerable to the hegemonic control of the ruling classes.

This vulnerability to ruling class hegemonic control draws our attention to yet another ugly feature of the situation in advanced capitalist societies – for that matter in all capitalist societies that those at the top of these societies, who have economic power, also come to acquire extraordinary ideological power over society through their control or domination of the diverse means and channels of communication that help make, really manufacture 'public opinion', and through (or against) which dissent, to the extent that it exists, must struggle and struggle really hard, for expression. The scientific and technological revolution of our times has increased this power hundredfold. Of course it has made for a degree of higher productivity and therefore more profits, as also for better policing of the workplace to extract more surplus from the working classes. As Gary Marx has informed us: 'Surveillance of workers on assembly lines, in offices, and in stores, has expanded with computerised electronic devices. Factory outputs and mistakes can be more easily counted, and work-pace controlled.... In some offices, workers must inform the computer when they are going to the bathroom and when they return... The CIA has reportedly used microwave lie detectors that measure stomach flutters from half a mile away.... the new surveillance technologies are an important factor in decreasing the power of the individual relative to large organisations and government'. But the new information and communication technologies have also added immensely to the power of those in command of mass media, advertisement and entertainment, the power to control popular consciousness, to turn whole people, like individuals glued to their TV sets, into what the German poet Hans Magnus Enzensberger has called 'secondary illiterates', those who need neither memory nor any thinking or learning to sustain themselves. These are of little worth to them, the passive subjects in a world where the reigning ideology is consumerism, with its exclusive concern for 'instant gratification' and 'contentment'. A market-driven 'mass culture' has come up which on the one hand aims at developing consumer instincts in the people to the utmost and thereby expanding markets for the greater glory of late-capitalist profit-making and, on the other hand, at ideological brainwashing of the people, diverting them from any advanced social ideals and implanting in their minds bland, illusory and often downright false and reactionary views of social and political realities.

A 'true idiot culture' Carl Bernstein has called it where for the 'first time in history the weird and the stupid and the vulgar are becoming our cultural norm, even our cultural ideal'. Even as a 'stupid and vulgar' culture is mass purveyed via television screens, tabloid newspapers, glossy magazines and similar other means, the tendency is to pitch all messages to the lowest level of mental capacity. Knowledge is reduced to slick, pre-digested, easy to understand capsules, inducing people to want simple answers to difficult problems. People's consciousness is transferred on to philistine, narrow-minded lines, and interest in truth which demands hard, complex and subtle exercise of mind, simply recedes into the background. The overall consequence is a dilution and dispersal of people's questioning spirit, their angry or combustible sentiments, an emasculation of their critical consciousness. There is general enervation of civil society, its members rendered incapable of 'Answering back' as C. Wright Mills once phrased it. According to Jean Baudrillard, the very possibilities of critical examination and reflection are destroyed. In other words, the inundations of consumerism and 'mass culture' leave the alienated individuals of contemporary late-capitalist society eminently vulnerable to capitalism's hegemonic control. Though oppressed and exploited, they are now more open to 'colonisation of the mind' – victims' internalisation of the cliché 'there is no alternative', their willing suspension of ideals and acceptance of a sub-autonomous existence in the interest of maintaining a secondary or even a tertiary position in the obtaining 'reality' – be it the capitalist society or for that matter the global capitalist system. For that is also what the 'third world mentality' is all about.

IX

A failure in the advanced capitalist countries, capitalism is even more a failure on the global scale, where capitalism's 'ugliness', its ravages or costs – natural, social and human – are nakedly visible in the vast areas of Latin America, Africa and Asia, in the stinking slums, shanty towns and barrios of the third world where hunger reigns. This is where the heedless logic of capitalism, its processes of capital accumulation, have exacted their heaviest price and where, therefore, its real and worst, as well as perennial victims are to be found (To these we can now add the newly arrived victims of Russia where return to the capitalist fold has meant a 'third worldisation' which has typically benefitted a tiny, and as a rule the most ruthless and corrupt section of the population, while callously exposing the overwhelming majority to hardship and sufferings of the worst kind).

The inhuman and marginalised existence of the overwhelming majority of the peoples of the third world, the conditions of poverty and destitution, mass hunger and starvation, of economic bondage and material degradation in which common humanity of countries of Asia, Africa and Latin America lives is well known and documented. We have touched upon the subject earlier (in the previous volume). Here I will only make a quick supplementing reference to the facts reported during the last decade – the decade of 'triumph of capitalism' – mostly by the United Nations, its allied agencies or programmes like the ILO or FAO and UNDP and international institution like the World Bank. Give or take a few percentages or odd millions here and there in the estimates, more than half of humanity today lives in poverty on less than 3 dollars a day, 45 per cent of whom, two and a half billion in the third world, live on less than 2 dollars a day, more than 1.3 billion – and their number is growing – live in absolute poverty, surviving on less than 1 dollar per day. Eight hundred and sixty million people go to bed hungry and 25,000 die every day due to hunger and poverty. Three-fifths of the 4.4 billion people in the so-called 'developing' countries are living in communities without basic sanitation, housing, health care or education – 'almost one-third are without safe drinking water, one-quarter lack adequate housing, one-fifth live beyond reach of modern health services, one-fifth of the children do not get as far as grade five in school'. We have a Fidel Castro asking 'a gathering of world health leaders to explain how, if the world economy has grown six times and the production of goods and services had climbed from less than $5 trillion to $29 trillion between 1950 and 1997, why do 12 million children under five die every year, why are 1.3 billion human beings living in abject poverty and why 800 million people have no basic health services'.

If over 100 million children of primary school age are not in school, about one billion adults cannot read or write. More than 100 million are homeless. Nearly one billion people around the world, a third or more of the world's labour force are either unemployed or underemployed, including a disproportionate number of women and youth; in advanced capitalist countries, with the highest unemployment levels since the Great Depression, nearly one in four young people are unemployed and elsewhere, in 'developing' countries, between 27 and 73 per cent of the unemployed are under 25 years of age. Tens of millions of workers in Russia are jobless and hundreds of millions in China's emerging capitalism are 'surplus to requirements'.

At the same time, accompanying it all is the gross maldistribution of income and wealth in the capitalist world, where the third world is its overwhelmingly large poor part. 'Between 1960 and 1991 the share of the richest 20% rose from 70% of global income to 85% – while that of the poorest 20% declined from 2.3% to 1.4%', and, 'in 1993, the top one per cent of the world's population received a larger share of the world's income than the bottom 57 per cent; the top five per cent had an income share approaching that of the bottom 85 per cent.' The net worth of the world's 200 richest people rose from 440 billion in 1994 to more than 1 trillion dollars in 1998 and the wealth of its 447 dollar billionaires exceeds the net income of half of the world's population. The top three billionaires in the world have now assets greater than the combined gross national product of all 48 least developed countries and their 600 million people. Today five per cent of the richest people of the world earn 144 times more than the poorest five per cent. The assets of 500 wealthiest people in the world amount to $1.54 trillion, more than the GDP of Africa or the total annual earnings of the poorest half of mankind. The gap in per capita income between countries with the richest fifth of the world's people and those with the poorest fifth increased from 10 to 1 in the first decade of the twentieth century to 30 to 1 in 1960, to 60 to 1 in 1990 and then to 74 to 1 at the end of the century. More than 80 countries in the third world have fallen below what they had as per capita income only a decade ago and the third world as a whole is now burdened with a crippling debt of more than 2.5 trillion dollars, owed to the rich capitalist countries of the world. 'The 20 per cent of the world's people in the highest-income countries account for 86 per cent of total private consumption expenditure – the poorest 20 per cent a minuscule 1.3 per cent'. While more than one billion in the third world countries eke out a miserable, sub-human existence at less than 1 dollar per day, hundreds of millions of dollars are daily spent on ice-creams, pet-foods, perfumes, business entertainment, etc. in the first world. This reality of the capitalist world is well captured by T.F. Homer-Dixon's metaphoric summation of the contemporary global situation: 'Think of a stretch limo in the potholed streets of New York City, where homeless beggars live. Inside the limo are the air-conditioned post-industrial regions of North America, Europe, the emerging Pacific Rim, and a few other isolated places, with their trade summitry and computer information highways. Outside is the rest of mankind, going in a completely different direction.'

It is not that the rich countries of the North are indifferent to the plight of the South. They cannot afford to be: direct economic interests are involved, there is the need for a stable world to better exploit it as also the ideological compulsion to fend off the challenge of socialism. Hence there have been regular declarations of 'war on poverty', especially in the 20th century. But the war has been equally regularly lost – lost above all because of the causal framework, the poverty-producing exploitative structural imperatives of capitalism.

It is interesting to note that, as the richest core countries of the global capitalist system are unable or unwilling to allocate even the miserable 0.7 per cent of GNP to which they had committed themselves in the mid-1990s for the purpose of reducing world poverty, and poverty in the world continues to grow, increasingly it is charity that is taking over and we have the spectacle of exploitation combined with charity beating all records of hypocrisy; as a commentator has put it: 'We impose our terms of trade, squeeze the third world beyond any possibility of repayment, precipitate the horrors of war and then rush to the rescue. And we show it all – obviously not the exploitation, but the starvation, death and the white knight in his tank – in full technicolour to the awed audience watching it throughout the world.'

Be that as it may, the important fact that needs to be recognised here is the causal connection between the structural logic of capitalism and poverty in the third world. This structural logic of capitalism, as Marx had pointed out, necessarily produces wealth and affluence at one end poverty and deprivation at the other pole of a capitalist society. With global capitalism, the major other pole are the colonial and ex-colonial countries of the third world. As its periphery and semi-periphery, these countries have been and remain an integral part of the world capitalist system, to whose present dismal conditions, the advanced centres of global capitalism have always and continuously contributed. Their mass poverty and underdevelopment is structurally related to the affluence and development of the more advanced part of the capitalist world. Apart from the loot and plunder of its original 'primitive accumulation' which involved even the slavery and massacre of indigenous populations, the capitalist system has throughout its history, and in recent years more and more, relied on imperialist exploitation of the resources of underdeveloped or so-called 'developing' countries. This is where metropolitan capital, on the basis of its global ascendancy, has always sought and still finds outlets for displacing its contradictions on to, and spaces for its countless expropriations against nature and human beings. The wealth and prosperity of the 'first world' rests on the poverty and exploitation of the 'third world'. The living standards, including the vulgar and ostentatious opulence of the west's rich, consumerist societies are ultimately paid for by the impoverished peoples of Asia, Africa and Latin America.

Within this global situation, the structural logic of capitalism is equally manifest in the more or less developed peripheral capitalisms that have come up in several post-colonial societies, often as a result or in the guise of 'national development'. They have signally failed to provide any kind of decent living to the common people in terms of their basic needs – food and clean drinking water, clothing and housing, education and elementary health care, etc. A small section at the top has certainly benefited, but the wealth and prosperity of the few in the capitalist third world has been quite compatible with the massive impoverishment, untold misery and suffering of the common people. Hundreds of millions of them continue to live in conditions of appalling deprivation, of hunger, ill-health, homelessness and illiteracy, and subject to different forms of class, race or caste and gender oppressions. In Latin America somewhere between two-fifths and three-quarters of the population live in poverty – and between a third and a half of them in extreme poverty. It is no better in most of Asia and much worse in Africa.

These capitalisms have, of course, their distinct country and history-specific features. But, subject to capitalism's logic of unequal and uneven development, they have all produced their third world versions of the 'two-third' societies of the capitalist West, where the 'two-third' consist of those living in appalling poverty and condemned to exclusion and marginality, while one-third live in affluence, enjoying the charms of economic well-being and now 'post-modernity'. The perverse logic of capitalism has, as elsewhere, created dual, even 'iceberg', societies, the very rich and the very poor at the two extremes, living socially, culturally, economically and ecologically in two entirely different social universes. Everywhere enclaves of high living and affluence, fully given to western consumerism have come up in settings of abysmal poverty of the masses, the 'first world' enclaves within the 'third world'.

Globalisaton of recent years and the 'structural adjustment programmes' imposed by the IMF and World Bank have only worsened the situation. They have put the third world all the more at the mercy of global capitalism, opening the way for still more ruthless exploitation by western multi-national corporations in association with the local, often comprador exploiting classes. There is mounting unemployment, further accentuation of poverty and widening of inequalities within and between nations. Whatever public education, health care or other social services existed in the third world have been undermined, adding to the penury and plight of the common people. In addition the third world countries are becoming the sites for polluting industries, 'dumping grounds' for nuclear and other wastes and, as friendly critics have pointed out, 'new deserts for the new poor' of the age of 'globalisation'. It may be added that when the movements based among the poor seek to challenge this state of affairs they are met, with the involvement or patronage of powers dominant in global capitalism, by merciless repression, death squads and fake encounters, and all kinds of military coups, bringing additional loss of life and still more suffering to the common people.

The third world today is a monument to the failure of capitalism in our times.

X

Capitalism has failed both at its centre, in the advanced capitalist countries, and at its margins, in the countries of the third world. For evidence we don't need to look backwards to the plunder and devastations of its original 'primitive accumulation' and early industrialism or more recent history of two world wars, world economic crisis of 1929 and recurring recessions, fascism and Hiroshima, innumerable colonial wars and the ruthless exploitation of the third world. Or appeal to the scholarly assessment of Immanuel Wallerstein: 'Perhaps as much as 85 percent of the people who live within the structures of the capitalist world-economy are clearly not living at standards higher than the world's population of 500–1,000 years ago. Indeed, it could be argued that many, even most of them are materially worse off.' The evidence is starkly visible in every part and aspect of contemporary capitalist world. It is visible in the impoverishment and immiseration on the rise just about everywhere in the world; in statistics on rates of unemployment, poverty, homelessness, and hunger; in the sullen slums of major cities of Western bourgeois democracies, proliferating urban ghettos of the gritty capitals of former Soviet bloc countries and the warrens of teeming tumble-down shanties of the peripheral South; in the gross inequalities of the world, the wretchedness of the impoverished and excluded within the rich Western societies and the huge mass of misery in the poorer countries; in the morally intolerable and socially unnecessary suffering – what Bourdieu has called *la misere du monde* – produced by capitalism everywhere.

Passing from one technological revolution to another, capitalism has certainly added to economic well-being and a pleasanter life of a few millions of the world's population. But billions of people on this planet are condemned to live in misery, hunger, untreated diseases and avoidable early death, crushed by unbearable and apparently unchangeable, dehumanising poverty. Self-complacent people like John Major may say 'socialism is dead, capitalism works'. But the question is: capitalism works for whom? Capitalism works very well indeed for people like him, for the privileged few of the capitalist society, but how does it work for the common people in Africa, in Latin America, or in India, Pakistan or Bangladesh? Or, for that matter, for the poor and the unemployed workers on the dole in the west? What of thousands of millions people all over the capitalist world who, subject to 'genocide through poverty', are finding it difficult to survive? Capitalism has not worked but failed miserably so far as overwhelming majority of humankind is concerned. And today, not to be dissociated from this failure is the fact of continued capitalist destruction of environment, the threat of a global ecological catastrophe that capitalism's accumulative logic now portends.

Socialism as they built it in the Soviet Union has failed. Elsewhere, capitalism too has been a failure. That both socialism as we have known it and capitalism as it has existed have failed in our times has, as suggested earlier, important implications for the present and future of humankind. Before we discuss these implications, it is necessary to look a little more closely at the *problematique* of capitalism today. However there is a most significant aspect to the double failure mentioned above which can and needs to be immediately stated. I would like to point out that while the failure of socialism was essentially the outcome of contingent human and historical factors, the failure of capitalism, far from being anything contingent, is the inevitable consequence of the basic law of motion, the structural logic of capitalism, its inner accumulative drive and contradictions which, even as they are essential to its enormously powerful and creative dynamic of growth, are also the cause of its destructive outcome in the world as a whole – a remarkable vindication of Karl Marx's analysis, even though he may have underestimated the developmental potential of capitalism as a global system or overestimated the revolutionary potential of its first victims, the European working class.

XI

The Soviet collapse and its immediate aftermath witnessed a great deal of talk about 'welfare capitalism' or 'capitalism with a human face', which most people saw embodied in the 'welfare state' of western Europe. Euphoria over 'triumph of capitalism' obscuring the fact that this 'welfare state' was at that time actually being dismantled in the west, 'welfare capitalism' or 'capitalism with a human face' was being touted as the alternative to the failed and discredited socialism. In deserting socialism, or what they believed was socialism, this is what

Gorbachev and his envious Soviet intelligentsia hoped for in the 'common European home'. This is also where not only the social democrats, but socialists in retreat all over the place, sought refuge in increasingly large numbers.

Since then the europhia has greatly subsided. Western capitalists have been loath to be accommodative towards the poor cousins in Russia – refused entry into the 'common home', they are savouring the long-forbidden pleasures of capitalism in their own native places. With the deepening crisis of capitalism and the continuing assault on the 'welfare state', the real, ugly, face of capitalism is visible as it has not been for a long time. Therefore not only has the original talk receded into the background, criticism of capitalism and talk of a humane society beyond capitalism have returned. But giving in to the barrage of bourgeois ideological propaganda, its endless rhetoric of TINA – 'there is no alternative' – many, even on the left, remain unable to think beyond capitalism. Even when critical of capitalism, they continue to believe that capitalism can deliver 'welfare' to the people. They continue to hope for 'capitalism with a human face'.

That transitory and severely limited possibilities apart, this belief or hope is unfounded should be abundantly clear from our argument and evidence so far. We have already, in more than one context, pointed out the failure of 'welfare capitalism', or the 'welfare state', in the advanced capitalist countries. This failure has been part of the general failure of capitalism worldwide. Much is made by apologists of capitalism that, deplorable as poverty still is in wealthy countries, thanks to the 'welfare state', the poor have been able to live better than their *immediate* forbears used to and their counterparts in less developed countries still do. This is not to be denied. The 'welfare state' has certainly been very much more than the proverbial 'trickle down' of capitalism, well described as feeding horses with oats so that some will pass through to the road for the sparrows. But, even at its best, 'welfare capitalism' has never ensured a socially beneficial utilisation of the immense resources which capitalism itself has brought into being. Even when all the necessary resources have been available, the 'welfare state' has nowhere been able to provide its citizens what could be regarded as a decent, humane existence, a life worthy of human beings, where there is freedom from exploitation and oppression, universal access to meaningful work, basic education, health care and non-polluted environment, leisure and opportunity to share in the rich cultural heritage of mankind, active participation of people in community and public life and, above all, where men and women live with a sense of empowerment and purpose. The productive capacity under capitalism has been and remains truly prodigious; and this provides the *basis* for humane societies. But having created that basis, capitalism itself has been, because of its structural logic, the greatest obstacle to the realisation of such societies.

Despite all evidence to the contrary, faith in 'welfare capitalism' persists, and in the debate over the crisis of socialism, 'the welfare state' continues to be flaunted as an example of the *success* of capitalism in the west. What is more, 'capitalism with a human face' is being hawked around as the salvation itself by the globalisation and market-infatuated elites in the third world; though there is a significant shyness about use of the word, 'capitalism' – 'liberalisation' or 'globalisation', 'structural adjustment' or 'market economy', 'economic reforms' or 'new economic policies', 'industrialisation' or 'economic development', anything but capitalism is the preferred expression these days. Another quick look at the 'welfare state', therefore, will not be out of place.

The 'welfare state' in the advanced capitalist countries of the west came into existence over the last hundred years as the practical consummation of the development, however slow, tortuous or belated, of 'social services', 'social welfare measures', or 'social policy programmes' of all sorts, to help the more unfortunate victims of the irrationality and exploitation of capitalism, and to provide, however inadequately, for some at least of the needs, private and public, created by unplanned industrialism and economic change, needs which the profit oriented economy of these capitalist countries has been, on its own, unable or unwilling to provide for. The forces behind this process of historical development of the 'welfare state' have been varied and complex. As Richard Titmuss has put them: 'Fear of social revolution, the need for a law-abiding labour force, the struggle for power between political parties and pressure groups, a demand to remove some of the social costs of change – for example, industrial accidents – from the backs of the workers and the social conscience of the rich all played a part.'

Of decisive political significance in this process were the continuous and often very bitter struggles waged by an increasingly organised and enfranchised working class through its political parties and trade unions, not only on its own behalf but also on behalf of other underprivileged sections of capitalist society. Of decisive economic significance in this process was the unprecedented expansion of material production in the west on a continuing capitalist or capitalist-cum-imperialist basis, especially in the post-Second World War period. The development of democratic rights and institutions – which again had to be fought for and won by the working masses – and of Keynesian theory and techniques also played a notable part in the historical evolution of 'the welfare state'. A contributory factor that needs to be specifically mentioned was, in Carlos Fuentes' words, 'a capitalism exposed to the critique of socialism and learning from it'. The fear of an alternative to capitalism that socialism, even as 'actually existing socialism' of Soviet Union, represented, the fear that it could spread, was an important civilising influence on capitalism. Without this 'danger', as it were, Western social democracy would never have been able to win or impose the 'welfare state'. The threat of socialism, enhanced by the economic and military accomplishments of the Soviet Union concentrated the minds of Western governments wonderfully on the importance of giving economic concessions to buy working class loyalty to the system, without in any way endangering it, that is, without the powerful and the privileged losing anything that was of fundamental importance to them.

As *Communist Manifesto* put it: 'A part of the bourgeoisie is desirous of redressing social grievances in order to secure the continued existence of capitalist society'. Securing 'the continued existence of capitalist society' is precisely the role played by the 'welfare state'. By altering some of its forms, by mitigating some of its worst manifestations through a patchwork of welfare measures, 'the welfare state' has smoothed over the class antagonisms, prevented the class-struggle from assuming sharper revolutionary forms and thus ensured a better functioning of the existing economic and social order, a strengthening of the basic institutions of capitalism. It has acted, in John Saville's words, as a 'shock absorber', and thereby contributed not to any transformation but only to the continued survival of the capitalist system. The system remains the essentially irrational and inhuman capitalist system it has always been.

The fact of 'welfare state', and its role in underpinning the capitalist system, does not, however, represent any success or triumph of capitalism, the way it is presented by the apologists of capitalism. On the contrary, the growing need of social welfare in capitalist society, in order to check the anti-social consequences of its market economy or secure some protection against the more obvious depredations of capitalism, demonstrates the failure of capitalist system. The gains of the welfare state rather represent the *limited* successes or triumphs of people *against* capitalism, forcing it to adopt 'socialist type measures', to 'work well enough', if it would survive as a capitalist system. The 'human face' acquired by capitalism has been forced on it by the sacrifices of countless working men and women who, as its victims, rejected its 'free-market theology'.

Success not *of* capitalism but *against* capitalism – such being the essential meaning of the 'welfare state', it is not surprising that capitalists have almost invariably opposed it as inimical to their immediate class interests. The more far-sighted leaders of the capitalist state, whose function it is to protect and promote the long term interests of the bourgeoisie as a whole, have, no doubt always recognised the value of the welfare state, its concessions or welfare measures, in sustaining the capitalist system and lending much needed legitimacy to the otherwise exploitative rule of the capitalist class. But, given their characteristic myopia where profits are involved, the capitalist classes themselves have generally opposed these concessions or welfare measures. In a reference to Roosevelt's welfare-statist New Deal programme in the US following the Great Depression, and capitalist opposition to it, Galbraith has pointed out: 'in our history, those favoured by power and position have frequently opposed the steps by which they and the system might be saved. Those of us, a diminishing band, whose memory goes back to the New Deal, remember the ferocity with which the mellowing reforms of that time were resisted. These reforms, we now agree – social security, farm price supports, public works employment, financial legislation, support to unions – mitigated the cruelties of capitalism and did much to save the system.'

Capitalist opposition also explains why reforms and welfare measures of the 'welfare state' have always lacked permanence. The capitalist classes always seek to reverse them whenever it becomes necessary or possible for them to do so. And history, as for example the history of the last two decades, teaches us, they are most of the time successful in doing so. This of course does not mean renouncing the struggle for reforms or social welfare within capitalism. Radicals or revolutionaries, Marx and Engels being among the most insistent of them, have always demanded from a reluctant and resistant capitalist power structure reforms beneficial to working people and other disadvantaged groups – reforms like a shorter working day, the banning of child labour, safety regulations, better education and better health care, unemployment insurance, etc. Precious gains have been won through such struggles. The point is that these gains are never secure within a capitalist system, as long as power remains with the capitalist classes. Their retention or enhancement has always been a matter of sustained struggle *against* capitalism.

Those who attribute some sort of inherent permanence to such welfare measures, are basically guilty of ascribing a crisis-free character to the capitalist system, which is simply false. Capitalism has been throughout its history a crisis-ridden system. And in a crisis, as their profits are squeezed, the capitalists resent the cost of the social welfare measures and press for their cutting down by the state. This is precisely what has been happening in the West in recent years with the return of a crisis in capitalism which has revived memories of the good old-fashioned slump of the 1930s. The 1980s onwards, initially well-exemplified by the Reagan and Thatcher regimes, the welfare state and its protections have been under assault in one country after another. There has been, as J.K. Galbraith has put it, a 'breaking of the social contract' which held that 'while some might be richer or some poorer, all citizens could expect both protection and a chance in the social system'. Instead there is 'the new ideological commitment' (with its damaging social effect) that seeks to eliminate or keep below obvious or urgent need 'the public support for voiceless poor of the great cities, for low-cost housing, for educational expenditure, for much-needed maintenance of roads, bridges, and other infrastructure (as regrettably it is called) for environmental protection and control', and so on. Under pressure of growing systemic difficulties – the need to cut costs and make the labour market more 'flexible' in order to stay competitive in the global markets – everywhere in the advanced capitalist societies the social welfare systems are being undermined by the capitalists, all the more boldly because of the new correlation of forces following the collapse of the Soviet Union and the retreat of socialism; they are, so to speak, now free from fear of any 'barbarians at the gates'. 'Globalisation' has meant a return to 'normal' capitalism, to raw and ruthless exploitation of 'carpet-baggers' vintage. There is an escalating crisis of social welfare, plunging living standards, a return to poverty wage and mass unemployment. The evidence is accumulating to prove that the post-Second World War prosperity that underlay the modern welfare state was no more than a blip in a general decline in living standards since the advent of capitalism. As the welfare state is being dismantled, there is mass unemployment, growing inequalities and, once again, poverty amid plenty as never before since the Great Depression. The working classes in the West will have to relearn their lessons in militant class struggles if they want to safeguard at least a part of the existing welfare measures. It is possible that in doing so they may well rediscover the need for socialism.

The argument for 'the welfare state', however, persists, and in the advanced capitalist countries one of its most consistent exponent and supporter has been G.K. Galbraith, who has been pressing for larger public support for social welfare in the US for more than three decades. The argument persists because the situation most desperately continues to demand it. Thus, in the United States today, the signs of a growing societal crisis can be recognised everywhere. Across the country, roads and railroads, bridges and urban transport, hospitals and schools and other essential services are, at times even dangerously, deteriorating. Education is in a mess, college graduates seem ill-prepared for work, high school students virtually illiterate. Major urban areas have been gripped by a cycle of poverty, drug-abuse and violence. Writes Galbraith: 'Our poor in the US have remained poor, and the number so classified has substantially increased, as has more markedly, the share of income going to the very rich. The condition of life in the centres of our large cities is – the word is carefully chosen – appalling. Housing is bad and getting worse. Many of our citizens are without even the barest element of shelter, their income at near starvation levels. Schools are also bad, and young and old sustained often by crimes, contrive a temporary escape from despair with drugs...' He adds: 'The English... are inured to suffering. It is accepted with comparative calm. In the US the urban underclass, now casually so designated, could be less patient. An explosion may be waiting to happen. And, in any case, it is a disgrace, which, when the history for the decade is written may well obtrude on the free enterprise ideology...'

Galbraith regrets the 'new ideological commitment' of the rich and powerful in American society; as in the past they could now too oppose 'the action so obviously needed to limit the worry and suffering from the current economic distress'. Given the urgency of the needs of infrastructural repair and social welfare, according to him, 'the only way to break the depressive equilibrium that does not depend on theoretical formulation is to move strongly on these needs'. Galbraith pleads for 'a larger, more effective, more compassionate role for the state', for 'a caring state' to ensure an 'escape from misery' for the poor and underprivileged of the capitalist society. Exactly as he did 30 odd years ago in his *The Affluent Society*, and has done throughout, Galbraith urges the state to perform better, to take the necessary remedial steps. But then adds rather pathetically: 'I urge these several steps with no great hope that they will be taken'! Concluding his recent (1992) plea in this regard, Galbraith writes: 'In the past, writers, on taking pen, have assumed that from the power of their talented prose must proceed the remedial action. No one would be more delighted than I were there similar hope from the present offering. Alas, however, there is not.'

Capitalism today simply disallows such hope. It is no longer a question of the utter inadequacy, in terms of needs and possibilities, of social welfare under capitalism, or its being always under threat of reversal by the capitalist class. It is that this 'welfare', indeed what was once thought of as the 'great transformation' – the mixed economy, Keynesianism, the welfare state, and above all the ideal of 'capitalism with a human face' – was a conjunctural anomaly for capitalism, an economic system quintessentially governed by an altogether unforgiving exploitative logic. The conjuncture having passed, the anomaly is fast disappearing to give way to capitalism as it normally functions as an exploitative system. The crisis of capitalist welfarism is so deep as to allow no room for any kind of welfarist politics, including the welfarist politics of Europe's now desperate-to-survive social democracy. Its much touted 'third way' is turning out to be 'a wishful fantasy', in practice a better than conservative defence of the established, but increasingly untenable, capitalist social order. In England, for example, the 'third way' of 'New Labour' has meant practice of even more severe anti-labour politics, imposition of policies which even Thatcherite conservative governments did not dare to introduce, cutting down of the welfare state to include even the precarious livelihood of the handicapped. Such is the reality of 'actually existing capitalism' today that it is rapidly eliminating all possibilities of a 'middle way' between capitalism and socialism.

Globalisation, let me repeat, is no 'great rupture' in the history of capitalism as the neo-liberal rhetoric has it; it is a return to capitalism at its most basic. What is more, as Ellen Meiksins Wood has written, 'the contradictions of capitalism are manifesting themselves in new and aggravated ways precisely because the old ways of pulling out of crisis are, as Marx said they would be, less and less available, in other words, precisely *because* capitalism is so universal.' The implications for the welfare state are obvious. If reliable and stable ways of humanising capitalism were never there, they are even less available today, which puts a question mark over even the old-style social-democratic 'humanising' of capitalism. For a humane social existence, socialism alone is the real alternative now – socialism as conceived by Marx which, as against the pitiful measures of the welfare state, allows for the fullest possible use of human and material resources for social well-being, for the maximum possible emancipation and self-realisation of the maximum number of human beings.

XII

The welfare state represents success such as it is, not of capitalism, but of struggle against capitalism. In its existence and possibilities, it is a response to capitalism's failure to deliver. This failure, the immediate subject of our discussion, is better understood if we take a look at the essential nature of capitalism, at the past and present of modern capitalism at the centre (now with the US at the top of the capitalist heap), and at the unprecedented crisis that has overtaken capitalism even as it has regained global dominance in the world. This will also light up the situation today in which humankind has to make its choices for the future.

About capitalism a couple of simplistic and erroneous notions need to be immediately rejected. There is a commonsense view of capitalism in which it really has no beginning. Capitalism's origins are traced back to the most primitive acts of exchange, in any form of trade or market activity; or it is seen as an almost natural process of technological development that has characterised human progress from the earliest times. Capitalism, so to speak, is taken for granted, either as the outcome of some perennial tendencies in human nature, or of natural laws when and where they are given a chance. Laws of capitalist economy are treated as if they are universal laws of human behaviour or production activity. Capitalism is virtually conceptualised out of existence. It is simply the natural state of material existence for humankind. Such views have the effect of denying or disguising the specificity of capitalism as an economic system. What gets lost in such views is the fact that capitalism, along with the capitalist market is a specific social form, the product of a dramatic rupture in historical development.

Again, it is necessary to be clear about capitalism in relation to the concept of 'development'. Capitalism is not a 'system of development' that might be opposed, for instance, to the 'socialist doctrine'. The concept of development is by nature ideological, suggestive of something desirable, for example, full employment, equitable distribution of income, rising living standards, etc. Capitalism or its expansion does not imply any result that can be justifiably identified in terms of development. Capitalism's definitive concern is with the production and accumulation of capital, guided by an unending search for profit. 'Accumulate, accumulate! That is Moses and the prophets!' This is how Max described the expansion-oriented and accumulation-driven essential logic or inner determination of capitalism. This logic or determination underlies both the formerly unimaginable dynamism and the most fateful deficiency of capitalism. Even as capitalism achieves miracles of productivity – 'miracles that (heretofore) slumbered in the lap of social labour', according to Marx – polarisation inherent in the dynamics of its capital-accumulation process results in the process getting stuck from time to time in the form of 'economic crises' with devastating economic and political consequences – including wars, big and small – which have been a distinctive feature of the history of our times.

As an economic system, the driving force of capitalism is not any desire to provide humanity with needed goods and services, nor even the desire of capitalists and other affluent citizens to increase their wealth and future incomes. It is the compulsion of capitalists, subject as they are to the laws of competition in the capitalist market, to produce and accumulate capital. This inner compulsion to accumulate capital, however, necessarily generates, through the behaviour of the market system itself, unequal income distribution in society so that if wealth and affluence grow and are increasingly concentrated in relatively fewer hands, there is at the other end growth of mass poverty and deprivation in society. This has important implications for the working of capitalism. For this means that even as capital accumulates and there is a growing productive capacity at one end, there is a progressive limitation of mass purchasing power at the other, so that the imperative to accumulate again and again runs up against a lagging demand for additional real productive capacity. The result is recurring 'economic crises', the crises of over production. 'In these crises', as Marx and Engels put it in the *Communist Manifesto*, 'there breaks out an epidemic that in all earlier epochs would have seemed an absurdity, the epidemic of overproduction.' These crises, 'by their periodic return, put on trial, each time more threateningly, the existence of the entire bourgeois society', and absurdly enough do so 'because there is too much civilization, too much means of subsistence, too much industry, too much commerce...' Marx and Engels had concluded: 'The conditions of bourgeois society are too narrow to comprise the wealth created by them.'

Capitalism, throughout its period of mature existence has betrayed a perpetual tendency to such crises, which periodically even get accentuated into pronounced recessions or depressions. Changes in form or pattern notwithstanding, this has remained a chronic *malaise* of capitalism. (For example, in the roughly two centuries since the US economy began functioning as according to the 'laws and principles of capitalism', recessions or depressions are known to have occurred at least every decade and often more frequently. In the half century since the Second World War there have been no fewer than nine. Another is currently on since 2001).

A historical function of class polarisation within capitalist economies, this recurring tendency towards economic crisis, depression or stagnation points not only to the historical limits of capitalist accumulation but even more to the increasingly irrational form of material production under capitalism from the standpoint of individual and collective needs of the common people. At a more basic level it is an expression of the most fundamental contradiction within the capitalist system – the contradiction between social production and private profit or appropriation.

Initially this contradiction was alleviated by periodic panics and depressions. But soon the ruling classes sought special development factors to support capital accumulation, new markets and new areas in which to invest, for example. An outstanding factor which counteracted depression or stagnation tendencies from the earliest days of capitalism has been the conquest and penetration of non-capitalist territories. In recent years, just as the capitalist state, through its welfare measures, has come in to take care of the consequences of the predatory logic of capitalism in order to save the system (which, incidentally, also help to create or shore up demand in society), it has, especially after the Great Depression of 1929-30, also learnt to intervene in the economy at crucial moments to block this purgative process or prevent it from going out of control, once again, to save the capitalist system from itself. Imperialism, the welfare state, Keynesianism, organised capitalism, state capitalism, transnational capitalism, technocapitalism, the consumer society and so on – all in their own ways have brought succour to capitalism in trouble. But the tendency to depression has always been there, and it still persists. So long as the accumulation process takes place smoothly or with only minimum interruptions, that is, so long as demand holds up, the system works and prospers. But when the accumulation process is seriously hindered or interrupted, that is, demand falters to block profitable investment of capital, the system falls on hard times, even collapses as happened in 1929 and thereafter. The business cycles, with their recurring periods of recession or depression, which have characterised capitalist development since the early 19th century, and which at times have meant long periods of stagnation, are only different forms or expressions of the malfunctioning of the accumulation process of capitalism. And, along with their consequences, they bear witness to the irrationality and failure of capitalism. This irrationality and the failure of capitalism as an economic system, I may add, is today more evident than ever before.

During the formative phase of modern capitalism, for a hundred and fifty years or so beginning in the second half of the 18th century – roughly the period of what is known as the Industrial Revolution – conditions for capital accumulation were extremely favourable. Whatever the devastation in human and material terms it otherwise caused, and despite the ups and downs, the system prospered and expanded mightily. The build-up of basic industries and infrastructure – including means of transportation and communication, particularly the railways – virtually from scratch provided vast and mutually reinforcing opportunities for profitable investment, so that even the periodic breakdowns of the accumulation process tended to be brief and were rapidly overcome. The demand for capital was enormous and growing, it tended to run ahead of the supply of capital which remained in perennial short supply. A self-reproducing and self-expanding process, marked by largely spontaneous recoveries from its periodic panics and depressions, capital accumulation and 'economic growth' reached a feverish pitch by the second half of the 19th century.

But this could not last for ever. The 1870s and 1880s witnessed a growing stagnation in the economy and by the early 20th century the process began to definitely taper off. With the basic industries in place and infrastructure, railroad networks, etc. practically completed, and the excess capacity produced by the intensified competition among capitalists contributing to the problem, the demand for capital began to lag. On the other hand, the accumulation process had generated immense new wealth in advanced centres of capitalism, leading to the emergence of a new aristocracy of finance in both Europe and America, disposing over pools of capital of unprecedented magnitude. The potential supply of capital was therefore enormous. Reversing the old relationship between demand and supply of capital, an unprecedented contradiction was emerging: a growing imbalance between shrinking demand and swelling supply, giving rise to the problem of finding profitable opportunities to absorb the growing flow of capital coming on the market. The accelerated imperialist expansion of the past half century helped, but only partially. The blocking of the accumulation process manifested itself in the severe economic crisis of 1907. But what might have developed into a prolonged period of stagnation was cut short by the First World War.

War was followed by the usual aftermath boom, additionally sustained by a number of special factors, most notably the first surge of the automobile revolution in the US with its ripple effects. The cyclical upswing of the 1920s, coming as it did in the context of the October Revolution, even promoted a debate over 'Ford versus Marx', with the bourgeois ideologues gleefully proclaiming victory for Ford. The glee however was shortlived as the old contradiction soon resurfaced to haunt capitalism again. Accumulation continued as of old for a while, but by the end of the decade it become clear that what was being produced, in one industry after another, was excess, underutilised production capacity. Accompanying it was a growing tendency for profits that could not find profitable outlets in real capital formation to be diverted into purely financial and mostly speculative channels. The result was the spectacular stock market boom and crash, and the unpredecedented breakdown of the capital accumulation process in 1929-30. The Great Depression of the 1930s was far and away the longest and deepest, worst ever crisis in the history of capitalism, with unemployment at one time bouncing up to 25 per cent of the labour force in the US, by then the leading capitalist country, revealing the full depth of the real problem of capitalism. Capital accumulation process and economic growth simply came to a halt. The entire society found itself in a profound crisis, and for the first time in the history of the United States the future of capitalism itself began to be questioned. (Incidentally, while the crisis gripped the entire capitalist world, its advanced countries as well as colonial regions, and they shared in its catastrophic consequences – stark economic desolation, tens of millions of jobs obliterated, derelict and abandoned factories and mines, mass burning or destruction of primary agricultural commodities on an unprecedented scale, etc. – it did not affect the Soviet Union. As Eric Hobsbawm has noticed, the trauma of the Great Depression was underlined by the fact that the one country that had clamorously broken with capitalism proved immune to the crisis. Thanks to its successful five-year plans, industrial production in the Soviet Union in fact more than tripled during this period, rising from 5 per cent of world manufacturing in 1929 to 18 per cent in 1938, and there was no unemployment – that scourge of capitalism economies – in the Soviet Union).

A brief and very limited cyclical upturn occurred in the mid-1930s (1933-37), mostly stimulated by state intervention, including such policies as New Deal in the US. But it was immediately followed by a recession within the depression, and before the end of the decade a new term had entered the vocabulary of mainstream economics: stagnation. The 1930s were a decade of profound stagnation which never really ended. Once again, it was a war which pulled the capitalist economy out of its deepest crisis ever. As J.K. Galbraith remarked some years later, 'the Great Depression of the thirties never came to an end. It merely disappeared in the great mobilisation of the forties', that is, it merged into the war economy of 1940-45. But while the Second World War superseded the stagnation of the 1930s and provided much-needed respite to capitalism in crisis, it did nothing to alter or supersede the underlying conditions, the internal logic of capitalism, that had produced such a dismal failure of the accumulation process. That the economy recovered and unemployment practically disappeared during the war, it should be obvious, was not part of any internal logic of capitalism.

The quarter century that followed the Second World War was indeed a period of vigorous expansion, reminiscent of the best days of capitalism's youth in the 19th century. The 1950s and 1960s were even described as the 'golden age' of western capitalist prosperity which led many ideologues to claim and even believe, that the crisis-ridden capitalism and its mass unemployment were now a thing of the past in the West, and the promise was held out even to the 'developing' nations that following the necessary stages of capitalist growth, they too could one day reach, as it were, a similar welfarist and consumerist *nirvana*. The reasons for this post-Second World War upswing of capitalism are not far to seek. But these reasons lie not within capitalism but in factors external to the essential internal logic of the capitalist system.

The Great Depression from which there was no spontaneous recovery, had established as nothing before had done that the normal condition of the mature capitalist system is stagnation. This is indeed what the internal logic of capitalism decrees. To the extent that this was not the actual state of the advanced capitalist countries in the quarter century after the Second World War, the explanation lies in factors external to this logic that offset capitalism's stagnationist tendencies during this period. The conditions at the end of war were exceptionally favourable for a resumption of capital accumulation. These conditions or factors, including those that have always made for economic booms in the aftermaths of serious military conflicts, were: a massive renewal of capital stock after a great depression followed immediately by a world war; a civilian economy, badly squeezed during the war, now holding accumulated savings and a huge pent-up demand for consumer durables; the near-global scope of the post-war reconstruction after the unprecedented extent of the destruction and disorganisation of the 1940–1945 years; the epoch-making stimulus provided by the second wave of automobilisation in the United States (also encompassing the expansion of the glass, rubber, steel and petroleum industries, the building of the interstate highway system, and the rapid suburbanisation of the United States); large pools of cheap labour and raw materials and new channels of trade and capital flows; technological spin-offs from war production, whole clusters of technological and organisational innovations bearing fruit in terms of productivity growth and consumer demand in the civilian economy; the large demand provided by a growing economic role of government in what came to be described as a welfare-warfare state, and so on. The wasteful expansion of advertising and 'sales effort', and the stability within international capitalism provided by the hegemony of the United States too helped in their own ways. Given these factors or conditions, a veritable cornucopia of attractive investment opportunities opened up at the same time that an enlarged pool of investible capital was becoming available.

These factors or conditions, however, were essentially temporary and, as had happened after the first world war, by themselves they could have at best sustained the boom for only about a decade, when in fact the boom this time stretched out into the 1960s, even early 1970s. A decisive additional stimulus lay in the fact that the war, like the stagnation that preceded it, never really ended. Just as the Great Depression, in Galbraith's words, merged into the mobilisation of the 1940s, so the Second World War merged into the Cold War of the succeeding decades. After a very brief immediate post-war interlude, 1947 onwards, the war economy, with its military reflation, continued through the Cold War, along with the hot wars in Korea and Vietnam and a number of smaller wars elsewhere, right through the 1980s. The military expenditure put a floor under the economy and eliminated the threat of a return to the low-level stagnation of the Great Depression. In other words, a military Keynesianism came to undergrid capitalism during this period. Stagnation was held at bay by wars, hot and cold.

As the Korean War got underway this, for example, is how one American business or financial journal after another reported it in mid-1950: 'the effect of the Korean crisis on business was salutary insofar as increased Government expenditures portend an indefinite continuation of our current high-level economic activity. Business was more assured of stability in the economy... than at any time in the past few years' (*Dun's Review*); 'war, even if localised, even if short, won't be followed by disarmament... Depression no longer need be a worry for as long as any one can foresee' – again, 'Armaments is the new industry that underwrites the boom... good times can be assured for a long time to come' (*U.S. News & World Report*); 'You Are Just Starting To Feel It – Contracts are just starting... Military spending will be the thing above all else that sets the pace for American business' (*Business Week*); 'While

Administration economists have never admitted this: there was plenty of evidence before June 25 that the post-war boom was becoming very tired indeed... Leaving out Korea, it is only too obvious that any sharp pruning of Government expenditures would have precipitated a first-class business decline' (*Journal of Commerce*). And this is how a recent Washington dispatch to the *Wall Street Journal* has it: 'It took World War II to pull the US out of the Great Depression, and if it weren't for American fighting in Vietnam the economy probably wouldn't have achieved a record nine-year expansion in the 1960s.'

As early as 1944 Charles E. Wilson, President of General Electric had declared that the United States needed a 'permanent war economy'. The Korean war was 'broken out' in 1950 and by the end of the Korean war build-up in the early 1950s, the foundations of such an economy, with a massive, permanent arms industry, were well and truly laid. From then on, for nearly four decades, the direct and indirect effects of military spending put a floor under the American economy, the war economy providing it with the areas of most profitable investment. The military factor thus exercised a powerful supportive and steadying effect on the basically vulnerable accumulation process, helping it to run relatively smoothly with only minor ups and downs. Whenever, during the recurring business cycles, the economy showed signs of stagnation – e.g. in the late 1950s and the early 1980s – the response was a new Cold War offensive and a sharp step-up of the military budget. Seen in the broad sweep of capitalist history, permanent war economy was doubtless the main reason why capitalism enjoyed a new lease of life in the post-war period.

It is thanks to this permanent war economy that the people in the West enjoyed their largely uninterrupted good fortune in the 1950s and 1960s. It is another matter that they, including most economists had uncritically come to identify this Cold War prosperity with the normal functioning of the capitalist economy.

This, however, could not last for long. Capitalism's laws of motion had only been modified, not repealed. The basic vulnerability of the accumulation process soon asserted itself to end this great and in some ways unprecedented post-Second World War prosperity. As the special, favourable, post-war conditions that fuelled it ran their course or otherwise exhausted their possibilities, and the long Cold War military build up began yielding diminishing returns in shoring up effective demand, a swelling tide of investment-seeking funds, unable to find profitable outlets because of general excess capacity, signalled renewed accumulation trouble. Stagflation surfaced in the early 1970s and a full-fledged recession, more severe than any of its post-war predecessors, returned to the economy in 1974-1975.

Stepping up the Cold War begun by the Carter administration in its last two years and, following the sharp recession of 1980-1981, pushed to new extremes by Reagan, helped but not very effectively. The other policies adopted to cope with the growing depression adding up to an onslaught mounted by capital on the working people, exemplified by the Reagan and Thatcher regimes, only worsened the situation, illustrating the contradiction that lies at the very heart of capitalism's accumulation process: its tendency to eliminate the demand that stimulates it. Aptly termed by Richard DuBoff as 'the corporate counter-attack' – its main aims were to weaken unions and get rid of the social wage in both the private and public spheres – it was a return to the raw capitalism of yore. Tax cuts in favour of the rich, union busting and dismantling of the welfare state, more 'flexibility' in the labour market, etc., even as they brought added profits and further prosperity to the top of the income structure, brought only increasing deprivation and insecurity to the lower levels. Capitalism once again had mass unemployment, poverty and even hunger and homelessness of the people amid the wealth and affluence of its rich beneficiaries. But this, instead of countering the trend towards the recession, only deepened it, for the simple reason that it is impossible to squeeze 'growing purchasing power' (required for a 'healthy' expansion and accumulation of capital) from the shrinking wages and the deteriorating standard of living of the working people.

The Soviet collapse had its political-ideological and plain plundering gains for the west but it brought little economic relief to the recession-beleaguered capitalism. The end of the cold war in fact coincided with the cyclical down turn or recession of 1990 which pushed US capitalism into one of its worst crises. With the Soviet collapse, the entire rationale for the cold war on which the relative prosperity of US capitalism and stability of the global capitalist system had depended for so long after the Second World War disappeared and with it the ideological-political underpinnings of the permanent war economy. But military-industrial complex and the politics allied with it were much too deeply rooted and powerful, imperialist interests abroad had still to be defended, and the world at large still required policing on behalf of capitalism, if necessary with the help of nuclear weapons, missiles and anti-missiles. The permanent war economy, therefore, stayed in place. Nevertheless the mechanism connecting economic crisis to the cold war, the rationale of rescuing the economy by continuous doses of military build-up had been badly damaged. The Gulf war was indeed a godsent, if ever there was one for American capitalism wracked by the post-cold war recession. The arms industries hummed again and in addition the supply of precious oil was secured and the image tarnished by the defeat in Vietnam was repaired. The reconstruction after the Gulf destruction meant ever more business, yet another area of profitable investment. More recent wars in Afghanistan and Iraq have been helpful in the same way. But whatever direct political or economic usefulness such little wars may have, they are not adequate enough, even in association with the extant war economy to shore up things and keep capitalism on an acceptable path of growth and stability. Ruled out by the ascendant neo-liberal ideology, no Keynesian state intervention has been forthcoming so far. But even if Keynesian strategies are given the credit for the post-war boom as some economists still do, it is obvious that they could not sustain it or stave off the recession. It is doubtful if they can do so now, that is, counter the current recession successfully. Thus, the recession that returned to the economy in 1974-1975 has continued – of course with cyclical ups and downs and regional variations and unevenness which have characterised capitalist development, including its crises, throughout.

The global economy has been in the grip of a prolonged crisis ever since the post-war boom petered out in the 1970s. There is retarded growth, precipitous fall of investment rates, soaring unemployment and intensified pauperisation. The decline of profitability resulting from the generation of chronic excess capacity and over production – 'an epic of overproduction of the means of production' as one description has it – continues to bedevil the economy. Recognising it as 'a serious threat' and typically hopeful about 'an orderly' way out, this is how the Bank for International Settlements reported it (in mid-1999): 'The overhang of excess industrial capacity in many countries and sectors continues to be a serious threat to financial stability. Without an orderly reduction or take up of this excess capacity, rates of return on capital will continue to disappoint, with potentially debilitating and long-lasting effects on confidence and investment spending. Moreover, the solvency of the institutions that financed this capital expansion becomes increasingly questionable.'

'An orderly' escape route is, however, ruled out, for what is involved is the structural logic of capitalism. Overproduction and excess capacity in the world capitalist economy, including American capitalism, have come to stay, pointing to the classic character of its current crisis wherein the build-up of overcapacity plays the central role. With the intensification of international competition, excess capacity is now appearing in industry after industry and on a global scale. It is virtually omnipresent in the manufacturing sector of the economy. The world output gap – between industrial capacity and its use – is approaching its highest levels since the 1930s, the utilisation rate of productive capacity is in fact plummeting down to the levels of those crisis years. Capitalism's natural tendency, the tendency of the investment seeking surplus (or potential savings) to rise relative to profitable outlets, is asserting itself as never before. The America of George W. Bush is perched on a mountain of unsold and unsaleable inventories. According to Inaba Seisakusho, one of Japan's leading industrialists: 'We are slashing capital investment because there is nothing to invest in. Even if we were to build a new factory, there is no prospect of seeing it generating additional demand.' The situation is only being worsened by the attempts made both by firms and states to reduce costs and improve competitiveness, which have the effect of exacerbating redundant production and reducing the growth of aggregate demand and thereby also reducing manufacturing profitability and inhibiting investment.

The new innovations that show up are failing to sustain a significant upsurge of capital investment. There is much hype over the digital revolution. The new technology of the information age has no doubt dramatically changed aspects of our personal and social life. But this is what all major technological revolutions over the course of capitalist development have done, each contributing its share in altering the way we live. In no case, however, did any of these earlier technological revolutions create a new economy. Nor has today's digital revolution. The economic laws of motion of capitalism remain in force. And it is these 'laws' which have eventuated in the current crisis of capitalism. The digital revolution has been, in its own way, certainly helpful, but it has failed to produce any leap forward for the economy, and now even the global telecommunications industry – the highest of high-flying sectors of the late 1990s upswing in the economy – is reported to be facing a 'black hole'. The enormous capital expenditures have created capacity that far exceeds demand. In other words, capitalism's crisis of overproduction and excess capacity remains as it was. Furthermore, as the crisis deepens and manufacturing profitability stays down, investment funds move with ever greater volatility around the world and there is unprecedented financialisation of the accumulation process. The situation is reminiscent of what happened at the end of the 19th century or during the late 1920s. And evidence is all the time piling up to confirm that the normal condition of mature capitalism – that is, the condition to which it tends in the absence of major extra-systemic factors, such as we have noticed earlier, is stagnation.

To continue with the argument, it is capitalism's deep-seated tendency to generate more surplus than it can absorb. As contemporary monopoly capitalism, it carries a contradiction within itself; on the one hand it generates a swelling flow of profits, on the other it reduces the demand for additional investment in increasingly controlled market: more and more profits, fewer and fewer profitable investment opportunities, with the consequence that capital accumulation and therefore economic growth which is powered by capital accumulation slows down. There is growing stagnation in the economy and a consequent augmentation of the role of finance in it. We have earlier noticed the double process of faltering real investment and burgeoning financialisation – a growing tendency for profits that could not find profitable outlets in real capital formation to be diverted into purely financial and mostly speculative channels – at the time of the Great Depression. Now with the intensified crisis of overproduction in the real economy we are faced with a similar but worse situation, indeed a 'financial explosion' – the vast expansion of debt, credit, and monetary and financial markets extending from the Wall Street to the third world – as capital, facing stagnation within production, seeks alternative outlets for itself. There is a new, intensified manifestation of the tendency of capital to direct itself not so much towards making useful goods and services as towards manipulating money and speculation, making money directly without the intermediation of a production process. This has counteracted stagnation to some extent but spelled greater and greater instability in the economy as the system takes on an increasingly speculative character. The problem is not confined to the advanced capitalist countries but extends in various ways through the medium of imperialism to the periphery itself. A manifestation of the crisis of global capitalism, it has been exploding as a financial contaclysm in country after country with a regularity which has ceased to surprise in Mexico (end of 1994), Brazil (1995), South Africa (1996), Eastern Europe (early 1997), Southeast Asia (late 1997), South Korea (early 1998), Russia and South Africa again (mid-1998), Brazil again (1998–1999) and Argentina soon after... Pundits are no longer asking *if* another country will be next, but *who* will be next.

It may be added that making money without the intermediation of a production process is nothing new for capitalism. As Marx has pointed out, the first forms of capital were really merchant capital, money increasing without production but through trade, which were superseded in the industrial period with its miracles of productivity, the historical achievement of capitalism. That at the end of its centuries-long development, capitalism has again entered a phase where, increasingly, money is transformed into more money unrelated to any real production, points to a certain exhaustion of its productive potentialities, its growing failure to subserve human material needs. A problematic way out of the accumulating difficulties and contradictions of capitalism – when productive self-expansion of capital is no longer readily available – this may or may not lead to the kind of collapse we have experienced before. But insofar as the problem here is located within capitalism's accumulation process itself, reform would be inadequate to redress it. A part of the structural problems of capitalism, it can only be redressed by the elimination of capitalism.

This is indeed the fundamental choice before us. Such is the crisis of capitalism today that it cannot afford even reformist solutions to its problems; it *of necessity* frustrates all attempts at interfering even to a minimal extent with its structural parameters. This, as we have argued, is the essential meaning of contemporary globalisation. Globalisation this time – with its deregulatory and export-led strategies, its 'economic restructuring' at home and WB–IMF decreed 'Structural Adjustment Programmes' abroad – is not just a new but an even more harsh and destructive chapter in the history of capitalism. A response to capitalism's most serious crisis since the Great Depression, it is a return to capitalism, including its imperialist logic, at its most basic. Which also means that capitalism's contradictions are now manifesting themselves all the more sharply so that at the moment of its greatest triumph, the whole world at its feet and the sense of alternatives more stifled than at any time in its history, capitalism finds itself in the words of billionaire speculator George Soros, 'coming apart at the seams'.

After the exceptional boom of the 1950s and 1960s the global capitalist economy has now endured more than three decades of seriously faltering performance, measured by overall growth in output, productivity, and full employment of resources. It has been marked by deep recessions and shortlived booms, as well as uneven progress of different national economies. Capitalism's recurrent crises have been exploding in shorter and shorter intervals of time. Even the privileged few countries of 'advanced capitalism' are going through recessions (and even 'double-dip recessions') at ever shortening intervals. The biggest capitalist economy, USA, moves, with but brief interludes from recession to recession, and the world's second largest economy, Japan, remains mired in seemingly endless stagnation or recession – which does not, however, rule out partial recoveries or cyclical upswings. That capitalism is now in a deep and perpetual crisis worldwide is widely acknowledged. The horrendous word, 'overproduction' is back in the discourses of economists and corporates and anxious reference to the Great Depression is not uncommon. Fears over the consequences deepen after every new manifestation of the crisis, though the system has avoided any large breakdown of the kind which occurred in the 1930s. What Kotibara, an eminent theorist at Tokyo University, says has relevance, not limited to his country: 'The words overproduction and crash were shunned because they were considered politically inappropriate; to many, they smacked of communist jargon. But things are changing so fast in our swiftly rotting economy and in people's violent reactions to the crisis. Take the case of a senior MITI civil servant declaring, without fear now of being rapped over the knuckles, that we are living through the biggest crisis of international capitalism since the end of the occupation and that we should read carefully the writings of Marx and shed our market dogmas.'

There has been no breakdown of the system. With the capitalist state standing guard over the system, breakdown in the future too is unlikely. But this should not prevent us from recognising the unprecedented, historically exceptional nature of the current crisis of capitalism. What we are facing is not a routine cyclical recession, a more or less extensive cyclical crisis of capitalism as experienced in the past, but the deepening structural crisis of the capitalist system itself, indeed a turning point in the history of capitalism. Earlier in its history – including the phase addressed by Marx – capitalist relations had only penetrated a small part of the world. Capitalism had its structural limits and contradictions which regularly erupted into crises – 'great thunderstorms' Marx called them – but they were followed by more or less normal recovery and relatively long expansionary phases. With the Soviet collapse the capitalist world system has reached, so to speak, the limits of its expansion and with this its structural limits and contradictions too have come into play with their devastating intensity. The contradictions of capitalism are manifesting themselves all the more sharply because, with capitalism become truly global, the old ways of 'displacing contradictions', of pulling out of crisis are, as Marx said they would be, less and less available. There has been growing frequency of recessionary phases tending towards a *depressed continuum*, as Meszaros has called it. And now this depressed continuum has come to stay. Once more or less temporary conjunctural and periodic crises of capitalism have turned into a chronic structural crisis directly affecting the whole of mankind. This is how Meszaros has described this crisis:

> the crisis of capital we are experiencing today is an all-embracing structural crisis. There is nothing special, of course, in linking capital to crisis. On the contrary, crises of varying intensity and duration happen to be capital's *natural* mode of existence: ways of progressing beyond its immediate barriers and thus extending with ruthless dynamism its sphere of operation and domination. In this sense, the last thing that capital could envisage is a *permanent* supersession of all crises, even if its ideologists and propagandists frequently dream about (or indeed claim the achievement of) nothing less than that. The *historical* novelty of today's crisis is manifest under four main aspects: (1) its *character* is *universal*, rather than restricted to one particular sphere (e.g., financial, or commercial, or affecting this or that particular branch of production, or applying to this rather than that type of labour, with its specific range of skills and degrees of productivity, etc.); (2) its *scope* is truly *global* (in the most threateningly literal sense of the term), rather than confined to a particular set of countries (as all major crises have been in the past); (3) its *time scale* is

> extended, continuous – if you like: *permanent* – rather than limited and *cyclic*, as all former crises of capital happened to be; (4) its *mode* of unfolding might be called *creeping* – in contrast to the more spectacular and dramatic eruptions and collapses of the past – while adding the proviso that even the most vehement or violent convulsions cannot be excluded as far as the future is concerned: i.e., when the complex machinery now actively engaged in 'crisis-management' and in the more or less temporary 'displacement' of the growing contradictions runs out of steam.
>
> To deny that such machinery exists and that it is powerful, would be extremely foolish. Nor should one exclude or minimize capital's ability to add new instruments to the already vast arsenal of its continued self-defence. Nevertheless, the fact that the existing machinery is being brought into play with increasing frequency and that it proves less and less effective as things stand today, is a fair measure of the severity of this deepening structural crisis.

What we are facing today is a *systemic*, truly *structural* crisis of capitalism – a crisis without end and with few avenues of escape. That some countries are doing well even in the midst of this crisis or have cyclical upswings, or that there are partial recoveries is something that has happened throughout the history of capitalism. It does not negate the reality of the current crisis which, in effect, questions the viability of capitalism itself as a social reproductive system and puts its transcendence and replacement on the agenda for our times.

XIII

The current crisis of capitalism, incidentally, is well reflected in the near bankruptcy of the mainstream 'economic science' in facing the problems posed by this crisis. The awareness of crisis is of course there in the business press and academic journals. But stagnation seems to have encroached upon economic thinking itself. This is nowhere more evident than in the refusal of orthodox economists to confront the issue of economic stagnation, despite nearly three decades of slow growth, rising excess capacity and financial explosion. The explanations have ranged from the trivial to the absurd. As for answers, appropriate measures being ruled out by capitalism's deeply entrenched special interests and ideological biases, inappropriate ones continue to be advocated which can only worsen the situation. A good example here is the repeated advocacy of the strategy of export-oriented competitiveness in a crisis-ridden global economy with an irreducible structural tendency to over capacity. With the crisis becoming daily more visible, the term 'regulation', forbidden till recently, has reappeared, but, however useful marginally, remains a rather impotent response to the crisis. Quite a few, including some in honest or simply opportunistic retreat from Marxism, can do no better than plead for a return to the failed strategies of yesterday to at least counter the more painful consequences of the 'deregulated economy' for its unfortunate victims in the world.

The crisis in economics, in fact, goes much deeper. Historically and traditionally, the subject matter of economics, as a form of meaningful inquiry, was a concern with trying to understand how economic systems work and with what consequences for human beings, as individuals, groups, classes, or communities. There has been a marked turning away from such a concern in recent years. With the reimposition of neo-liberal orthodoxy and its 'free market' recipes, Marx and Keynes have been erased from economic thought. So many of the younger economists have been busy only devising ways and means of understanding and managing the minor ups and downs of the economic system, while others in pursuit of a purer and nobler 'science' have taken refuge in a world of mathematical models having no relation to the operations of real people and real systems. The 'theoreticians' of 'pure economics' have replaced analysis of the real world with that of an imaginary capitalism – at times it is almost witchcraft taking the place of rationality – 'Pure Economics, or the Contemporary World's Witchcraft', Samir Amin has called it. For quite a few seniors, reflecting an important aspect of the contemporary crisis of capitalism – the enormous increase in the relative importance of speculative finance in the economy – catering to the needs of the speculators, providing 'new tools for weighing the risks and rewards of different investments and for valuing corporate stocks and bonds' (according to the *New*

York Times) has become one of the loftiest goals of 'economic science' – and they themselves are now 'heroes to a generation of money managers and corporate financiers' (as *Business Week* has put it) while others, regardless of systemic interconnections, concern themselves with 'family budget' and 'individual preferences'. (These shifts have been well reflected in recent Nobel prize awards in economics, even as concern for the future of the system has also prompted propping up of reborn 'Keynesianism' or 'developmentalism', with its pleas for 'safety nets', for better education and health care for the poor, especially in the third world, or honouring criticism of IMF–WB policies, of course, from within the system). That it has failed to confront the reality of contemporary capitalism, the deep structural crisis it is facing today, is writ large over contemporary bourgeois economics. Reporting a recent year-end annual meeting of the American Economic Association, *Business Week* said it all in a terse headline: '7000 Economists – and no answers'. This failure of bourgeois economics, in its own way testifies to the fact that capitalism is objectively ready to be transcended.

XIV

To argue that capitalism is in crisis and that its transcendence is now objectively necessary is not to suggest that this transcendence is imminent, though incipient rebellions against the present socio-economic order are brewing worldwide. Again, though matters can get out of hand and 'violent convulsions' cannot be entirely ruled out, a breakdown of the system is also not likely. The capitalist class has learnt well one of the lessons of history of the last century – how to use the state to protect its own from such a disaster. The capitalist state is always there to save capitalism from itself or its enemies. This apart, capitalism has proved to be an exceptionally resilient system. Helped by the state, its class power and hegemonic ideology, and by means as diverse as violence or war, deeper penetration of the periphery, laying the burden on the working people (employed as well as unemployed) and so on, it has survived crisis after crisis in the past. Capitalism as a social order is oppressive and generates its own opposition, which it then has to channel and control. It has been eminently successful at this. As a system it has shown an uncanny knack of co-opting or neutralising opposition within the parameters of its own economy and politics, co-opting and accommodating even revolutionary leaders of the subaltern classes through a mechanism that Gramsci describes as '*transformismo*'. It has been regularly able to so co-opt its opponents as to make *them* run *its* system and, at times, even help save it. And then, it always has its 'Prize-fighters' as Marx called them. Therefore, the crisis notwithstanding, capitalism's capacity to survive is not to be underestimated.

In other words, crisis is not to be confused with any so-called 'breakdown' or 'impending breakdown'. Capitalism will not collapse by itself. A nuclear war or environmental disaster may lead to barbarism or worse. Otherwise the rule of capital will end when it is overthrown by other classes. Hence, uncertainties of the situation notwithstanding, the need for socialists to put class struggle at the centre of their politics. And to be truly anti-systemic, it has to be a struggle for both reform and revolution, with the former subordinated to the latter as enjoined by Marx. 'An antisystemic movement', as Wallerstein has said, 'cannot neglect short-term defensive action, including electoral action. The world's populations live in the present, and their immediate needs have to be addressed. Any movement that neglects them is bound to lose the widespread passive support that is essential for its long-term success. But the motive and justification for defensive action should not be that of remedying a failing system...' Apart from seeking to prevent the system's negative effects from getting worse in the short run, defensive actions (or the struggle for reform) should be so conducted as to subserve the long-term, revolutionary aim of a transcendence of the system itself.

XV

Whatever the future may hold for humankind, a socialist transcendence of capitalism, or barbarism or worse that capitalism in crisis now portends, the important thing to note in the immediate context is the failure of capitalism explicit in the current crisis and consequences of capitalism. Capitalism's pursuit of profit and accumulation of capital not only has an inherent tendency to depression and regularly runs into crises, these crises intensify the exploitative and oppressive consequences flowing from the predatory structural logic of capitalism which, accumulating wealth and affluence at one end, creates and continuously refreshes the sources of poverty and inequality at the other end, domestically as well as globally. This poverty and inequality are not the residue of a backward system getting better, as the apologists for capitalism not unoften argue, but are the contemporary products of a system of production that creates such marginalisation of the people everywhere. The accumulative logic of capitalism simply breaks the linear connection between economic development and social well-being. The recurring crises of capitalist accumulation process only make matters worse for the people. The costs of 'recovery', whatever there is, indeed of all successful 'restructuring' of capitalism in history, are invariably passed on to the weaker sections of society, to the unemployed and the welfare-dependent at home and to the poor in the third world. Given the systemic, truly structural nature of the current crisis, polarisation of wealth and human misery, within capitalist societies and worldwide, has now asserted itself with a vengeance. The incidence of material deprivation today is unprecedented. Globalisation has been fortunate for some. For the vast majority, subjected to capitalism's boundless appetite for profit, it has been a disaster. The protracted crisis in advanced capitalist economies may not signal a terminal decline, or eventuate in a breakdown, but it most obviously indicates that these economies have exhausted their capacity to survive without depressing the living and working conditions of their own populations – let alone the less-developed countries which they continue to exploit, and not only as sources of cheap labour and the bearers of debt. 'Economic restructuring' at the centre has meant, shrinking expenditure on education, health and social assistance, mass unemployment, sharply enhanced insecurity, and emergence of 'the new poor' alongside the old ones. While 'social demolition' continues in the now globalised former Soviet Union, 'economic reform', the unilateral structural adjustment policies have intensified the misery and chronic underdevelopment in the vast periphery and semi-periphery of global capitalism. The failure of capitalism is today evident everywhere, in every part of the world. Setting this failure in historical perspective, Istvan Meszaros has written:

> In the course of the last century capital has certainly invaded and subdued every corner of our planet, little and large alike. However, it proved quite incapable of solving the grave problems which people must confront in their everyday life all over the world. If anything, the penetration of capital into every single corner of the 'underdeveloped' world only aggravated these problems. It promised 'modernisation', but after many decades of loudly trumpeted intervention it only delivered intensified poverty, chronic indebtedness, insoluble inflation, and crippling structural dependency. So much so in fact that it is now highly embarrassing to remind the ideologists of the capital system that not so long ago they nailed their flags to the mast of 'modernisation'.
>
> Things have significantly changed in the last few decades, as compared to the expansionary past. The displacement of capital's inner contradictions could work with relative ease during the phase of the system's historical ascendancy. It was possible to deal under such conditions with many problems by sweeping them under the carpet of unfulfilled promises, like modernisation in the 'Third World' and ever greater prosperity and social advancement in the 'metropolitan' countries, predicated on the expectation of producing an endlessly growing cake. However, the consummation of capital's historical ascendancy radically alters the situation. It is then not only no longer possible to make plausible new sets of vacuous promises but the old promises too must be wiped out of memory, and some real gains of the working classes in the privileged capitalist countries must be 'rolled back' in the interest of the survival of the ruling socio-economic and political order.
>
> This is where we stand today. The triumphalist celebrations of a few years ago now sound very hollow indeed. The slanted development of the last century brought no solutions on the model of 'mobile property's civilized victory' (Marx), in that it simply multiplied the privileges of the few and the misery of the many. However, a radically new condition has emerged in the course of the last few decades, gravely affecting the prospects of

> development in the future. For what is particularly grave today from the point of view of the capital system is that even the privileges of the few cannot be sustained any longer on the backs of the many, in sharp contrast to the past. As a result, the system as a whole is being rendered quite unstable, even if it will take some time before the full implications of this systemic instability transpire, calling for structural remedies in place of manipulative postponement.

This was Marx's own perspective on capitalism which is coming into its own in our times.

XVI

Capitalism has extraordinary productive achievements to its credit – Marx and Engels had themselves paid eloquent tribute to it in the *Communist Manifesto*, at the very beginning of modern capitalism: 'The bourgeoisie, during its rule of scarce one hundred years, has created more massive and more colossal productive forces than have all preceding generations together.' Capitalism has produced even more 'miracles' of productivity of social labour since then, putting a vast amount of actual and potential economic surplus at the disposal of society. But the capitalist class has proved signally incapable of rationally managing this surplus today available in the economy. The crucial failure of the capitalist social order lies precisely in the fact that it is unable to make the best use of the immense resources that capitalism has itself created, that is their use for human welfare. Capitalism, even as it has provided for a consumerist economy for the few in the affluent capitalist countries and their counterparts elsewhere, condemnd sizeabl sections within these countries and the vast masses in the third world to a life of penury and destitution, hopelessness and despair. And the failure here is not the result of any wrong economic policies but essentially the product of classic tendencies inherent in capitalism. The scientific and technological revolutions of our times have made this failure of capitalism even more stark. Never was the gap between society's potentiality and society's performance so immense as it is today in a world of global capitalist domination.

Under capitalism, the resources become available through the scientific and technological revolutions turn into 'excess capacity'; they cannot be fully used, or when they are used it is not for the benefit of the people but in a wasteful pursuit of profit and capital accumulation, as is evident in the way the new production and communication technologies are catering to the consumerist appetites of the few and military requirements of global capitalism. Marx's notion that capitalism at a certain stage of its development becomes a 'fetter' upon the productive forces may not have come true literally. But capitalism imposes upon the production process priorities dictated by the striving for private profit rather than humane and rational ends, and thus capitalism *has* come to be a fetter upon the most beneficent use of the productive forces, the immense resources it has itself brought into being. That capitalism today cannot make 'full' and/or 'good' use of the available productive resources graphically illustrates the contradiction between the highly developed forces of production and the existing capitalist relations of production, and even more the contradiction between *social* production and *private* appropriation that Marx had emphasised as lying at the very foundation of capitalist production process – each in its own way pointing to the need and necessity of supersession of capitalism as a mode of production.

Capitalism, to go over this argument a little differently, while stimulating the technological inventiveness of humankind, then turns its achievements not into a new and better life for the people but into profits and unemployment. The gap between the rich and mighty on one side and the poor and outcasts on the other, far from narrowing, widens even in the privileged countries of advanced capitalism. That is how the development of technology today, as it grows into the so-called Third or even Fourth Industrial Revolution, is in its own way contributing to the marginalisation of the working population in the advanced capitalist countries, having an impact similar to that of the steam engine at the time of the Luddites in England. It is as if supplementing the neo-liberal ideological attack of laissez faire, free trade and monetarism, capitalism is mounting a technological attack too on the working classes. The dominant new technologies are both labour and capital saving. Unlike those characteristic of the earlier industrial and transport revolutions, they do not absorb vast amounts of capital and tend to eliminate more jobs than they create. The inventive gains – automation, micro-electronics, robotisation, etc. – hold the prospect of rendering millions of working people in the developed countries unemployed. The process has indeed begun and we already have this new unemployment or redundancy of human labour, and the consequent deterioration of living conditions, a dehumanising subsistence on the dole of an increasing number of even young workers. The founder of automation Norbert Wiener had said in 1950: 'The automatic machine is the precise equivalent of slave labour. Any labour which competes with slave labour must accept the economic conditions of slave labour.' We have almost approached the situation foreseen by Norbert Wiener: it is already there as a part of what scholars have written of as 'Latin-Americanisation' of the developed countries of capitalism, including the United States – massive poverty, unemployment and immiserisation, the degradation and degeneration of vast segments of population, widespread hunger, malnutrition, and child labour, whole areas polluted to the point of saturation and treated as dumping grounds for toxic wastes, everything the same as in the underdeveloped countries in the periphery of global capitalism. If the process of closer integration of the global capitalist system has, promoting a limited and distorted growth, created enclaves of vulgar affluence for certain segments at the top of society in the underdeveloped poor countries, it has also led to the emergence of mass privation and different forms of human degradation at the base of the developed, rich and super rich countries of the capitalist world, with technology playing its own role in the process in ways other than the one generally recognised.

Technology, as we have noted on more than one occasion, is never free of its socio-economic context and uses. Bourgeois ideologues' hype over it notwithstanding, new technology remains subject to capitalism's structural logic and its polarising consequences. To reproduce an earlier argument with a borrowed addition: Prophets are promising a 'new age of prosperity' where the work would be done by computers and robots. If so, the beneficiaries would surely have all the 'leisure time' to indulge themselves: 'Surfing' the internet? 'Eco-tourism' in Brazil? 'Virtual reality' video games and sex? 'Cyber-shopping' from home? The choices would be endless and available, as always in capitalism, to the fortunate few. But ordinary people would continue to do the work if and when they get it, as they have always done in capitalism. While millions would have been unceremoniously kicked out of the labour force and millions more new arrivals will share their fate, the rest would continue to work at low-wage, part-time, unstable and insecure jobs in capitalism's 'technological utopia'.

XVII

Capitalism's failure, or at least declining legitimacy which surely reflects it, is evident in several more or less important features capitalism has acquired in recent years. I will here refer to only two of these which are noticeable for their everyday conspicuousness. Though not important in directly structural terms, corruption has today become a distinctive feature of contemporary capitalist societies. Corruption in business transactions is, of course, a practice as old as human history or, at least, as old as trade and commerce. But its rise to significance in the economy to become an almost integral part of the contemporary capitalist systems is something altogether new – corporate scandals have never before hit the ceiling in such an embarrassing manner and the scandal sheet is lengthening. Enron, World Com, Adalphia, Xerox Tyco and Global Crossing, and numberless other companies in the US have been accused of fraudulent financial deals, tax evasion, misuse of corporate funds, false declaration of pre-tax profit and any number of other similar crimes. One CEO after another has been embroiled in accounting scandals. Italy's richest businessman, Silvio Berlusconi, who also happens to be its current prime minister, is enmeshed in a number of bribery and other legal cases. And he is not alone among Europe's and America's businessmen-politicians. Of corruption in capitalisms of Russia and the Third World, less said the better. Says Alan Greenspan, Chairman of the US Federal Reserve and a leading ideologue of capitalism of the current phase of globalisation: there is 'no increase in human greed, just an increase in the opportunities for greedy behaviour'! A brief comment on the phenomenon, therefore, will not be out of place.

It has been pointed out that practices we now call corrupt have been, throughout much of human history, the normal and legitimate means of not only doing business but, even more importantly, conducting the affairs of state. In the immediate pre-capitalist past, for example, when it was harder to distinguish the public functions of the state from private appropriation, a feudal lord or a state official would, and was expected to, use his political, judicial, and military powers not only to perform his 'public' functions – whether the conduct of war or the adjudication of legal disputes – but also to extract surplus and line his own pockets. That was a normal way of appropriating surpluses from direct producers, especially from peasants. The rise of capitalism involved and coincided with a clearer distinction between the 'political' and the 'economic', the 'public' and the 'private', where capitalists, unlike feudal lords or absolutist officials, don't appropriate surpluses by directly exercising some kind of official or pubic power, but do so, that is accumulate profits, through the mechanisms of the market, and the conduct of public business is supposed to be separate from the process of private appropriation, so that such appropriation in this sphere, that is, the normal and legitimate practices of the earlier era, is nothing but so much corruption. Capitalism as it came up not only disapproved of such corruption and sought its outlawry but was also propelled forward by a morality of its own. This period had its 'robber barons' and financial swindling in collusion with ministers and politicians. But, on the whole, capitalists' pursuit of profit was governed by the protestant ethics. God was the 'Great Taskmaster' watching from above to see that they acted as proper capitalists in the market place. 'To get rich not by production but by pocketing the already available wealth of others' was an aberration which, as Marx said, violated 'the bourgeois laws themselves'. That however was long ago, during the period of ascendancy of capitalism. As crime itself has become big business in the economy, where, according to a United Nation's report, the turnover of 'crime internationals' today surpasses the combined GNP of more than 50 of the least developing nations of the world, capitalist societies have come to be characterised by an all-pervasive corruption or kleptomania in which not only businessmen but presidents, prime ministers and their cabinet colleagues, members of parliament and bureaucrats, and politicians of all sorts are all entangled, not only in the advanced capitalist countries of the west but in the more or less developed capitalist countries of the third world, including India, as well. Even 'Communist China' has long ceased to be an exception. That its socialist marketeers have acquired this deviant art so early in their turn to the market only testifies to their country's rapid progress along the road to another capitalism of our time.

Corruption is a conspicuous presence everywhere in contemporary capitalism. Its systemic importance, however, is not to be exaggerated. Its conspicuousness must not make us overlook the much wider range of repugnant behaviour or practices within capitalism through which far more serious damage continues to be *invisibly* inflicted upon living human beings and the natural environment. Even so, viewed as a questionable aberration once, but become an almost normal behaviour or practice today, reflecting a breakdown of capitalism's preferred morality itself, corruption does signify a certain loss of legitimacy of capitalism as it has come to exist today.

This is far more the case with another – already noticed – recent feature of capitalism, which is not only conspicuous but also systemically most important: the dominance that financial-cum-speculative capital has come to acquire in the economy. Quintessentially a system of capital accumulation, capitalism accumulates through a regular generation of additional profit in the real economy, the one that produces goods and services that enable people to live and reproduce. But the very structure that yields these profits to capitalists puts strict limits on the incomes, and therefore purchasing power, of the underlying population. They are barely able to buy what has been produced – goods remain unsold and excess capacity comes to mark the economy. There is therefore no profit to be made from expanding the capacity to produce the goods that enter into mass consumption. To do so would be to invest in excess capacity, a patent capitalist irrationality. What then are capitalists to do with their profits? This is a problem which has dogged capitalism throughout its history. During its period of ascendancy, as capitalism grew and expanded at home and abroad, even as it regularly produced excess capacity and ran into crises of overproduction, new opportunities continued to become available for profitable investment in real productive assets. With capitalism becoming increasingly, and now truly, global, such opportunities have become scarce. Investment in financial assets has been capitalism's answer to its old problem. The process began with the stagnation of the 1970s and accelerated during the following decades, with the consequence that the old structure of the economy, consisting of a production system served by a more or less important financial adjunct now stands replaced by a new structure in which a vastly expanded financial section has achieved a high degree of independence and sits on top of the underlying production system. The capital accumulation process has come to be pre-eminently financialised. One consequence is that capital, no longer able to sustain maximum profitability by means of commensurate economic growth, has come to rely more and more on simply *redistributing* wealth in favour of the rich, and on increasing inequalities, within and between national economies with the help of the 'neoliberal state'. The other consequence is that cut loose from its origin and moorings in a real economy of production, financial capital has, almost inevitably, become speculative capital geared solely to its own expansion, accompanied equally inevitably by all sorts of speculative frauds and manipulation of financial institutions. A long time ago, with the experiences of the 1920s and 1930s in mind, Keynes had warned: 'Speculators may do no harm as bubbles on a steady stream of enterprise. But the position is serious when enterprise becomes the bubble on a whirlpool of speculation. When the capital development of a country becomes a by-product of the activities of a casino, the job is likely to be ill-done.' Not only has the warning come true – the speculative bubble has so expanded on top of the economy that productive enterprise is very near being a 'bubble on the whirlpool of speculation' – the bubble, reflecting a serious contradiction at the heart of contemporary capitalism, the disconnection between the productive base of the economy and the financial superstructure, has been regularly bursting in one Third World country after another, devastating the lives of the peoples concerned and garnering new gains in capital and assets for the plundering multinationals. Such is the reality of capitalism today. Its dire consequences for the people are visible on all sides, from mass unemployment in the advanced capitalist countries to deepening poverty and destitution in the third world and unchecked ecological deterioration everywhere. But the point to be noticed in the immediate context is that the financialisation of capital accumulation distorts and negates what is the ultimate purpose of any economic system, the satisfaction of human needs – which puts an additional question mark over capitalism's legitimacy as an economic system for our times.

XVIII

The two conspicuous features of contemporary capitalism we have just discussed in their own way point to the growing failure of capitalism as an economic system. This failure is of course most evident in capitalism's inability to use the vast productive resources it has itself created for human welfare. Its structural logic inevitably leaves it incapable of doing so. But a closer look will reveal another aspect of its failure, which again is a product of its structural logic – the wastefulness and destructiveness of capitalism even at its best and most prosperous. What I have in mind are not just aspects or factors which we have already noticed in one context or another: capitalism's structural logic which makes for a crisis-ridden economic growth, with familiar disparities and marginalisations within societies at the centre and economic backwardness and barbaric living conditions in countries of the periphery; or the indifference of a market economy to its external costs, which it regularly off-loads on to the social and natural environment; or the rampant consumerism, a market-stimulated produce or perish frenzy for newer and newer consumer demands, for ever new fashions and models and styles in products with zero use-value and high exchange value, which has virtually turned global capitalism into a gigantic and highly efficient machine for the production of junk; or the corruption which is eating up increasing amount of resources in contemporary capitalism; or the stagnation of real production process whereby capital investment has come to be biased away from industry or manufacturing towards commercial, real estate, and financial speculative ventures, a shift most evident in the US, and even more so in Japan, so that the direction of the whole economy, in fact of the whole society is increasingly determined by financial and trading rather than industrial capital. These factors and more are all there. What I now want to underline is that capitalism has increasingly become, in a very specific sense, a system of economic waste, waste of actual and potential human and natural resources. As already noticed, it is a deep-seated tendency of capitalism in its modern, most developed form to fall increasingly short of producing what it is capable of producing owing to a lack of purchasing power in the hands of workers, farmers, and the unemployed. The human need is there, but not the purchasing power to back it; therefore, it is no domain for profitable investment. At the same time capitalism's accumulation process, profitable investment elsewhere, generates ever increasing productive capacity so that there is a vast potential overflow of the economic surplus in society which, under the circumstances, means underproduction, underconsumption, and under-investment, or what is the same, underemployment of men and women, underutilisation of productive capacity, and depression. The only remedy for this persistent malaise that is available to capitalism is the multiplication of the already present waste in both the private and the public sectors of the economy in order to ensure a somewhat more efficient and smooth working of the capitalist system. The very survival of capitalism has been now increasingly dependent on its squandering of resources in diverse ways, above all, on the wasteful extravagance of consumerism – where, a system gone berserk in its profit-driven dynamism is catering to the ever new market-created wants of the few with purchasing power, when it cannot meet the basic needs of the vast numbers who cannot translate these into what an economic reason grown cynical calls 'effective demand' – and, even more, on armaments, preparation for war and war itself, so much so that, recognising the centrality of the military public sector to the prosperity of the post-war 'golden age', scholars have been speaking of the modern capitalist state as 'welfare-warfare state' – though 'welfare' has been steadily disappearing in recent decades, leaving the 'warfare' part all the more important. Indeed, the inherent irrationality of capitalism, particularly of modern monopolistic and oligopolistic capitalism, and its ultimate failure is today nowhere more evident than in the fact that it has increasingly become 'an economy of waste', an economy of 'institutionalised wastes' where automatically expanding waste in the private or business sector (ever-proliferating sales organisations – there are now more people employed in selling goods than those engaged in producing them – tremendously expanded and expensive advertising and publicity campaigns, 'acceleration of obsolescence', etc.) goes hand in hand with deliberately organised waste in the public or governmental sector (ever-increasing arms expenditure, sky-rocketing military budgets, prosecution of imperialist or counter-revolutionary wars – in Korea, Malaya, Kenya, Algeria, Congo, Vietnam, Afghanistan, the Gulf, etc. – proxy wars and armed interventions the world over and capitalism's own hegemonic warfare in the midst of the uneasy peace between rival capitalist powers). It has been pointed out that, since 1945 alone, there have been more than 150 wars, large and small, mostly in the third world countries, fought with armaments supplied by the advanced industrial nations, as an essential item in their balance of payments. The manufacturing of arms constitutes a guaranteed 'substitute market' which is of importance to capital as a whole, confronted as it is by recurring crises of market outlets and overaccumulation. The immense 'military-industrial complex' in the US does not merely account for one-third of the national economy, but also insulates it from the unwelcome frustrations and uncertainties of the market.

Already in the 19th century Marx had pointed out the utility of fighting a war for capitalism, not as a prescription for its armed defence but as a possible strategy the capitalists would be forced to adopt in order to survive economically. As V.G. Kiernan has told us, militarism has been the shepherd of capitalism throughout the 20th century. War is terrible but it is also, as Lenin once said, 'terribly profitable'. Profitable both in its destruction and the reconstruction to follow, it is good business all the way. The act of destruction generates a demand for weaponry, and in turn stirs up the output of *material* and goods, revs up the economy. The subsequent act of reconstruction hopefully does the same. Both activities in effect illustrate a most crucial aspect of demand management under global capitalism. Thus, though on a modest scale, the recent Iraq wars were classical capitalism: create demand through destruction of Arab lands and Arab people and then follow it up by creating demand, a second time, through activities which would pass as reconstruction. The wastefulness of it all is obvious. Dig a hole, John Maynard Keynes had once said, and fill it up, that is the art of saving capitalism. Or, if you prefer, get the country regularly bombed by terrorists. For this is precisely how a leading spokesman for Indian capitalism had it in the aftermath of the terrorist destruction of the World Trade Centre in the USA. For him it was the answer to the problems of American economy in distress. As he put it in an interview to *The Times of India*: 'Billions of dollars will be spent on reconstruction and re-development. Normally, slowdown could have continued for another year or one-and-a-half years. But with this pump-priming, the US economy will revive faster. The medium term outlook will be better on the economic front – much better than what it was before terrible Tuesday.'

It can be, and has been in fact, argued that the capitalist-democratic state, interested in the stability and smooth functioning of the system as a whole, can, aided by Keynesian techniques – whose efficacy up to a point is not to be denied – use the economic surplus generated by a capitalist economy rationally and purposefully, to ensure not only work and livelihood but also a fuller and more meaningful life for men and women at home and abroad. To be sure, a logically coherent plan can be devised along these lines. But it would involve a drastic redistribution of income and wealth and a basic reordering of the way society's economic surplus is utilised – something which no bourgeois politician or political party would be willing to countenance. This argument – that a full and beneficent use of resources is possible under capitalism – is really no more than saying that if capitalism were something other than what it actually is, there would be no need to change it. I may add that capitalism being what it actually is the reason why the much-hoped for post-Cold War 'peace dividend' never materialised in the USA. Policy makers did not switch to beneficial social spending over military expenditure as a means of utilising the available surplus or stabilising the economy. Arms spending was the rational option to the ruling class, since it brings healthy profits and does not have the drawbacks, from capitalist standpoint, of redistributing income and enhancing the social confidence of the working people. Military spending thus remained high even after the disappearance of the Soviet Union. This, incidentally, also showed that the tremendous expenditure on armaments during the Cold War was not a burden imposed by the 'red peril' but an indispensable part of the existing economic system.

What Paul Baran said on the subject four decades back still holds true. Writing of the United States, 'the principal citadel of capitalism', then as today, Baran drew attention to its ever-expanding waste in the private sector: 'tremendously expanded (and expensive) sales organisations, advertising campaigns, public relations programs, lobbying schemes...a continuous, relentless effort at product differentiation, model variation, and the invention and promotion of fancier, more elaborate, more sumptuous, and more expensive consumer goods'. But pointing out that not all the recklessly multiplied waste of the business sector and the rampant growth of the system's unproductive sector are able to provide sufficient drainage for the overwhelming economic surplus generated by today's vastly-developed forces of production, Baran wrote:

> Nor are other more or less automatically functioning mechanisms of surplus absorption – capital exports, corporate outlays on research and development, and the like – powerful enough to solve the problem. A conscious effort at utilisation of the economic surplus is indispensable if its congesting effects are to be kept within tolerable limits, if depression and unemployment are not to be allowed to assume major proportions and thus to endanger the stability of the economic and social order. Such a conscious effort can be undertaken only by the government. The government in capitalist society, however, is not constituted in a way to promote the purposeful and sustained employment of the economic surplus for the advancement of human welfare. The powerful capitalist interests by which it is controlled, as well as its social and ideological make-up, render such a policy most difficult if not entirely impossible. It is unable to control the practices of Big Business, let alone invest directly in productive enterprise, since this would be manifestly in conflict with the dominant interests of monopolistic and oligopolistic corporations. It is barred by the values and *mores* of a capitalist society from large-scale spending on welfare objectives (at home and abroad). Thus even a liberal, progressive administration tends to seek salvation in military spending, adding in this way deliberately organised waste in the government sector to automatically expanding waste in the business sector.

To the wastefulness of capitalism must be added the ecological devastation that capitalist industrialisation has wrought on a world scale. Capitalism's quest for profit, its wars and rampant consumerism have meant a reckless despoilation of natural environment, widespread pollution and poisoning of earth, air and water, fast wasting of the unrenewable resources of the planet and the destruction of global ecological equilibrium. Nature's reprisals can be already heard even if only as the quiet ticking of time bombs. This is how Sweezy and Magdoff summed up the situation with capitalism at the end of the 20th century:

> Capitalism, Marx and Engels emphasized a hundred and fifty years ago, unlocked the huge productive potential of the human species. But with the burgeoning of monopoly and imperialism towards the end of the nineteenth century, capitalism increasingly directed this potential into destructive and anti-human channels. The beneficiaries were and are a tiny minority of owners and exploiters at the top. The rest – victims of wars, depressions, oppressions, and misdirected development – constitute the vast majority of humankind. Nothing in the history of the twentieth century lends credence to the belief that capitalism can change its nature and become a force for the good. And now, as the century draws to a close, the realization is growing that capitalism – production for profit and accumulation of capital as opposed to the production to meet the needs of the people – is at the heart of the problem of ecological degradation which is rapidly becoming a clear and present danger to the very survival of human civilisation.

More recently Istvan Meszaros has written:

> (A) basic contradiction of the capitalist system of control is that it cannot separate 'advance' from *destruction*, nor 'progress' from *waste* – however catastrophic the results. The more it unlocks the powers of productivity, the more it must unleash the powers of destruction; and the more it extends the volume of production, the more it must bury everything under mountains of suffocating waste. The concept of *economy* is radically incompatible with the 'economy' of capital production which, of necessity, adds insult to injury by first using up with rapacious wastefulness the *limited resources* of our planet, and then further aggravates the outcome by *polluting and poisoning* the human environment with its mass produced waste and effluence.

XIX

The 'actually existing socialism' – which was not Marx's socialism whose possibility remains open – has of course, failed. But, surely, the 'actually existing capitalism' – which is the only kind of capitalism possible – has not been the success it is made out to be. In any objective judgement, capitalism too has been a failure in our times. Other considerations apart, capitalism has been a failure in terms of possibly the most legitimate criteria for assessing the performance of a social system: 'fullness of employment' and 'goodness of employment' of the actual and potential resources available in society. Never before in human history has the gap between society's potentiality and society's performance been so immense as it is today in capitalism's current stage of development. Evidence is there, as we have already noticed, in the extraordinary productive capacity that three successive industrial revolutions have put at the disposal of humankind *and* the poverty and illiteracy, squalid slums and homelessness that are the lot of millions of families in the wealthiest countries of the capitalist world and the hunger and misery of hundreds of millions of people, living out their empty and barren lives in the hovels of the peripheral or semi-peripheral poor countries of the third world.

Capitalism's failure has a dangerous dimension which needs to be explicitly stated. Schumpeter, the eminent liberal economist used to characterise capitalism – in fact praise or idealise it – as a system of 'creative' or '*productive destruction*'. This was, on the whole, true of capital's ascending phase of development. Today, by contrast, we have reached a stage when it would be much more correct to characterise it as ever-increasingly a system of '*destructive production*'. Throughout its history, the capitalist system has done damage, and sought to restrict any efforts to limit the damage it does, to people and nature. But now the logic of the system seems to have reached the point where the destructive force of capitalism is pre-eminent, outstripping whatever capacity it ever had to repair or compensate for the damage it inflicts. Under the conditions of capitalism's structural crisis its destructive constituents have come to the fore with a vengeance, almost getting out of control. Capital, it should be remembered, is driven as much as it is driving. It is being driven by its accumulative logic, by the unrelenting competition between capitals in each sector of the economy as well as by the global capital or financial markets, with consequences that are both dramatic and unpredictable. Even 'experts' cannot predict when or where the next economic or financial crisis will strike, or the next 'natural' disaster. The fanciful notions of 'planned capitalism' or a new technocratic industrial elite coming to manage the economy remain the fanciful notions they are. Instead, *Communist Manifesto's* image of the capitalist as 'the sorcerer, who is no longer able to control the powers of the nether world whom he has called up by his spells' captures all too well what is happening in the global capitalist economy. Capitalism's 'destructive production' is not only proceeding on a frightening scale, its uncontrollability foreshadows self-destruction both for the capitalist system itself and for humanity in general. I may add, the way things are going we have only a few decades, certainly not centuries, to bring to a halt this destructiveness of capitalism.

XX

Capitalism came up in a 'little corner of the world', as Marx described Europe of his times. Marx analysed this capitalism's internal contradictions, the irrationality inhering in its recurring crises of overproduction, and saw it as preparing the ground, the necessary objective and subjective conditions, for its own supersession by a more rational economic system, socialism. Marx recognised, better than anyone else before or after him, the universalising tendency inherent in capitalism and took note of capital's early expansion into non-capitalist spaces, internally as well externally, as also the fact that this expansion into 'much larger terrain' helped save capitalism from its internal contradictions. Marx's recognition of this early period of capitalism's historical ascendancy as a global system is full of brilliant insights vindicated by the later development of capitalism. But Marx never raised the question whether a fully globalised capitalism, that is, with no more non-capitalist space to move into, would be viable. This was not his problem. Besides, he expected capitalism to be overthrown and superseded by another system, namely socialism/communism, long before it spatial limits had been reached. It was left for Marx's followers to wrestle with this and related questions. Most outstanding here have been the attempts of Rosa Luxemburg and Lenin – one, focussing on global capitalism as a whole, postulated that the ultimate using up of the non-capitalist space would bring on a final crisis from which there would be no escape, the other, focussing on global capitalism as a collection of units, their uneven development, and imperialist rivalry for control of the remaining non-capitalist areas, postulated the beginning of an era of wars and of revolutions from below. The writings of Rosa Luxemburg and Lenin are of seminal importance for understanding contemporary capitalism. But these writings, or the tortuous development of capitalism as a global system is not what I am immediately concerned with. Capitalism *has* become a truly global system today. It is a couple of issues relating to this reality that I would like to mention or re-emphasise.

Capitalism, as it developed, used to escape its internal crises by moving outward, into new markets and colonies. Today, having become a truly global or universal system, it no longer has the same scope for external expansion which used to save it from its internal contradictions. Expressive once of capitalism's *relative* limits, which could be overcome or displaced temporarily with further expansion, these contradictions, the way they are now manifesting themselves, point to capitalism having reached, as it were, its absolute limits, when the ways of overcoming or displacing them are almost exhausted. So deep is the crisis of capitalism today that a scholar has even suggested, 'global capitalism risks falling apart in a replay, at once tragic and farcical, of the trade wars, competitive devaluations, economic collapses and political upheavals of the 1930s'.

Capitalism, however, has not fallen apart, so far. However failed a system, capitalism continues to exist and dominate the world. True, capitalism is in deep crisis which is not a momentary occurrence to be soon superseded as in the past, but a structural crisis with precipitations or 'dips' of varying intensity, tending towards 'a depressed continuum', as Istvan Meszaros has called it, where one recession follows another. This, however, is not to suggest the approach of any so-called 'the final crisis' – which would simply be a radical version of millennial madness. It is of course possible that in the end internal contradictions of capitalism become explosive and state regulation of economy and other ways of displacing, temporarily, these contradictions prove inadequate or get exhausted. The 'depressed continuum' is in the long run an untenable situation and for that reason a social transformation may become feasible. But social systems do not merely collapse and disappear on their own. The Soviet system came closest to having done so but even here external pressure and complicity and desertion of local rulers were important factors in its 'self-destruction'. More generally, the social systems linger on, unless and until some internal or external force – revolution or invasion – topples them and puts a different system in their place. That this may be the ultimate fate of capitalism is certainly possible. But at the present time this seems to be no more likely than a healthy resurgence of the system. The worsening conditions of living of broad layers of people, including low income and middle classes – expressed, for example, in massive impoverishment, social marginalisation, growing inequality, unemployment, personal insecurity – has not resulted so far in any significant shift of population towards options involving *political* opposition to the incumbent governments of the ruling classes. There is widespread social protest no doubt, any number of 'new social movements' are going on, but there is a *disjunction* between these protests or movements and politics, especially radical politics which goes to the root of the problems and aims at an alternative system. Old-style revolutionary politics, stagnant and in disarray for long, seems to have finally exhausted itself. New revolutionary politics is emerging but is not yet strong enough to make its presence felt except in a few places. The immediate prospect, therefore, is for an indefinite crisis-ridden survival of capitalism – a survival with millions unemployed and living on the dole, many more wallowing in the garbage of consumer society in New York or New Delhi, gasping for air among the super-plenitude of automobiles, the ultimate 'convenience', in their streets, and the overwhelming majority condemned to their life of poverty and degradation, every new 'triumph' of capitalism generating new victims, new exploitation and new discontents, bringing immeasurable suffering and premature deaths to hundreds of millions throughout the world. The 21st century may well overtake the 20th in its quota of capitalist depredations.

Capitalism continues to exist. But this by itself, or the absence or weakness of any movement for radical change against it, in other words, the failure of its irrationality and inhumanity to give rise to forces seeking its overthrow and transformation into a more rational and humane social order, cannot be seen as a proof of the rationality, an argument for the desirability, or a sign of the progressiveness of the capitalist order, much less as any sort of 'triumph' of capitalism. 'That position', says Paul Baran, 'is no more defensible than would be the view that an inability of the human body to resist tuberculosis, however caused, furnishes a proof of the harmlessness or even usefulness of that illness.'

He adds: 'The failure of an irrationally organised society to generate internal forces pressing towards and resulting in its abolition and replacement by more rational, more humane social relations results necessarily in economic stagnation, cultural decay, and a widespread sense of despondency. Such a society – even if once the most advanced in the world – loses its position of leadership, slides into the backwaters of historical development, and turns into a breeding ground of reaction, inhumanity, and obscurantism.' This is indeed the case today, not only in the United States but increasingly in the other so-called advanced societies of late capitalism.

The US leading, these societies are, in a profound sense, to a greater or lesser degree, sick societies. Concerned scholars have written of the phenomenon of 'alienation' in these societies, their citizens' growing sense of anomie and estrangement, of isolation, hostility and frustration. They are sick with these and a hundred other social and psychic ailments born of prolonged living under an essentially irrational system, sick with apathy and boredom, with 'other-directedness' and conformism, with fears, insecurities and neuroses of all kinds. Their sustained social regression is reflected as much in the reaction and obscurantism they breed, their frivolous consumption and culture of drugs, and even guns, as in the debilitating barrage of fraudulent politics, barren culture and stupefying entertainment, inspirational rackets and demoralising press, and comic books, to which their people, even otherwise ill-educated, are exposed all the time. Societies in the grip of crises which they cannot resolve, they are inevitably producing deep pathological deformations which manifest themselves variously in different places as racism, sexism, anti-semitism, xenophobia, ethnic or national hatreds, fundamentalism and intolerance, even as plain cruelty and aggression. Poverty, unemployment and insecurity-related crimes and associated phenomena – ill health and suicides, alcoholism and drug addiction, racist discrimination and criminal violence, violence against women and child abuse, etc. – are on the rise everywhere. In many of these 'advanced' societies marginal indigenous populations are rapidly being wiped out for one reason or another. By their very nature profoundly immoral societies, based as they are on domination and exploitation of man by man, along with humanistic values and culture and all human relationships, even their professed moralities and principles now stand devastated by the morality and values of 'the market'. And, most significantly, there is the near-absence of ideals in these societies, of any concern for a better future to strive for, that has been the motive force of all human progress in the past. The instruments of communication and discovery invented by their technological genius have become the means of debasing people's understanding and preventing them from looking beyond the capitalist horizon.

Indeed, the sickness of these so-called advanced societies, the spiritual disarray of the capitalist civilisation they represent, is nowhere more evident than in their cynical idealisation of capitalism as it exists and utter lack of any vision of a secure and more satisfying life beyond their 'consumerist heaven of instant gratification', a life which would be satisfactory of basic human needs – decent livelihood, knowledge, solidarity, cooperation with fellow human beings, gratification in work and freedom from toil – and provide the possibility of men and women appropriating the world with all their glorious *human* senses. It needs to be added that these societies are all the more sick societies because they need to change the existing state of affairs but are unable to generate the necessary social forces for carrying out the revolutionary change they so badly need.

I may digress a little here to make a brief reference to mainstream scholarship on the subject which has tended to argue for exactly the opposite of what I have just stated. How they have done it makes it an interesting illustration of how descriptive and explanatory language in social sciences invariably carries its load of values and political preferences with it. Scholarly studies of revolution (by Crane Brinton, Chalmers Johnson *et al*) are replete with such words as 'fever', 'symptoms', 'suffering', 'acute condition', 'convalescence', 'relapse', etc. as also 'immune' and 'vulnerable'. For those who know the rules of the game, such words are, as E.H. Carr put it in another context, 'manifestos of a political affiliation and of a particular interpretation'. To treat the study of society and revolution as analogous to the study of pathology, even 'mental illness', to speak of societies as being 'immune' or 'vulnerable' to revolution, shows an obvious conservative bias in the analysis: the implicit assumption is that a 'healthy society' is 'immune to revolution'. But an analysis why revolutions do or do not occur carries no logical implications of approval or disapproval. As a matter of fact a *much* stronger case can be made for the view that 'sick' societies are precisely those which are 'immune to revolution', which need a revolution but cannot make it, that is, generate social forces capable of carrying out the needed revolutionary change. I would suggest that such indeed is the case today with the societies of global capitalism; they are truly 'sick' in their inability to make the revolutions they need, at the centre and even more in its peripheries.

The continuance of capitalism as 'sick' societies of advanced capitalist west has an important implication. In a sense socialism arrived a little before its time, attempted as it was first in Russia, a society that was not prepared to build it. The Bolsheviks had to contend with the problems of a backward, underdeveloped capitalist-feudal social order, problems which caused grave distortions and contributed to the ultimate failure of their attempt to build socialism. Those who may be called upon to build a late-arrived socialism in advanced capitalist countries will have to contend with equally difficult but *different* problems of an 'overdeveloped' capitalism – a capitalism living beyond its time as it were, beyond the period of its historical legitimacy. This, however, is no reason to think that they too will fail. There was no *necessity* about the failure of socialism in the Soviet Union. It was a contingent, human failure. What was needed, above all, was a truly creative practice of Marxism to cope with the entirely unanticipated tasks. Much the same holds true for the socialist experiments of the future whenever and wherever they are made and, again, there is no reason to think that they shall not succeed.

XXI

It has been a long, at times repetitive, argument about the nature, history and the present situation of capitalism to establish its failure as a socio-economic system. I will sum it up with one last word on capitalism and socialism and then conclude with a discussion of 'the basic issue', as I have called it: the condition in which humankind finds itself consequent upon the failure of both capitalism and the attempt to build socialism in our time, and the options that lie ahead.

Capitalism today continues to be and has again achieved exclusive domination in the world. The ideologues have proclaimed its final victory. But does it mean that capitalism has ceased to be the system it has been, that its appetites will be any different in future, that it will no longer be producing poverty amid plenty and unemployment even during times of prosperity, or, more generally, will not continue to produce inequality and uneven development, consumerism, moral and cultural degradation, and deterioration of personal and social life, that its world would no longer be a world of rich and poor, hunger and war, that two-thirds of humanity will not continue to live in the 21st century as they did in the 20th, starved, semi-starved and destitute, or that capitalism will not abuse its technological capacity to destroy which wars in the Gulf and Afghanistan demonstrated and 'war against terrorism' threatens to do on a continuing basis. There is no reason to believe that the leopard has changed its spots, that future with capitalism will be any different from the past, that given its logic of profit-seeking and private accumulation, capitalism will cease to be 'the predatory system' – as Einstein called it – that it has always been, or cease to be the irrational market-governed system so that even a society like the US, with the capacity to feed, clothe, house and provide health care for all its members many times over, nevertheless has mass poverty, homelessness, malnutrition, health care costs that most people cannot afford, and a system of education that leaves many functionally illiterate, and a Castro is compelled to point out: 'Never before did mankind have such formidable scientific and technological potential, such extraordinary capacity to produce riches and well-being but never before were disparity and inequity so profound in the world'.

Though globally dominant as never before, capitalism remains the system it was, beset with the problems of a world divided into a minority of very rich countries and a great majority of the poor, of polarisation of wealth and control over resources within and between societies, of unemployment, mass poverty and a growing gap between the rich and the poor, of wealth concentrating in fewer and fewer hands as the poor in the first world get daily more marginalised and hunger grows daily more desperate in the third world, and now of a new imperialist war without limits – problems to which it has no answer because for the most part it is capitalism itself which has created these problems. It remains incapable of rational and equitable use of productive resources. Whatever benefits it may be bringing to the few, for the overwhelming majority of humankind, there is no future in capitalism, national or globalised.

Again, while accumulation of the powers of ultimate destruction continues and nuclear annihilation remains a near possibility, adding to this threat of 'the modern Dark Ages' is the problem posed by the ongoing destruction of the eco-systems and the biosphere. The sheer exponential growth in production and pollution accompanied by ecological degradation is making the world increasingly uninhabitable by the human species. Capitalism is *by its very nature* committed to unlimited economic growth. 'Sustainable development' simply cannot work through the market; to be at all successful, it must work *against* it, that is, by planned use of natural resources and not their use for profit-making and free consumer choice in the market.

Yet again, there is the overarching question as to what kind of society we, as human beings, want to have, given the productive potential and therefore the possibility, such as humankind never had before, for a civilisation of reasonable well-being for all. Surely it is people and not 'economic growth' or productivity that must come first in such a society. It has to be a humane society that fosters cooperation, solidarity and respect for universal ethical values, and makes for a non-alienated, 'truly rich human life' that Marx spoke of. Of course such a society is impossible without basic material security and need satisfaction. But to believe that you can assure need satisfaction through greed, private acquisitive drives, universal competition and strife – the values of capitalism – and yet hope for a humane society of cooperation and solidarity is utopianism of the worst kind. Subordinating humanity to economics, to imperatives of the market, capitalism commodifies life and undermines and rots away the relations between human beings which constitute societies. Its ethos of the marketplace – competition, egoism, aggression, alienation, universal venality, in short the rat race – creates a moral vacuum in which nothing counts except what the individual wants and can grab, here and now. At the end of it all, even when wants are satisfied, the people are ever more subordinated, ever less free, ever more flattened and made passive by the dictatorship of consumerism, that arbitrarily shapes values, imposing on them the heavy burden of uniformity. The values of difference, individualisation (not individualism), all-sided development of man, of human freedom itself, disappear in the marketplace which is proclaimed to be free. As *human beings*, people simply don't fit into capitalism, which is a quintessential market society. For a truly humane society to come into existence, capitalism has to go.

This illustrative reference to a few important issues makes clear capitalism's essential incapacity to solve the problems facing humankind today. Capitalism is simply not answerable to the sort of social control which is necessary and which socialism alone can provide. For socialism involves a decisive replacement of capitalist economy governed by the predatory imperatives of the market with an economy of socially planned production and distribution of goods and services, based on a social ownership of the means of production which alone makes it possible to direct economy towards social-ethical ends. As Einstein, in his own way, put it: 'The real purpose of socialism is precisely to overcome and advance beyond the predatory phase of human development.'

Of course it is foolish to claim that socialism has all the answers or solutions to the problems we face. But socialism, a systemic change from production for profit (capitalism) to production for the satisfaction of human needs (socialism) does give us, all of us, a chance of confronting these problems successfully and building a better future for humanity. Socialism holds, not the certainty, but the possibility and promise of building not just a 'better kind of society' but a different kind of society in which people can live lives worthy of human beings, not just in comfort, but together and in dignity.

From the very beginning, it is humanity's experience with capitalism that created the cause of socialism, indeed the necessity for it. Marx, with Engels, only put it on a firm basis as the negation of capitalism. One hundred and fifty odd years later, the practical and moral case for it remains as, if not more, valid and powerful as when it was formulated by Engels in his *Anti-Duhring*, of course in the idiom of his time. He had written:

> The appropriation by society of the means of production puts an end not only to the artificial restraints on production which exist today, but also to the positive waste and destruction of productive forces and products which is now the inevitable accompaniment of production...Further, it sets free for society as a whole a mass of means of production and products by putting an end to the senseless luxury and extravagance of the present ruling class and its political representatives. The possibility of securing for every member of society, through social production, an existence which is not only fully sufficient from a material standpoint and becoming richer from day to day, but also guarantees to them the completely unrestricted development and exercise of their physical and mental faculties – this possibility now exists for the first time, but it *does exist*.

> The seizure of the means of production by society puts an end to commodity production, and therewith to the domination of the product over the producer. Anarchy in social production is replaced by conscious organisation on a planned basis. The struggle for individual existence comes to an end. And at this point, in a certain sense, man finally cuts himself off from the animal world, leaves the conditions of animal existence behind him and enters conditions which are really human. The conditions of existence forming man's environment, which up to now have dominated man, at this point pass under the domination and control of man, who now for the first time becomes the real conscious master of nature, because and insofar as he has become master of his own social organisation. The laws of his own social activity, which have hitherto confronted him as external, dominating laws of Nature, will then be applied by man with complete understanding, and hence will be dominated by man. Men's own social organisation which has hitherto stood in opposition to them as if arbitrarily decreed by Nature and history, will then become the voluntary act of men themselves. The objective, external forces which have hitherto dominated history, will then pass under the control of men themselves. It is only from this point that men, with full consciousness, will fashion their own history; it is only from this point that the social causes set in motion by men will have, predominantly and in constantly increasing measure, the effects willed by men. It is humanity's leap from the realm of necessity into the realm of freedom.

XXII

The argument for socialism remains valid and the world's need for a socialist transcendence of capitalism was never more urgent than it is today. But the fact has to be recognised that the effort to build socialism in the Soviet Union and Eastern Europe has failed. What was built there as socialism has, after a long period of degeneration collapsed back into capitalism. Korea is no example of a socialist society as it should be, and in China and Vietnam, unwilling or unable to find answers to their problems within socialism, to invent newer forms of social property and socialist democracy, the two being intimately connected, communist parties still in power have opted for their own roads to capitalism. Cuba alone continues to struggle in defence of its socialist inheritance and the future remains uncertain. Elsewhere, in most places, forces committed to socialism or radical social transformation are in retreat. However one looks at it, the immediate prospects for socialism in the world are rather bleak. The issue therefore is settled, at least for the time being and no matter how one qualifies the proposition, at the end of its seventy years' long struggling existence, socialism can be legitimately said to have failed in our times.

But, as we have argued, capitalism too – whether flowering or in crisis – has been a failure in our times and this fact too has to be recognised. John Major and his ilk may declare with smug self-complacency that 'capitalism works', but it has certainly not worked for overwhelming majority of the world's population who remain condemned to a hand-to-mouth existence even after five centuries of capitalist expansion and domination in the world. The failure of socialism (such as it was) does not make it any kind of success or triumph of capitalism. It has rather left the world all the more a world of mass deprivations and oppressions, of injustices and inequalities, with capitalism's sole superpower, the US, standing guard over it as a frighteningly well-armed, foolishly arrogant and bully-like policeman, threatening the world with more of the same in the name of fighting 'terrorism' spawned by its own economy and politics, or defending or promoting 'freedom' and 'democracy' as it has recently done in Iraq, in the Balkans and in several other places in the Middle-East and Africa!

In the midst of capitalist triumphalism following the collapse of the Soviet Union, David Harvey had written: '...we live in an age of political celebration of the virtues of entrepreneurial capitalism and individualism, in an era when our technological confidence appears unbounded... and when spatial barriers are crumbling. Yet it is also an era... (which) reflects a crisis of capitalism of the deepest magnitude – a crisis that flexible accumulation has not resolved given its paltry rates of growth, the painful devaluations, the increasing class polarisations, the increasing political tensions – all in the midst of extraordinary instability, insecurity, fragmentation and change.' The crisis has only deepened since then and the new century has opened in the midst of an all-pervasive economic, moral, cultural and intellectual disarray and a consumerist deterioration of individual and social life. The collapse of socialism has made the unacceptable consequences of capitalism all the more visible and vicious, and exposed the inadequacy of different variants of social democracy as well as the irrelevance of the dominant theories of growth and development, their 'assorted medications' for economic and social ills that are now chronic at home and abroad. There is widespread political and social instability, economic chaos, corruption at the highest levels of society, and above all '*a shrivelling of the spirit*' as it has been described. Science, reason, progress, the entire inheritance of the age of Enlightenment and the great revolutions is being questioned and abandoned, the predominance of morally destructive consumerism is accompanied by a fashionable post-modernism's nihilistic relativism concerning matters of truth, knowledge, or morals. And the world over there is the rising incidence of xenophobic nationalism, racism, religiosity and fundamentalist revivalism, religious and ethnic strife, tribal and national conflicts, and the exhibition of raw power in both private and public spheres. There is pervasive lament over the sorry shape of things in the world, east or west. A sign of times, scholars have turned to Toynbee and his discourse on the disintegration of civilisations whose cause, according to him, lies in 'schism of the soul', in the 'personal crises of behaviour and feeling and life which are the true essence and origin of the visible manifestations of social collapse'. They have been discussing both the causes and symptoms of disintegration in the countries of Western Europe and its offshoot on the other side of the Atlantic, the United States. Decades ago Lewis Mumford had written of 'a blankness, a sterility, a boredom, a despair' that had, at deeper levels, come to characterise modern, that is capitalist society. Today all this has surfaced with a vengeance in the alienated societies of capitalism. We have the lament of Leszek Kolakowski: '....Whatever area of life we reflect upon, the natural instinct is to ask: What is wrong with it? And indeed we keep asking. What is wrong with God? With democracy? With Socialism? With art? With sex? With the family? With economic growth?.... It seems as though we live with the feeling of an all-encompassing crisis without being able, however, to identify its causes.' Gramsci had once written, of course of a different historical juncture: 'The old is dying and the new cannot be born; in this interregnum a great variety of morbid symptoms appear'. These 'morbid symptoms' are, to a greater or lesser degree, there all over the advanced and less advanced capitalist countries today, as good an evidence as any of the deep crisis of the capitalist civilisation, of the ultimate failure of capitalism in our times.

The new interest in Toynbee and Gramsci's observation is suggestive of what is possibly the most meaningful way of understanding the problem of capitalism and socialism in our times, namely, locating it in the problematic of epochal transitions, in this case from capitalism to socialism/communism. Of course there is no such thing as a general theory of transition between social systems, above all, because each such transition is a unique process, typically occupying and defining a whole hitorical epoch. It has to be analysed and explained as such. The important point however is that in understanding epochal transitions in a world historic scale of centuries we must not look for simple, straightforward rise and fall of social systems, a grand march through te classic modes of production from lower to higher. On the contrary, each transition, never brief or simple, is always a curious zigzag – wherein a multi-dimensional movement in one direction may turn back on itself, in some places the reversal may be prolonged, conceivably even permanent, the movement resuming a forward direction on a new basis, there itself or elsewhere, and so on. Such perspective on transition to socialism was always implicit in classical Marxism. In a reference to the Paris Commune, Marx had written: 'The working class know that they have to pass through different phases of class-struggle. They know that the superseding of the economic conditions of the slavery of labour by the conditions of free and associated labour can only be a progressive work of time....' Rosa Luxemburg always viewed socialist revolution as a worldwide phenomenon, spread over an entire historical period, and involving advances and retreats, victories as well as defeats. Such was also the perspective of Lenin as he confronted the unanticipated task of *beginning* the socialist transition in Russia. This is how I myself put it in mid-1989 as the gathered clouds were darkening over Eastern Europe:

> ....in a Marxist understanding of transitions between historical epochs, the transition from capitalism –via 'socialism' which Marx never saw as a distinct form of society in its own right – to a communist civilisation, is not to be viewed, nationally or internationally, and at any stage, as a peaceful or unproblematic, unilinear process, free of contradictions and conflicts, social or class antagonisms, something impelled forward entirely by the forces of 'scientific and technological revolution'. On the contrary, in some ways comparable to the passage, through centuries, from the feudal to the capitalist civilisation, though qualitatively different from it in its exceptional revolutionary character – history's 'most radical rupture' Marx called it – this transition is bound to involve, as it already has, even wars and civil wars, revolutions and counter-revolutions. In general, it should be viewe as a long period, 'the period', in Marx's words, 'of revolutionary transformation of the one (capitalism) into the other (communism)', characterised at every stage by bitterly fought class struggles, with their inevitable victories and defeats, retreats and advances, ups and downs o all sorts – provided, of course, that the irrationality of continued existence of capitalism does not in the meantime plunge mankind into a new barbarism, that of an ecological disaster, if not of a nuclear holocaust itself. The issue, indeed, remains 'socialism or barbarism'.

What we are indeed witnessing today is the end of an epoch, the epoch of transition to capitalism. Over these five hundred odd years, as capitalism expanded to structure and restructure an unequal world of core, semi-periphery and periphery regions in terms of economic strength and benefits, at each stage of this expansion, capitalism was able to overcome its permanent contradictions, but not without worsening the situation for itself for their overcoming in future. Now with a possibility of further expansion virtually exhausted, these contradictions are difficult to overcome as in the past. They are manifesting themselves all the more violently with truly disastrous consequences for the people that suggest the passing away of the epoch of capitalism's domination. Even at its best capitalist development has been a process of 'creative destruction', to use Schumpeter's famous phrase. As accumulation takes place, competition forces firms to be creative in order to survive, those firms that are not creative are destroyed. In a world of markets and competition, winners are matched by losers, and creation and destruction become one and the same. Losers, however, have not been simply impersonal firms or abstract inefficient technologies. In the real world, losers have been people, sometimes capitalists, but always working people, individually and as communities. 'Creative destruction' has meant the unemployment of real workers, the destitution of real communities, devastation of the environment, and disempowerment of the people. The destructive aspect of capitalism's 'creative destruction' has now reached a point where the historical *raison d'etre* and justification that capitalism, as a mode of production, once had, has disappeared and we can legitimately speak of capitalism living beyond its time, beyond the period of its historical legitimacy.

Capitalism's achievements are now all in the past, its future promises only disasters for humankind. In the *Communist Manifesto*, Marx and Engels had written of class struggle ending 'either in a revolutionary reconstitution of society at large or in the mutual ruin of the contending classes'. The great class struggles of the 20th century have obviously not resulted in 'a revolutionary reconstitution of society'. What Marx and Engels saw as 'the common ruin of the contending classes' is already on in the world. Economies everywhere in shambles; obscene wealth alongside abject poverty and wanton waste of resources; widespread collapse of law and order; senseless regional and ethnic conflicts; new wars between or within nations almost on a daily basis; spread of weapons of mass destruction and threat of terrorism on a global scale; an all engulfing ecological crisis – all this in fact points to the common ruin of more than the contending classes as a very realistic prospect in the historically near future.

Elsewhere, in his *Grundrisse*, referring to the macroscopic quality of the capitalism system, the uncontrollable nature of its accumulation process, Marx had pointed out that 'capital as such is absolutely incapable of limiting itself, irrespective of the consequences even for the total destruction of humanity'. Marx's understanding of the dangerous potentialities of capitalism later came to be formulated in Rosa Luxemburg's famous poser: 'socialism or barbarism'. In Luxemburg's time, her warning had a still indeterminate temporal character. In our day, with socialism having failed, barbarism is already a reality in much of the world. Barbarism has appeared not only on the fringes or periphery of the capitalist system – in Russia, Africa and Middle-East, in the former Yugoslavia and in Columbia or India – but at its centre as well. It is rapidly assuming global proportions. Walden Bello in his *Dark Victory* writes: 'Barbarism stares us in the face in many guises – in clean-shaven technowarriors who manage, from Washington, the death of hundreds of thousands in Middle Eastern battlefields that they experience as sanitized digital images in electronic monitors; in Christian Serbs who rape Muslim women en masse and depopulate Muslim villages in the name of "ethnic cleansing"; in neo-Nazi German Youth who burn down the homes of Turkish guest labourers; in French rightists who advocate mass deportation of undocumented Third World workers to preserve the "purity" of French culture; in American fundamentalists who have declared moral and cultural war on blacks, Third World immigrants, the women's movement.'

Capitalism living beyond its historical time indeed spells a future of barbarism for humankind. It could be a nuclear holocaust that its politics has threatened for half a century or the almost certain ecological disaster which – the noise over so-called 'sustainable development' notwithstanding – capitalism's accumulative logic now portends. Barbarism of sorts is in fact already creeping upon us – what with the irrationalisms, fundamentalisms and fascistic ideologies and demagoguery of various hues, racism, xenophobias and chauvinist nationalisms, terrorism and 'cult of violence', jingoist 'greatest nationism' with its 'crusades', 'infinite justice' and 'bombing enemies back into the stone age', and much else of the same sort, already arrived in tandem with ruined environment and high technology. The danger from the continued existence of capitalism really goes beyond the barbarism it has already spawned or threatens in future. Capitalism has now become so destructive and dangerous that the question is not whether we can expect a better or worse world from capitalism, or even whether it is going to be a barbarised world, but whether we would be left with a world at all. Modifying Rosa Luxemburg's dictum in relation to the dangers we face, Meszaros has suggested adding to 'socialism or barbarism', '"barbarism if we are lucky" – in the sense that the extermination of humankind is the ultimate concomitant of capital's destructive course of development.' Such an outcome, 'the extermination of humankind' is implicit in the uncontrollable accumulative logic of capitalism. It has been rightly pointed out that the truth about capitalism today is not that it is the 'end of history', as the bourgeois ideologues want us to believe, but that its continued existence can really bring on the end of human history. The epoch of capitalism may well end up in 'the total destruction of humanity', the possibility predicted by Marx in 1845.

Socialism may have failed for the time being, but it remains *the* alternative if humankind would survive and hope for a safe world and life worthy of human beings. It bears repeating that the unacceptable economic, moral and ecological consequences of capitalism, its failure ranging from unemployment, poverty and inequalities to barbarisation, at home and abroad, are not aberrations of the system or 'negative' effects produced by specific circumstances or 'mistaken' policies. They are the product of capitalism's unreformable and uncontrollable systemic or structural logic, the logic of exploitation and polarisation immanent in the system itself. Therefore these 'effects' are permanent, even though they are diminished in certain phases and increased in others. They are thus essentially irremediable. In other words, the failure of capitalism in our times has a systemic or structural necessity or inevitability about it. In contrast, there was no systemic or structural necessity about the failure of socialism in the Soviet Union. With politics commanding the economy, socialism simply has no structural logic or 'laws' similar to what market-based capitalism has. Socialism failed primarily due to the inadequacies of theory and practice, to the mistaken *choices* that the Communist parties in power made. Apropos the failure of communist regimes (and Social Democracy in Europe), Gabriel Kolko has written: 'Their consistent failure to redeem and significantly (as well as permanently) transform societies when in a position to do so is testimony to their analytic inadequacies and the grave, persistent weaknesses of their leadership and organisations. It is this reality that has marginalized both social democracy and communism in innumerable nations since 1914, providing respites through the century to capitalist classes and their allies that otherwise would never have survived socialist regimes that implemented even a small fraction of the reforms outlined in their program.' While this may be bending the stick too far the other way, the important point is that socialism's was essentially a human failure. Which had nothing inevitable about it. The lessons learnt from this failure will help whenever or wherever the attempt is made next time. Socialism, therefore is not just *the* alternative to capitalism, it remains a real choice for humankind.

XXIII

As suggested above, taking 'the longer view' of things, the present day defeats and reversal of socialism are best viewed as part of the zigzag that the epochal transition from capitalism to socialism is bound to be.

The 20th century opened with global capitalism's total domination of the world. Then, as anticipated by Marxian analysis, indeed by Marx himself, came the socialist revolutions of the 20th century – the European revolutions in the aftermath of the First World War (of which only the Russian Revolution survived), in Eastern Europe after the Second World War, and then in China, Korea, Cuba, Vietnam and elsewhere – taking approximately a third of world's population and territory out of the capitalist system. Socialism, as pointed out earlier, does not take root and grow within the confines of capitalist society, as capitalism had done under feudalism. It is a new beginning, a society best built on the material basis provided by capitalism.

But now these poor and backward countries were called upon to build socialism where this basis hardly existed. It was a task for which they were most ill-prepared. Even so, as these countries struggled to build, and other revolutionary regimes and movements professing Marxism and committed to socialism emerged in Africa and elsewhere, for a long time the contest between capitalism and its post-revolutionary rival claiming to be socialist seemed to be close and of uncertain outcome. After the events of the recent past, it may be that the visible future belongs to capitalism. But such perspective is relatively new. For most of the century, it was far from clear that capitalism would survive into the third millennium. Now it is the post-revolutionary rival claimed to be socialism that has failed even to last till the end of the second millennium. This, however, is not any end of the earlier perspective. The Soviet experiment in socialism has failed because the conditions, both objective and subjective, were most unfavourable for it. There was the initial economic backwardness, then internal class war and armed and unarmed foreign intervention, global capitalism's continuous effort to prevent any successful construction of socialism. Decisive in its own way were the factors of inadequate and often erroneous theory that guided, or misguided, this experiment and poor political leadership. But it is important to recognise that what has been tried and failed is not socialism but history's first serious effort to build socialism. The reasons that produced the cause of socialism as well as the revolutions aimed at its achievement are still very much there. There is no reason to presume that new revolutions, surprising as ever for the dominant capitalism, will no longer take place and new efforts to build socialism will not be made. And even less reason to presume that given favourable circumstances, more adequate theory and better political leadership, such efforts will not succeed.

Capitalism, an older, more deeply rooted, vastly richer system, one in control of most of the world's natural resources and with much greater lasting power and the will to use it, has no doubt survived the revolutions and socialism of the 20th century. But it remains loaded with contradictions and conflicts within itself, both nationally and internationally. It was indeed an irony of history that the presence of Soviet socialism in its own way helped mollify these contradictions and thus contributed to this survival of capitalism. The fear of socialism persuaded the capitalist governments to curb the predatory logic of capitalism to a greater or lesser degree and thus pre-empt the emergence of an effective revolutionary challenge to the capitalist system itself. At the same time, the political and economic deformities of Soviet socialism, its negative example, lent a certain legitimacy to capitalism, and made it all the more acceptable to people because of its association, however tenuous, with liberal democratic political forms. Again, the very existence of Soviet-led 'socialist bloc', helped prolong the life of modern capitalism by providing a pretext for the Cold War and, therefore, an excuse for military Keynesianism, where armament production provided massive opportunities for profitable investment of economic surplus, an almost ideal method for priming the economic pump and keep the capitalist system going. Now all such 'advantages' have been eliminated. The counter irony provided by the collapse of Soviet socialism is that a triumphant capitalism must now confront its own internal contradictions as never before, contradictions which have always been much more dangerous and lethal than any challenge posed by alternative social systems. Already a recession, more deep-seated and prolonged than any since the Second World War is underway, reminding many of the Great Depression of the 1930s. Not that a collapse is likely, although it is certainly not impossible. But more to the point is the fact that the contradictions and conflicts of capitalism not only gave rise to economic crises and wars both small and large in the past – two world wars and a Great Depression in the last century – but also the great revolutions of the 20th century. There is no reason why it should be any different in future. Even with the inhibition of the social imagination that has occurred consequent upon the collapse of Soviet socialism, it is absurd to think that capitalism, which is, from the perspective of *la longue duree*, a mere moment in human history, has already used up all the possibilities available to the future. No failures or defeats, no matter how great and tragic, can extinguish the human aspirations and forces pressing for a better life. There is no reason to presume, I may repeat, that the causes which produced revolutions and the effort to build socialism will not continue to do so in future too, and that, in the epochal transition of our times, these new efforts to build socialism, learning from the failures of the past will not succeed.

XXIV

Here a look at capitalism's emergence and spread, the transition from feudalism to capitalism can be quite instructive. This transition, it is important to remember, itself took four to five hundred years and is still incomplete – feudalism still persists in large parts of the world and even otherwise vast populations, strictly speaking, still remain outside the 'market economy', beyond the 'sovereignty of global markets'. It is now agreed that both the decline of feudalism and the beginning of capitalism can be traced far back into the Middle Ages, that is to say, into a period when there is no doubt that the dominant European mode of production was feudal. During the epochal transition that followed, we can see several incipient capitalisms emerge and subside time and again, in Venice, for example, or Bohemia under the Taborites. Oliver Cox has indeed argued very persuasively that Venice in the Middle Ages was already a thoroughly bourgeois city-state, completely oriented towards profit-seeking commerce, with significant capitalist production (e.g. in ship-building) and a typically bourgeois political and ideological superstructure.

Pointing this out Sweezy has suggested that 'the same can be said with even greater certainty of a considerable number of Italian and Northern European cities in the later feudal period' and that 'the discovery of America and the opening up of sea routes to the Far East in the fifteenth and sixteenth centuries generated a burst of activity (including plunder and piracy as well as trade) which by no stretch of the imagination could be called "feudal".' The late Middle Ages thus witnessed not one but several promising yet false starts for capitalism. But weak and divided, they lacked the stamina to survive in the hostile, predominantly feudal environment of the period. Smothered by surrounding feudalism, the emerging capitalism, simply failed to catch on. It was not until centuries later that a new conjuncture emerged in which a budding capitalism, benefiting well from its earlier abortive appearances, could take root and grow powerful enough to fend off its enemies and survive, to finally arrive as it did in England and other Atlantic societies. Once arrived the struggle with feudalism still continued, a struggle between two actually existing social formations for supremacy, i.e. for state power (monopoly over the means of coercion) and the right to organise society in accordance with their respective interests and ideas. Moreover the process was a prolonged one in which the 'new' social formation had ample time to prepare itself, both economically and ideologically, for the role of undisputed dominance. It is thus that capitalism grew and developed into the globally dominant system of our times, till socialism made its first efforts to make a breach into it, an effort which has now failed.

But the failure of history's first socialist effort does not mean that more successful future efforts are impossible. The evidence of history suggests otherwise. As we have just noticed, it was only after many centuries of turmoil through a long process of advances and retreats that capitalism established itself as the dominant world economic system. In the centuries-long struggle between feudalism and capitalism, there were many 'triumphs of feudalism', but in the long run, capitalism finally prevailed. So in the case of the transition from capitalism to socialism, the struggle may continue for centuries. There have been, and undoubtedly will be, other 'triumphs of capitalism', but in the end socialism may yet prevail. By historical standards, a few centuries is not a long time and socialism has existed for only a very short time. It is certainly mistaken and premature to superficially extrapolate from the developments of the recent, historically limited, past and speak of the ultimate failure of socialism, to take an entirely bleak view of its future prospects. It is certainly not justified to regard the Soviet effort as only a 'heroic but tragic experience', 'an abortive search for an impossible short cut', a 'parenthesis' or 'interlude' in the history of capitalism, or, as in Stefan Heym's phrase, merely a 'footnote in history', and so on. Rather dismissive in nature, such assessments tend to suggest a failure of socialism as such. On the contrary it is far more legitimate to argue that in view of the epochal nature of the transition involved, the Soviet collapse does not mean the end of socialism but only the end of the world's first large-scale attempt to transcend capitalism and build a socialist society. In the larger perspective of next century or two, the developments since the 1920s can be better understood as a disastrous but still educative false start and the current crisis of socialism as a period of temporary retreat in the epochal transition to socialism. Therefore, if we believe that capitalism needs to be negated in socialism, that the underlying ideas and ideals of socialism provide the only possible framework for a decent human society, we certainly don't have to abandon hope simply because the first attempts to realise them in practice – under very difficult and unfavourable conditions, it should be noted – proved unsuccessful. We can and must still hopefully struggle for socialism and refuse to accept capitalism as the inescapable destiny for humankind. It is thus that the contest between these two approaches to human social development is still unsettled. Its outcome remains open. In a long-term historical perspective, 1917, as Goethe said of 1789, may yet mark the beginning of a new epoch in the history of humankind.

But this 'long-term' is today loaded with a problematic. Once available to capitalism to emerge, consolidate itself, and grow dominant, *time* is no longer so available to socialism, which incidentally, also has most serious implications for the future of humanity. The reason lies in the growing ecological crisis in the world where capitalism's systematic or structural logic now threatens the very existence of humankind on the planet earth. This suggests not only the urgency of a socialist negation of capitalism but also that once a promise of liberation socialism has now become a question of survival too. Human species today needs socialism not only to realise its potential but even to survive. In other words, the chances of survival and realisation of the potentials of both human species and socialism have come to be interlinked today. Which also means that the future of socialism is as bleak or bright as that of humankind.

APPENDIX: ON THE WELFARE STATE*

Even friendly critics have been compelled to recognise the glaring social inadequacies of the so-called 'welfare capitalism' and the utterly irrational composition and social direction of production and distribution under it. J.K. Galbraith, for example, writing in *The Affluent Society*, of the wealthiest country of capitalism today, the USA, notes its obvious 'failure to invest in people' because of the gross 'social imbalance' of its economy: its strong bias towards production of private consumer goods, no matter how frivolous or even injurious, and away from public services, no matter how necessary or beneficial, resulting in a strange combination of starved community services with extravagant private consumption, of public squalor with private opulence.

It is really interesting that in order to remedy this situation all that Galbraith offers is a call to scrap the old outmoded economic theories and ideas, the 'conventional wisdom' as he calls it, born of a period of economic scarcity, for new ideas suited to the needs of 'the affluent society', which demand the diversion of resources from production and distribution of private consumer goods or frivolities to provision of public services that satisfy vital social needs. This, obviously, is easier said than done. There is no doubt, of course, that capitalist economy may on occasion – in order to ward off a crisis or to sustain its prosperity or to maintain its growth rate, etc., – accept such and similar ideas and make necessary institutional and ideological adjustments. In times of crisis even far reaching concessions may very expediently be made to them. But this does not last for long, nor ever go deep enough to touch the basic irrationality of the system, which as a whole continues to function on the basis of 'conventional wisdom', that is, the central motivating principle of profit-making. As a *capitalist* system, it can function on no other basis. And what Galbraith calls 'conventional wisdom' is not merely a set of outworn ideas and prejudices, which the capitalist class is itching to get rid of

---

* An extract from the author's *Reason, Revolution and Political Theory* (1967).

on the advice of the well-meaning liberals. It is rather the ideological mask of very powerful vested interests, 'the fighting creed', as Sweezy and Huberman once put it, 'of a class-conscious minority which understands the nature of its privileges and means to protect them'. What is more, this minority has truly formidable means of doing so.

What the situation, therefore, demands is far more than a setting up of new ideas, however eminently reasonable or intrinsically valid they might be. It demands the decisive breaking down of the entrenched power of the interests behind the old ideas. This means socialism. Only socialist ownership of the means of production can help break decisively with the value system of private profit-oriented ownership, and alter in a fundamental manner the irrational and inhuman priorities of capitalism. Only thus will it become possible to make a rational and purposeful use of the productive resources, 'their studied and rational use' as Galbraith says, which ensures that our production and distribution satisfy the real, truly human, needs of men in a modern society.

For a critical comment on Galbraith's argument see Michael Lipton, 'The Mythology of Affluence', *New Left Review* No. 35, January-February 1966. Suggesting that the Galbraithian attitude is 'unsound in its theoretical basis, careless in its empirical analysis and harmful in its political consequences', and that Galbraith 'buries theory and fact in a half-baked mythology of affluence', Lipton particularly underlines the fact that in holding 'that wrong doctrines, not sectional interests, are the main cause of social evils', Galbraith ignores 'the realities of power', 'the power structure that perpetuates proved abuses, stifles industrial democracy and numbs social feeling'. For a fuller discussion of the subject see Tom Kemp, 'Galbraith as Prophet of American "Neo-Capitalism"', *Science and Society*, Vol. XXIX, No.4, Fall 1965. Commenting on Galbraith's argument in defence of capitalism, Kemp points out that Galbraith 'leaves out of the picture altogether the exploitative nature of capitalist society and the political consequences which flow from it', that he 'refuses to make a full qualitative assessment of American society' and that he 'avoids a deep analysis of power relations'. Arguing that 'the relevant problems with which Galbraith does not deal, by reason of his limited perspective, are legion', Kemp underlines the 'apologetic' character of Galbraith's argument as a whole: 'Scientific method and science itself are renounced in favor of comforting sophistries and evasion of the main case against capitalism'.

To criticise the argument of Galbraith, however, is not to deny that even within the limits of capitalism itself much more can be done to mitigate the economic and social consequences of its irrationality, or that a better 'balance' can be achieved – Sweden is a case in point – between social and private needs. For the sake of argument, one could go still further and concede the possibility of acceptance, by the oligarchy which controls the resources and surpluses of society under capitalism, of the proposal recently put forward by the authors of 'The Triple Revolution' in the USA who, making a powerful indictment of America's present sorry situation, of its poverty amidst affluence, have suggested that in view of the 'Cybernation Revolution' now underway, society should guarantee 'an adequate income as a matter of right' to all its members. But it is not difficult to see that given the *essential* irrationality and inhumanity of capitalism and the *mores* and values of a market society, even this would mean not the much hoped-for social and moral regeneration but only a streamlining of the present patchwork of welfare measures, which would still further dull men's striving for a more rational and humane social order and reconcile them with a society which even at its best, and no matter how productive it becomes, must remain one of class division and exploitation, of social and cultural deprivation, of inequality at once culturally degrading and morally repulsive, and of alienation. It would thus serve, as religion often does, only as an opiate of the people tending to strengthen the *status quo*. And its beneficiaries would still remain really the victims of an irrational and unjust social order, men alienated from their *human* essence, from their rightful inheritance of freedom, of happiness and justice, of knowledge, enjoyment and creation. If happy, they will be 'happy' only as willing slaves are; if cheerful, they will only be 'cheerful robots' as C. Wright Mills would describe them (see *The Sociological Imagination*, ch: 'On Reason and Freedom').

See also Erich Fromm, *The Sane Society*. Fromm points out how 'alienation and automatization' are already leading 'to an ever-increasing insanity. Life has no meaning, there is no joy, no faith, no reality. Everybody is "happy" – except that he does not feel, does not reason, does not love.' Fromm writes: 'In the nineteenth century the problem was that *God is dead*; in the twentieth century the problem is that *man is dead*. In the nineteenth century inhumanity meant cruelty; in the twentieth century it means schizoid self-alienation. The danger of the past was that men became slaves. The danger of the future is that men may become robots' (p. 360).

This is the reason why it is all the more important today to affirm the necessity of a socialist transcendence of the capitalist limits of the welfare state, the necessity of socialism in the sense of a *socialist* ownership and use of the means of production. This is an absolutely necessary condition, though admittedly not a *sufficient* condition, of being able not only to fully develop and utilise the expanding productive resources for the benefit of whole society, but also to go beyond it to realise for all men the conditions of genuine *human* existence, to realise a productive, cultured community of free and equal human beings in which, as Marx and Engels once put it, 'the free development of each is the condition for the free development of all' (*Manifesto of the Communist Party*, p. 72).

Index of Names

Index of Subjects